The Evolution
and Future
of High Performance
Management Systems

THE Evolution AND Future OF High Performance Management Systems

GLENN BASSETT

QUORUM BOOKS
Westport, Connecticut • London

Library of Congress Cataloging-in-Publication Data

Bassett, Glenn A.
    The evolution and future of high performance management systems /
Glenn Bassett.
       p.   cm.
    Includes bibliographical references and index.
    ISBN 0–89930–813–9 (alk. paper)
    1. Industrial management. 2. Industrial productivity. I. Title.
HD31.B369448   1993
658—dc20   93–12992

British Library Cataloguing in Publication Data is available.

Library of Congress Catalog Card Number: 93–12992
ISBN: 0–89930–813–9

First published in 1993

Quorum Books, 88 Post Road West, Westport, CT 06881
An imprint of Greenwood Publishing Group, Inc.

Printed in the United States of America

∞™

The paper used in this book complies with the
Permanent Paper Standard issued by the National
Information Standards Organization (Z39.48-1984).

10 9 8 7 6 5 4 3 2 1

For my sons,
John and Glenn Jr.,
Exemplars of High Performance

Contents

Exhibits

Acknowledgments

Attempting the dual objectives of expositional clarity and scientific accuracy in any book is not an easy task. The first objective demands smoothness of flow and adequate interpretive commentary to make the facts lively and interesting. Offering a clear critique of prevailing management theory requires both a special degree of factual accuracy and a willingness to cut through the popular rhetoric with pointed and pithy argument. There is always the hazard of cutting away some theoretical muscle in the process.

A number of colleagues and friends responded to my call for critical review of the material in this book to assure clarity and accuracy. They deserve recognition for their effort. Chapters on Frederick Taylor, Hawthorne and motivational theory were critically reviewed by Ed Locke. Peter Peterson reviewed the material on Taylor and Ford, and Denis Organ reviewed the Hawthorne section. Victor Vroom reviewed the chapters on quality of work life and participative management. John Baldwin, former chief negotiator for General Electric Corporate Relations, critiqued the material on Boulwareism; Ed Giblin of the Institute for Advanced Compensation Research did a critical reading of the pay chapter; and my long-time colleague and mentor Herb Meyer reviewed the chapter on selection methods and policy. I would only wish that Ed Ghiselli were alive to add his critical commentary, but his influence is, nevertheless, present on many of these pages.

The good offices of these scholars and managers have kept me from gross error in the matters of fact and illuminated my perspectives constructively. This does not necessarily mean that all are in agreement with my arguments and conclusions. Scientific management continues to enjoy strong advocacy by management scholars, and suggesting ideological narrowness or naivete among adherents of the human relations movement seems unduly harsh criticism of sincere scholarly intentions to others. If management science is to be reformed on a critically sound foundation, though, it is necessary to develop and articulate these arguments as clearly as possible. This has been my objective.

Introduction

The competitive edge of modern-day business emerges from creation or discovery of a high performance management system. A system that increases efficiency, decreases cost or enhances quality confers immediate competitive advantage on its creator and sets a standard for the rest of the industry to follow. But once disseminated across the field of competition, it becomes the standard. Now a new, yet more innovative, high performance system must be discovered that once more creates competitive advantage for its inventors.

The history of industry since the mid-nineteenth century is traced through the discovery and implementation of successively more sophisticated high performance systems. It begins with centralization of productive capacity in the modern factory system. Prior to the invention of factories, each community was a system of independent craftspeople and farmers who enjoyed an idyllic communal existence formed around specialization of craft. The factory system was the product of engineering temper and skill in a globally competitive world. The first high performance factory systems were organized around the disciplines of industrial engineering to exploit intercontinental commerce. Frederick Winslow Taylor created the high performance factory system that has been dubbed "scientific management."

Henry Ford used scientific management as the foundation of his engineered, moving assembly line and created the next phase in high-performance management systems—a phase that has dominated most of the twentieth century. It became the target of assaults by another arm of science, human relations theory, which campaigned first as the human relations movement, then in the guises of a quality of work life movement, participative management rhetoric and a variety of guerrilla thrusts under the battle cry of motivation theory. The Ford system, though, was too robust to yield to mere humanistic rhetoric. Indeed, the sheer success of Ford's personal vision of scientific management raised Western productivity to unparalled heights and rendered America the "arsenal of democracy" in World War II. Simple management humanism could hardly compete with that.

Without question, scientific management, especially in the form of the moving assembly line, lacks much in human and humane values. It invites criticism. But attempts to invent high performance systems on humane foundations that outperform the earlier successes of scientific management have fared badly even as they gathered greater numbers of ideological adherents. The great human relations movement that followed World War II has foundered in the swamps of its own rhetoric. It has gone nowhere.

As the twentieth century eases toward closure, there are indications that new high performance systems are aborning. Somehow, they seem to cannibalize the best from old systems to weave the new. They leave behind the lock-step work flow of the engineered assembly process and abandon the narrow specialization of work that characterized it. In its place there is flexibility for the system to redesign itself around a multiskilled work force, trained and empowered to make production decisions formerly reserved solely for production engineers. This is one current variety of emerging high performance system. But it is probably only *one of many* new kinds of high performance management systems with potential to emerge in this age. Indeed, the pace of technological change may open the door to a variety of high performance systems, each suited to its particular industry or market, each with its own character. Management in the twenty-first century appears destined to face the challenge of creating and re-creating ever more competitive and effective high performance systems. Doing so will require understanding and appreciation of the evolution of high performance systems through the nineteenth and twentieth centuries and understanding the basic elements that made them successful. We may begin with an historical review of high performance systems and build to the present, identifying the characteristics of such systems as we progress.

The first stirrings of modern shop management practices appear within the discipline of industrial engineering. The dominant personality in this field unquestionably is Frederick Winslow Taylor, the universally acknowledged father of scientific management. Taylor's accomplishments and his personality are vividly impressed onto the fabric of modern management theory and practice. Once discovered, this imprint can be seen again and again in current-day organization practice. Taylor's own words in the form of his treatise before the Society of Mechanical Engineers on "Shop Management," his summary of "The Principles of Scientific Management," and his "Testimony Before the Special House Committee" are contained within his book, *Scientific Management* (1947). This is the proper historical foundation of scientific management.

A large proportion of present-day organizational and operations practices can be traced directly to Ford and Taylor. The shape of modern mass production methods as built around Taylor's industrial engineering methodology was dominantly formed by the personality and engineering genius of Henry Ford. Ford invented the modern moving assembly line with all its grand efficiencies and cruel excesses of worker overspecialization and lost worker dignity. He is the model and epitome of the twentieth-century captain of industry. Without appreciation for the contributions of these larger-than-life personalities, it is hard to understand present-day management practice. Ford's life and accomplishments are summarized by Lacey (1986) and Nevins and Hill (1957). Ford's own summary of his industrial philosophy is found in *Today and Tomorrow* (1988).

Organized labor resisted the factory system almost from its inception. The contradiction of industrial autocracy in juxtaposition with popular democracy was inevitably enacted in the labor movement. The human relations movement of the twentieth century arose as much out of opposition to the militancy of industrial democracy as out of disgust with the inhumanities of scientific management. Reaction to the excesses of efficiency wrought through Taylor's and Ford's methods is most clearly evidenced in the classic Hawthorne studies conducted at Western Electric's Hawthorne plant in Chicago between 1924 and 1932. Early efforts to undercut labor warfare and reform industrial practice around a core of human relations research began with Hawthorne. The blending of political ideology with science evidenced at Hawthorne influenced the character of organization theory for nearly a half century, proceeding independently and in parallel with the traditions of Ford and Taylor.

The effect of Hawthorne on scientific management was dominantly that of standing in ideological opposition to the less humane qualities of Taylorism. Overemphasis on the ideological "good feelings" agenda at Hawthorne, unfortunately, deterred the more substantive potential of human relations research for a half century or more. Hawthorne offers an opportunity to see how ideological rhetoric and sound management practice were confounded to create a confusion of management theory that still prevails. The Quality of Work Life movement of the 1970s flowed directly from the Hawthorne tradition, and the antiauthoritarian rhetoric of worker participation represents another branch of human relations ideology that has run in parallel with quality of work life.

The complex and sometimes confused rhetoric of motivational theory offers an example of theory evolving in a disciplined, scientific way, arriving ultimately at a point where the ideologies of both quality of work life and worker participation are largely refuted. Out of the rigorous research on worker motivation has come modern goal-setting theory, which has already begun to reform management practice. Emphasis on goals within a context of management by objectives and sound management strategy is emerging as a core element of modern high performance management systems.

The role of worker compensation in high performance systems arises at many points in the evolutionary course of high performance systems and is ultimately summarized in its own chapter because of the centrality of pay rhetoric to cost and efficiency. The divorce of craftsperson from customer in a factory economy laid the foundation for conflict over the distribution of industrial wealth, making pay as much a political as a market issue. As a result, science-based arguments for or against various pay systems are likely to be confused, baffling and irrelevant. Sorting these arguments out requires radical reformulation of the theory of compensation. Such limited research as exists is reviewed. The largest part of the argument, though, is logical refutation of the prevailing rhetoric of pay as a motivator. High pay, we will find, is typically an essential support to a high performance system, but it cannot generate high output in the absence of that system.

A rich and largely overlooked body of research evidence on productivity, fatigue, rest periods and total hours worked is recovered from the earliest part of this century as the basis for examination of the prevailing habit of an eight-hour workday and forty-hour workweek. *Industrial Fatigue and Efficiency*, written in 1921 by H. M. Vernon, a medical doctor and investigator for the British Industrial Fatigue Research Board during World War I, details research that establishes a foundation for the efficiency of a shorter workweek. It is an astonishing work that offers opportunity for reconnection with the historical roots of work schedule policy in industry. Analysis of this potential for design of modern high performance systems is detailed in the chapter on work schedule and hours of work.

Modern high performance systems appear to require reemphasis on individual uniqueness and breadth of skill through broad-based multiskill training within a context of a robust and supportive work culture. Indeed, one of the best paths to high performance at the turn of the twenty-first century appears to be in systematic, purposeful construction of a high performance culture formed around the selected skills and attitudes of individual workers, augmented by intensive training within a high performance culture. Attention to relevant individual differences and to work group values is indispensable to creation of such a culture. Indeed, an argument for the necessity of discriminating good from poor potential workers probably turns on the individual's potential to the shape and quality of organization culture. Ultimately, the robustness of a culture is determined by the clarity, honesty and openness of its communications. These are issues that must also be visited.

The unpopular success of scientific management; the failure of a popular human relations ideology; a long, sometimes confusing and unproductive search for new principles through behavioral science; and an emerging view of modern high performance systems, often stimulated by competition in the global arena, will trace the course of this exposition. The evolution of past high performance systems and a study of likely elements of tomorrow's high performance cultures is our focus here.

The Evolution
and Future
of High Performance
Management Systems

Chapter One

Taylor and Ford: The Age of Scientific Management

Frederick Winslow Taylor and Henry Ford were contemporaries. Taylor was born in 1856, Ford in 1863, only seven years apart. Both began their careers as engineers with machinist apprenticeships. Each learned his trade and tested his knowledge in the crucible of hard, personal experience. As youngsters, both were imbued by their mothers with strict moral values and habits that they followed faithfully throughout their lives. Taylor and Ford both broke into the national public limelight in a narrow span of time from 1901 to 1912. Ford raced his own auto design and won in 1901. Taylor presented his first major treatise on scientific management, entitled "Shop Management," in 1903. Ford perfected the design for and produced his Model T in 1908 and by 1910 it was the most popular car in America. In the following three years, sales of the car doubled annually. Scientific management became a catchword in the popular press in 1911 when Louis Brandeis employed it as a defense against railroad rate increases in testimony before the Interstate Commerce Commission. Then Taylor himself made news in 1912, testifying before the Special House Committee investigating scientific management. Each was canonized by his followers and vilified by his detractors to the maximum within their respective lifetimes. Their combined influence on the shape of twentieth-century industrial practice has not been matched by any two hundred other men from their or succeeding generations. They were, perhaps, the two most famous engineers/managers of their time, if not of all recent history. Yet there is no record of their ever having met face to face.

Frederick Winslow Taylor was born in Philadelphia in 1856. His parents were of Puritan and Quaker backgrounds, inured with all the self-discipline and industry that those heritages suggest. Franklin Taylor, his father, was a Princeton graduate who subsequently studied law and practiced before the Pennsylvania bar. Emily Winslow Taylor was a serious student of language and the classics who personally supervised the education of her three children.

Frederick followed the pattern expected of his family's station and the times. He prepared for Harvard at Phillips Exeter Academy, and passed the Harvard examinations with honors. The severe discipline of the Exeter program was demanding. His eyesight began to fail him and he was prevented from pursuing a planned career in law. Advised that advances in optical science could correct much of the problem, he was nonetheless instructed to take a long rest from reading. Filled with an energy that had no ready purpose, Frederick entered a pattern-making and machinist apprenticeship in a small Philadelphia pump manufacturing company owned by friends of his family. For one who was said to hate to work with his hands, it was a strange and fateful decision. He would later acquire a Mechanical Engineering degree through evening study, then a Doctorate of Science and go on to become a towering name in the field of industrial engineering.

Upon achieving his journeyman's papers as a pattern-maker and machinist, Taylor applied for and was offered a job with the Midvale Steel Company as an ordinary day laborer. He was no ordinary employee, though. In the short span of eight years, Taylor rose through the ranks to the position of assistant to the chief engineer. On the way up he worked as a gang boss and foreman, where his theories of scientific management began to form.

THE EVOLUTION OF AMERICAN INDUSTRY

Taylor entered American industry as it was concluding its transition from a phase dominated by the individual craftsperson to one characterized by great, consolidated industries founded on massive capital bases. The small craft shops of the eighteenth century dependent on water and animal power to supplement human energy gave way as transoceanic commerce, and later the logistics demands of a vast American Civil War, created the modern "factory" system of production. Steam energy from wood, coal and, ultimately, petroleum powered machinery of previously unparalleled productive capacity. Ownership of tools, once wholly in the hands of craftspeople, passed to the new class of capitalist entrepreneurs.

The more traditional roles of workers and owners, though, were slow to catch up with the changes that consolidated production brought to this new nation. Workers still approached their work as if they were independent craftspeople, learning the uses and limitations of their tools through experience on the job, passing on experience and knowledge to one another in a quasi-apprenticeship fashion. Owners functioned like landlords, taking their share of the wealth produced without direct involvement in organization or management of the work. Workers were now divorced from contact with their customers. Owners' agents sold the produce of factories, collected the sale price and forwarded it to the plant owners. Owners took their rent off the top and paid workers their wages from the residual. The age-old subjugation of renter to interests of landlord replaced the craftsperson's traditional independence as the financial side of the business now came firmly under control of plant owners.

Response of workers was, naturally, distrustful and defensive. Financial yield on these new, energy-intensive, grandly productive tools was certainly far superior to any return ever possible from an independent craftsperson's shop, but the lavish, quasi-royalty life-style of newly rich owners advertised how profitable a consolidated production system could be. Conflict over the division of revenue was unavoidable. Owners, seeking higher return on investment, applied whatever economic or social pressure they could to support their demand for ever higher production, while workers held back as much as they could—without directly jeopardizing their jobs—as protest over their share. Workers controlled the shop floor while owners controlled the cash. Owners cajoled and threatened, while workers produced the minimum. Piecework incentive pay plans were widely popular as devices for increasing production. Workers soon concluded, though, that piecework was a trap; once workers took the bait and raised production, thereby establishing new standards of output, the rates would be cut by owners. As long as workers alone knew how to work the production floor, as long as owners were content to focus on the product distribution and financial side of the business, it was a standoff. Gains were more easily won by owners through investment in improved plant and equipment, while gains for workers were more surely obtained through the threat of withholding their labor and letting costly capital investment stand idle.

A FAIR DAY'S WORK FOR A FAIR DAY'S PAY

As the fates would have it, Taylor, a morally idealistic, upper-middle-class young man, still grounded firmly in the Puritan-Quaker heritage of colonial America, would blunder blindly and ignorantly onto this impasse. Working with his hands in the factory, a role, which, by all the logic of the age should never have befallen him, he discovered the waste and sloth that prevailed among workers. In his roles as a laborer and machinist, he grudgingly accepted the informal restraints on his output required by his fellow workers. But his moral standards were deeply offended. Here was opportunity for vastly greater output—he knew how much more work he personally was capable of. But it was an opportunity wasted because workers would not produce what they were capable of and owners would not pay a consistently fair wage for higher output. The arena of conflict for Taylor was that of industrial engineering. Armed with an M.E. degree from Stevens Institute of Technology, he went forth to slay the dragons of industrial waste and sloth. His sword was scientific management. From this crusade would emerge the first truly high performance industrial systems.

TAYLOR'S ATTACK ON SOLDIERING

Taylor had served an assignment as clerk of the machine shop at Midvale early in his career. There he observed and recorded the extent of output restriction or, as he referred to it, "soldiering," that characterized workmanship. As a gang boss he was determined to stop the systematic soldiering that pervaded the machine shop. He boldly announced that he fully intended to get more production from them. The opposition was total and bitter. He predicted resistance and demanded absolute support in his efforts to raise production from plant management. Without that support, he promised he would not lift a finger to increase output in the shop. Management assured him of its full support. Thereupon he set new, higher standards of work output. If a worker balked, he would take over the machine and demonstrate to the resisting fellow how the standard could be achieved. Failing to find cooperation, he issued a stern warning to the entire shop that "if I have to take this step, it will be a durned mean one!" These were men he had worked beside as a machinist, and he had sympathy with the causes of their resistance, but he was determined to prevail in the interest of increased output.

Taylor began by recruiting an especially intelligent, ambitious group of laborers and training them personally in the best machine methods. He extracted an advance agreement that, in return for instruction in the machinist trade, they would do a fair day's work for him. Once trained, though, these trainees bowed to the pressures of the experienced machinists and refused to work any faster than the group standard. Taylor expressed his understanding of their situation, but announced that since they had broken their agreement with him to deliver a fair day's work, he would henceforth treat them entirely differently from the machinists. He announced to trainees that all their rates would be cut in half on the day following. "All you have to do is turn out a fair day's work and you can earn better wages than you have been earning." The group protested angrily to higher management, charging that Taylor was a tyrant. They received no hint of sympathy. Then, overnight, they gave in and met Taylor's output requirements.

Journeyman machinists responded with passive resistance. Every time Taylor won over someone to his higher work standards, they would intentionally break a machine part. Taylor had anticipated this form of resistance and had prearranged for management support in the extraordinary response he made to it. He imposed a fine on any man breaking a machine for *any* reason. The fines were paid into a workers' mutual benefit fund and actually went back to the workers themselves, but the fines were individually imposed and had the effect of reducing individual income. Taylor stuck to his system of fines, continued to proselytize workers to do a fair day's work and, after three years of struggle and resistance, prevailed. His crew accepted the requirement that they perform a fair day's work. By sheer dint of personal will, Taylor created a high performance management system at Midvale. He would call it scientific management.

In later years after Louis Brandeis had turned scientific management into a politically hot subject through use of its principles to fight increased rail tariffs, Taylor testified extensively before a Special House Committee on the meaning of scientific management. Hostility of organized labor toward the spread of Taylor's methods and principles generated political opposition to his movement. The premise of the investigation was congressional concern over application of the principles of scientific management at U.S. Army arsenals.

Taylor was called on to defend his theories and was questioned by Congress about his early battle for production at Midvale. He was asked if his men might not have been justified in their resistance to his demands for fear of "ultimate exhaustion." Taylor (1947) responded, matter of factly and perhaps a little wryly:

In working on the average machine tool, of necessity the greater part of the day is spent by the man standing at his machine doing nothing except watch the machine work. I think it would be safe in saying that not more than three hours of actual physical work would be the average that any machinist would have to do in manning his machine..

He had never, indeed, asked anyone to do what he, himself, could not easily and comfortably do. Taylor's concern was to end the destructive practice of withholding output, whereby the worker cheated the owners, the customer and himself of the full potential for payoff from their productive plant.

PRINCIPLES OF SCIENTIFIC MANAGEMENT

The heart of Taylor's scientific management is easily summarized: set high standards of performance, train workers to meet them, enforce them strictly and pay fairly for high output. It is a model that remains viable and relevant to the present day. Taylor's emphasis on clearly articulated, difficult goals, indeed, has been reverified as a sound approach to performance motivation through goal-setting research. Emphasis on performance against difficult goals is perhaps one of the most enduring and significant elements of high performance systems. The followers of Taylor, however, were inclined to emphasize the technical, engineering methods of scientific management such as time and motion study, work process analysis and piecework pay.

The technical specifics of Taylor's system are summarized in Exhibit 1–1. Testifying before Congress, he summarized and condensed his theory into four general principles. Like most broad principles, they are more than a bit abstractly enigmatic standing by themselves. They need to be interpreted in light of Taylor's methods and actions in the plant setting.

The first principle is that managers must "develop a science for each element of a man's work." This principle encompasses *all* of the methods he had introduced to support high standards of output and work efficiency. It includes time and motion study, cost analyses, piecework pay systems, functional foremanship and work process planning. Here Taylor challenges owners to take control of the shop floor and set work standards for all workers. He also is effectively announcing the end of the worker as craftsman, independently self-sufficient in carrying out his work. It is a principle that places industrial engineering at the pinnacle of workplace management. A further result has been to make work standards the skirmish line along which industrial guerrilla warfare has continued to be chronic as Taylor's battle to set higher output standards has been repeated a hundred thousand times over in factories worldwide.

Exhibit 1-1
Techniques of Scientific Management: Specific Methods on Which
Scientific Management Is Founded

Cost Center Accounting:
> Allocation of specific costs to each product line or work activity.

Piece-Rate System:
> Wage payment based on the individual's amount of work output.

Time Standards:
> Measured time for accomplishing a task, typically established by
> observation of an industrial engineer with a stop watch.

Motion Study:
> Analysis of specific, elemental work motions required by each task.

Functional Foremanship:
> Sub-division of supervisory and support activities into specialties:
> Gang Boss -- Allocates labor and machinery to available work.
> Speed Boss -- Assures maximum efficient methods are used.
> Inspector -- Assures that all work is properly finished.
> Repair Boss -- Responsible for all maintenance and housekeeping.
> Shop Disciplinarian -- Administers discipline and keeps the peace.

Planning Department Specialties:
> Work flow and routing.
> Documentation of and instruction in efficient job methods.
> Time and cost record keeping.

The second principle is to "scientifically select and then train, teach and develop the workman." Taylor (1947) adds parenthetically that "in the past, he chose his own work and trained himself as best he could." Responsibility for maximizing work skill is shifted from worker to manager. Again, there is an abridgement of the workman's independence. Taylor's personal emphasis on intelligence in selection of workers augured the overuse of intellectual ability as a universal selection criterion in the first half of the twentieth century. His more soundly conceived proscription to train, teach and develop has largely been ignored and overlooked in favor of the narrowest possible specialization of tasks through which to reduce training time and cost in the name of maximum cost efficiency. Taylor long went unheard on this principle.

Principle number three calls for management to "heartily cooperate with the men so as to insure all of the work being done in accordance with the principles of the science which has been developed." It is a strangely stated principle which suggests the personal discomfort Taylor experienced at having to impose a science of work top-down on employees. It would be much more easily understood if proposed as a demand for cooperation of workers with the science he had developed for their tasks. Alternatively, had he called on management to make imposition of this science on workers as palatable as possible through sympathy and understanding, we would readily grasp his intent. As stated, though, it stands as a surprisingly weak call for a "mental revolution" offered to Congress as central to the proper implementation of scientific management. A clarion call to revolution fizzled into a penny-whistle whimper for peaceful change.

Finally, he calls for "an almost equal division of the work and the responsibility between management and the workmen. The management take over all work for which they are better fitted than the workmen, while in the past almost all of the work and the greater part of the responsibility were thrown upon the men." Taylor hints at the injustice of demanding increased work output when management will not develop the skill or exert the effort to properly support their efforts. The possibility is bypassed that workers were happy having the greater part of work and responsibility "thrown" onto them as long as they were free to do the work as they chose. Taylor here envisions a new role for management in designing, planning and coordinating operations throughout the plant. Merely engineering the plant and tools is no longer sufficient; management must now be accountable for designing and coordinating work tasks. It is the death knell for the worker as craftsperson. It is also the birth of the manager as shirtsleeve doer alongside the worker in the plant. It is an organizational revolution that would inevitably eclipse the mental revolution called for by Taylor as a foundation for implementation of his ideas.

In a span of some thirty-five years, Taylor created and implemented the operating structures that have dominated industrial order down to the present day. It was, perhaps, a natural step for engineering to move from development of the materials and tools of production to design of its methods and standards. Taylor saw an opportunity for a high performance production system and moved to fill it. He effectively reformed the factory into its present-day structure. In doing so, he opened the door for the era of worker as robot by abridging the self-sufficient independence of the crafts-styled worker and focusing on efficiency as the central measure of work effort. Carried to its logical limit by such as Henry Ford, scientific management would diminish the craftsperson role to near eclipse. Taylor had intended and hoped for much better. His was a utopian vision. And while his methods effectively drove the productivity of labor to previously unknown heights, they minimized the laborer's role to the lowest degree of power possible.

FORD'S CONTRIBUTION TO AND CORRUPTION OF SCIENTIFIC MANAGEMENT

Despite the absence of direct personal contact, Ford could not help but be influenced by Taylor. At the turn of the twentieth century, Taylorism was as much on the air in Detroit as were the dust and smoke from the factories of this frontier boomtown. Taylor in 1909 spoke before the assembled management of the Packard production plant about his theories of scientific management, offering a four-hour presentation of his ideas. Time and motion studies as the basis of labor standards for production were already standard for most heavy industry. The simple, basic tools of scientific management and modern industrial engineering were so widely infused into the culture of heavy manufacturing by 1910 that they were impossible to miss.

By the turn of the twentieth century, Taylor had made his indelible mark on modern industrial culture. At that same point, Ford would begin making his. The baton would invisibly pass as the new century came onto the stage of history. If Ford's methods had any influence on Taylor, it was brief and came too late to make a difference for Taylor. Ford's first moving assembly line, a triumph of engineering efficiency designed for the production of spark-generating magnetos, was implemented in 1913. Taylor was dead two years later. He never had an opportunity to observe the extent to which the high principles and exacting practices of his scientific management movement would be corrupted by the pragmatic mind of a Henry Ford. Ford's edge over Taylor was one of longevity as much as of engineering ingenuity. He survived thirty-two years beyond Taylor's passing.

THE SHAPING OF HENRY FORD'S CHARACTER

Henry Ford was born in Dearborn, Michigan, a bucolic farming community east of Detroit. Tradition has it that in his twelfth year he encountered a wagon-mounted steam engine employed to power farm machinery. Such engines were by no means uncommon, but this one exhibited a unique design feature. Most such devices were hauled by horses, but this one had a chain that was used to drive the rear wheels of the wagon. On arrival at the workplace, the chain was replaced with a belt used to power farm machinery. Here, indeed, was a primitive "auto-mobile" in the most literal sense of that term. Henry was more than a usually impressionable farm boy in his twelfth year. His mother had only just recently died and he was open to the special drama of such an event. In later years, he would recount this experience with a self-driven steam engine as an encounter with his life's destiny.

Ford apprenticed at Flower Brothers' Machine Shop in Detroit, then returned for more than a decade to farming as his occupation. Later he obtained employment with the Detroit Edison Company as a maintenance mechanic. His first car, the quadricycle, built while still an employee of Detroit Edison, was little more than two bicycles harnessed as a team powered by a simple gasoline engine taken from a magazine plan. It was lightweight and capable of speeds up to 20 miles per hour, but it was not very sturdy and steered badly. For a beginning, though, it was auspicious.

Automobiles were the technical rage during the last decade of the nineteenth century. The development of automobiles between 1890 and 1910 was the technological parallel of the development of personal computers between 1975 and 1985. The first passenger auto was built by the German engineers, Daimler and Benz, in 1886; then the Duryea Brothers entered with their U.S. design in 1893. The first U.S. car race was run on Thanksgiving Day 1895 with the winner posting a speed of 6.66 miles per hour. In five years, that top speed would rise by a factor of ten.

With the quadricycle experience behind him, Ford designed his next generation car, learning from the lessons of the first. Prospective backers challenged him to demonstrate a sixty-mile test run on rural roads as a condition for taking the enterprise seriously. The trial run was a success, and the Detroit Automobile Company, capitalized at a hefty $150,000, was born sometime late in 1899. Early demonstrations for the benefit of reporters yielded poetic rapture for this new technology in the pages of their newspapers. But success for Ford was yet some distance off. He was still a tinkerer. He could build one automobile, but not a batch of them. Production was organized in one-at-a-time machine shop fashion with no plans, no formal designs, nothing but an idea in Ford's head. He did not know how to get from design to quantity production. He spent less and less time in the shop. With little more than a year behind their venture, backers dissolved the company. Henry blamed the greed of his backers for the failure, grousing a little for good measure about his own lack of authority to realize his ideas. Clearly, though, Henry was not yet ready to produce cars. The most celebrated production manager of the twentieth century had struck out ignominiously on his first try at bat.

Ford did not lose his luster altogether with his backers. They had lost money, but that is part of the start-up game. He could still find money to build *a* car, especially if it was a racing car. Henry prepared to race in October 1901 against the proven machine of a Cleveland manufacturer, Alexander Winton. Winton was the favorite and, when a third competitor dropped out with mechanical problems at the starting line, it looked like a shoo-in for Winton against the untried Henry Ford entry.

Before a crowd of nearly 8,000 spectators at the Grosse Pointe course, the duel began. Ford's inexperience on the turns cost him in the first six laps, but he learned as he went—a quality that was already a Ford trademark and would carry him upward more than any other. On the seventh lap, he passed Winton, then pulled ahead as Winton's vehicle developed engine problems. The local entry began to look like a winner; the crowd went wild. Ford was demonstrating that he could compete with the best and win on his machine's performance reliability. It was a smashing triumph. Within five weeks, the Henry Ford Company was born, capitalized at $60,000, which included a $10,000 equity valuation on Ford's designs and know-how. But within only four months, his backers, disillusioned by lack of progress with production, sacked him again.

Ford quickly found backing for his next race car, the "999," named for a famous express train of the era. Alexander Winton was due back in Detroit for a rematch and Ford was ready. This time, though, he sought for an experienced cycle racer, Barney Oldfield, to pilot the massive open power-plant that propelled the 999. Oldfield carried the day for Ford, and the Ford machine was again supreme. But Henry, it would seem, could not maintain a business relationship with any backer; he sold the racer design to his partner and went off on his own again, complaining of "sneaky tricks" that had been played on him by his latest associate.

Ford's persistence was not to be denied. In the summer of 1902, he formed a perilously undercapitalized partnership with a new backer, Alex Y. Malcomson, under the name of Ford & Malcomson Ltd. Still a partnership, the firm would subsequently become the Ford Motor Company under Articles of Association to facilitate attraction of additional capital. With two attempts at founding his own corporation, a failed partnership behind him, and less than three years' experience at company-building under his belt, Henry Ford was about to make his first real beginning on the spectacular motor car manufacturing company that was to be.

BEGINNINGS OF THE FORD MOTOR COMPANY

Ford's first design for the company that was to become his own was dubbed Model A, not to be confused with the later, 1928 auto of the same designation. Ford contributed a reliable new two-cylinder engine design and the mechanical prototype to the firm. Malcomson's role was to find financial backing—not an easy task with Ford's track record. Malcomson's most significant endowment to the new business was a no-nonsense bookkeeper, James Couzens, who brought the basic business discipline to the firm that Ford had heretofore lacked. When, later, push ultimately came to shove between Malcomson and Ford and Malcomson attempted to take on an active management role in the new company, the very backers whom Malcomson had successfully recruited would stick with the productive partnership of Ford—the engineer and his bookkeeper—as the indispensable team for continued success. In the political and financial maneuvering that followed, Ford gained majority control over the company, accumulating 58.5% of its stock. He at last owned his own successful auto manufacturing company. It was his show, and he would soon make that clear to everyone. No one would ever again tell Ford how to make cars.

Once secure in his control of the Ford Motor Company, Ford was free to enact his personal values and character in the structural design of his cars and his company. From here on, it is all pure Ford—successful, dominant, dogmatic entrepreneur Henry Ford. Certainly, he had learned some valuable lessons in his progress through companies he could not dominate. As early as 1903 he is quoted as having observed that "the way to make automobiles is to make one automobile like another automobile . . . just as one pin is like another pin when it comes from a pin factory." From the success of his first Model A and the nagging of Couzens, Ford extracted the first principle of efficiency in simple mass commodity production: uniformity.

Ford's description of pins from a pin factory is most likely a reference to Adam Smith's classic illustration of efficiency of production in the manufacture of pins, taken from his 1776 economic treatise on "The Wealth of Nations." The specific quotation that caught Ford's attention is probably the segment of Smith's work reproduced here as Exhibit 1–2. Smith's point was that narrow specialization of labor's functions is the source of maximum efficient output. It was a principle that Henry would soon put into practice. If Taylor shut out the worker as craftsperson by seeking maximum output with scientific management's rigorous work standards, Ford was about to usher in the age of worker as robot, programmed to serve the newly invented high-performance moving assembly line.

Auto production was still a one-at-a-time proposition in 1905 when Ford took control of his fledgling company, and would remain so for almost another eight years. Standardization of parts was improving but cars were put together individually by crews that frequently modified

Exhibit 1-2
From Adam Smith's *The Wealth of Nations*

To take an example, therefore, from a very trifling manufacture; but one in which the division of labour has been very often taken notice of, the trade of the pin-maker; a workman not educated to this business (which the division of labour has rendered a distinct trade), nor acquainted with the use of the machinery employed to it (to the invention of which the same division of labour has probably given occasion), could scarce, perhaps, with his utmost industry, make one pin in a day, and certainly could not make twenty. But in the way in which this business is now carried on, not only the whole work is a peculiar trade, but it is divided into a number of branches, of which the greater part are likewise peculiar trades. One man draws out the wire, another straights it, a third cuts it, a fourth points it, a fifth grinds it at the top for receiving the head; to make the head requires two or three distinct operations; to put it on, is a peculiar business, to whiten the pins is another; it is even a trade by itself to put them into the paper; and the important business of making a pin is, in this manner, divided into about eighteen distinct operations, which, in some manufactories, are all performed by distinct hands, though in others, the same man will sometimes perform two or three of them. I have seen a small manufactory of this kind where ten men only were employed, and where some of them consequently performed two or three distinct operations. But though they were very poor, and therefore but indifferently accommodated with the necessary machinery, they could, when they exerted themselves, make among them about twelve pounds of pins in a day. There are in a pound upwards of four thousand pins of middling size. Those ten persons, therefore, could make among them upwards of forty-eight thousand pins in a day. Each person, therefore, making a tenth part of forty-eight thousand pins, might be considered as making four thousand eight hundred pins in a day. But if they had all wrought separately and independently, and without any of them having been educated to this peculiar business, they certainly could not each of them have made twenty, perhaps not one pin in a day; that is, certainly not the two hundred and fortieth, perhaps not the four thousand eight hundredth part of what they are at present capable of performing, in consequence of a proper division and combination of their different operations.

pieces and forced their fit as needed. Some workers chased parts, others assembled them onto the chassis at various points around the car. The chassis itself sat in the center of the floor, surrounded by parts and workers. An element of the old craft shop still pervaded auto manufacture in the earliest decade of the century. The design of a new model itself was almost entirely a craft-styled effort. Parts were designed and machined as the design emerged. The model for a design was, after 1905, usually executed in wood by a pattern shop. Auto designs changed frequently, a pattern that would soon become standard in the industry, but one that was still at this early stage of the industry driven by the innovative engineering design spirit exemplified in Henry Ford.

Design changes were also driven in part by the need to test the market for its best sales opportunities. Ford tested his notion of a popular, low priced market by mass producing the Model N. It was a smashing sales and financial success that yielded the first million-dollar annual profit to the Ford company in 1907. Discovery of a new vanadium alloy steel, the dream of a mass market and Ford's native populism combined to push design experimentation forward.

In 1907, riding the crest of sales success, Ford assembled a team of designers, walled off a room in a corner of the factory and began to design what was to become the Model T. It was an auto that was to be full of dramatic innovations. High-tensile-strength vanadium steel, developed at Ford's initiative and expense, gave the new design its lightweight strength in body, chassis and mechanical parts. A single cast engine block with the top sliced off made for an improved, lower cost engine. The "planetary" transmission, a magneto to replace the dry battery that supplied an engine spark, and a simplicity of design that invited maintenance by the most casual of amateur mechanical talent were all pioneered in designing the Model T. It was to be lightweight, serviceable and low cost, though initially not as cheap as later assembly-line methods would make it.

Announcements of the Model T were first sent to dealers in the spring of 1908. Fearing that announcement of such dramatic breakthroughs as the Model T represented would immediately kill sales of cars in stock, most suppressed the news. When the product appeared in the fall of 1908, customer response was extraordinary. In less than four months, hard cash orders were received, which filled existing plant production capacity of 10,000 cars through the following summer. Subsequent orders had to be returned to disappointed customers.

The Model T was a major breakthrough in technology and performance reliability. It was a high-quality, utility vehicle that was suited to rutted, unpaved farm roads of the time. Its planetary gear permitted the driver to rock the vehicle out of a deep rut merely by alternating depression of the reverse and forward pedals. By jacking up one rear axle and attaching a power belt, the Model T was converted into a power source for every kind of belt-powered machinery, common in that time. Farmers and laborers could drive to the work site, jack up a wheel, attach the drive belt and operate machinery used in their work, then reconvert the Model T to an automobile ready for the drive home. In technologically elegant form, it was the reincarnation of that self-propelled steam engine Ford had encountered as a twelve-year-old boy, now reborn as Henry Ford's marvelous internal-combustion-powered machine. Customer excitement was well-founded. Once introduced to the motoring public, the Model T would dominate the automotive market for nearly two decades.

Ford's problem now was to exploit the success of his creation. Had any rational business planner projected the future sales of the Model T against such an auspicious beginning, he would certainly have concluded that it would become impossible to satisfy the emerging demand without exceeding the available labor supply, overreaching the capability of production tools and falling short of enough plant capacity ever to catch up with it. Ford's capacity to learn in the heat of heavy competition was prodigious. The competition now was with rising demand—the best kind—and he would apply himself to the challenge with great insight and energy.

From 1908 to 1913 the Model T's sales surged ahead, followed closely by equivalent rises in the manpower employed to assemble the cars. In some years, both sales and plant employment doubled. Ford and his staff searched the land for advanced machine tools that would increase productivity. Labor was scarce, machines were plentiful. Anything that offered an advance in efficiency was immediately purchased, irrespective of the value of machinery it displaced. Couzens, meantime, caught the wave of Taylorism spreading through industry, and focused on stopwatch measured work standards. The notion of the pin factory with its vast efficiencies in narrowly specialized labor probably recurred for Ford periodically until, sometime in 1913, he was ready to experiment with work specialization on a small scale.

Continuous process production lines were not original to Ford, but they were rare, and, certainly, nothing on the scale of Model T assembly had ever previously been attempted. The site of the first test was the magneto assembly department. Until now, each worker, surrounded by all the parts needed, built a complete magneto. The operation was composed of twenty-nine distinct elements, which required some logical sequencing even when accomplished by a single operator. Specialization of work functions in the style of Adam Smith's pin factory implied a flow sequence of operations from start to finish, which called for movement of materials and the partially finished magnetos through a logical series of workstations. The seed of a moving assembly line was inherent in the idea of work specialization from its beginning even though never articulated as a necessary support of the idea. The impelling concept was specialization of tasks to improve labor productivity. Continuous flow based on sequence precedence followed almost automatically.

Initially, the engine flywheels on which magnetos were installed were slid along a shelf in front of workmen. Each workman manned an assembly station responsible for one or two of the twenty-nine required operations. Component bins for each station rested below the shelf. Crude as it was, an immediate improvement in assembly time was obtained. From fifteen minutes' completion time for a single worker handling all steps before the change in method, per magneto production time dropped a little over 12% to thirteen minutes, ten seconds. With further refinements in the flow system, which included a motor-driven conveyer belt, time eventually fell to five minutes—a 67% reduction. The work formerly done by three employees could now be done by one. There was a clear savings in labor cost and in labor utilization. The two surplus men could be assigned elsewhere, easing the requirement to recruit added labor as production expanded. Narrow specialization of task functions allowed replacements for lost or promoted workers to be trained faster and less expensively. The price of the vehicle could be reduced and the profit made on it could increase. It was an impelling idea whose time had clearly come. Economies of mass scale from continuous, uniform, scientifically engineered work flow were on the threshold of taking the industrial world by storm.

The idea quickly spread through the plant. Couzens' production records calculated the average time for assembly of a completed car from component parts at twelve and a half hours. A crude assembly line was implemented on which each chassis was pulled by winch and rope down the floor while operations, logically sequenced and serviced by parts close to their expected point of use, were carried out by specialist workmen at stations along the way. Again, an improvement in time standards for output was immediately apparent. Time plummeted from the previous twelve and a half hours' labor time per car to just under six hours—a more than 50% saving. One man was now doing the work formerly done by two in assembling Ford's spectacularly popular Model T. As implementation of the assembly-line method spread through the Ford plant from 1913 to 1914, output of cars doubled while the size of the workforce fell by 10%. With efficiencies and cost savings like that available, the sky was the limit. Ford's imagination would certainly be equal to the opportunity.

ORGANIZATIONAL INNOVATION AT FORD

But the labor shortages that had always plagued Detroit and the farming frontier were becoming too severe for even efficiencies like these to overcome. And, although task specialization on the moving assembly line both improved manpower utilization and reduced labor skill level and training cost dramatically, from the first it offered fragmented, uninteresting, unchallenging, mind numbing, machine-paced work to workers who were accustomed to the easier pace of varied tasks. Turnover was high. Not that it wasn't already high among assembly crews as a result of the explosive expansion of production. But the crews could at least allocate available skill to the tasks at hand and use spare time for informal training of newcomers. Labor turnover on the new moving assembly line could easily become so high that production flow could never stabilize and poor quality would perennially be a serious problem. The grand success of the Model T and moving assembly processes created new problems in recruiting and holding experienced, competent production labor, relatively unspecialized though it might be.

Ford's solution was to buy a stable manpower force with the promise of high wages. Simultaneously, he cut the work day from nine to eight hours at the new, higher day's wage. Reducing work hours was a sound measure that was ahead of its time. Supported by the theory and principles of Taylor's scientific management relating to fatigue, cutting work hours was probably accompanied by the expectation of a full day's production from each worker in eight hours. With production efficiencies rising as rapidly as they were in 1914, it was a fair redistribution of some of the gains to labor even if output did fall slightly for a shift's work. The principal reason for the eight-hour day, though, was increased use of the available plant capacity. An eight-hour day permitted scheduling of three shifts a day, thereby permitting round-the-clock production.

As radical and dramatic as the new wage and hour package was, the wage part was a bit of a swindle as well. Ford grandly announced that the implementation of a $5.00, eight-hour workday applied to the lowest level worker. The press was initially overwhelmed at his magnanimity. Such humane generosity toward the average workingman was unprecedented. It almost sounded too good to be true. And in a number of respects, it was. Ford's base wage, formerly paid for a nine-hour day, remained at $2.34. The $5.00 rate was arrived at by supplementing the base with a $2.66 bonus. But a long list of conditions limited those who could share in Ford's largesse. For starters there was a six-month service minimum to qualify. In addition, no one under age 22 could draw the bonus unless they supported a widowed mother or other next kin. Female employees were excluded. Workers meriting the bonus were required to lead a clean and sober life subject to inspection and enforcement by a company "sociological department."

The impact on job seekers in those economically depressed times, though, was awesome. From 10,000 to 15,000 job seekers came to Ford's employment office gate on any given day in succeeding weeks, many from substantial distances, drawn by the notoriety of Ford's pay scheme. Desperate, hopeful, they milled about, fighting with one another and trading rumors. The company needed several thousand workers to man its new third shift, but this crowd was overwhelming. In the icy cold of midwinter, the crowd grew angry and surly. Ultimately, it charged the gate, only to be turned back with fire hoses. Responsible businessmen and news editors throughout the United States, astonished and frightened by the expectations that such an announcement could raise among working people, had predicted unrest and chastened Ford for his foolishness. Ford was unfazed. Demand for the Model T and rising plant efficiency were so great that he could afford to pay several times $5.00 an hour and still thumb his nose at the entire world. Unrepentant, he was content to go on tinkering with the desperate hopes and abject fears of a faceless work force of human robots to find the motivating forces that improve the working of his marvelous high performance production machine.

The industrial legacy of Henry Ford endured through the better part of the twentieth century, largely unchallenged until the Japanese discovered the flaws of his production methods. General Motors, Chrysler, Studebaker, Nash, and a dozen other market followers mimicked his lead slavishly. They, along with most other mass production operations in the world, faithfully applied the lessons of narrow worker specialization, tight, scientifically measured work standards, technical and financial domination of organizational decision making at all levels, very large-scale continuous production supported by a complex moving assembly line, and high pay to keep an army of industrial robots working consistently at their tasks until the blessed release of death or retirement. The partnership of Henry Ford and James Couzens still shapes the fundamental functional power balance of many industrial organizations. The efficiencies of the moving assembly line undergird the productive power of virtually every commodity-producing factory. Modern, efficiency-minded managers still seek quiet, pliable, cooperative workers who will carry out orders unquestioningly, accepting high pay to forget they are thinking, feeling humans while they satisfy their life's dreams through purchase of efficiently produced commodity products and services. But the age of high-volume, engineered-flow, assembly-line output has passed. Engineered assembly process is now more often an impediment to high performance than at its cutting edge.

SUCCESSFUL EXAMPLES OF SCIENTIFIC MANAGEMENT IN APPLICATION

It would be incorrect, though, to suggest that scientific management has failed or been discredited as a viable path to high performance management systems. Taylor's principles as originally articulated are potentially as powerful today as they were almost one hundred years ago. The error in his approach appears to lie mostly in overemphasis on technical and engineering expertise in designing systems or setting standards. When corrupted by Ford's excessive emphasis on narrow worker specialization, it is an error that killed the craftsperson's initiative and barred his experienced contribution to creation of a high performance system.

Two present-day companies exemplify the effectiveness of scientific management as a foundation for exceptionally high performance by scrupulously avoiding these flaws. They are the Lincoln Electric Company in Cleveland, Ohio, and Nucor Steel of Charlotte, North Carolina. Both companies are standouts in their industries. Lincoln Electric dominates the market in arc-welding equipment, enjoying a reputation as the highest quality producer that consistently underprices its competition (Lincoln, 1961). Nucor is a highly profitable producer of steel from scrap metal, using minimill technology to prosper in an industry where large, integrated steel producers like USX (formerly U.S. Steel), LTV, Inland, Armco, Wheeling and Bethlehem have consistently lost money (Kirtland, 1981; Isenberg-O'Loughlin & Inmace, 1986).

Both Lincoln Electric and Nucor Steel appear to have successfully demonstrated Taylor's claim that the best management strives for low labor cost and pays high wages to its work force. Cost structures in each case lead the respective industry. Lincoln Electric outstrips all its competitors in cost and price, while Nucor's cost structure per ton of output in 1985 came in behind only a single Japanese producer, Tokyo Steel, averaging 981 tons per employee in the new and competitively brutal worldwide competition in steel. Wages at Lincoln Electric and Nucor are 80% to 100% above the average day rate for similar work in their industries. They are stunning examples of scientific management in application.

How do they do it? The patterns of management followed by Lincoln Electric and Nucor Steel display a number of commonalities, most of which are straight out of Taylor's book. Work is exactly measured and standards are carefully set for work output. Development of a science for each task is fundamental in these companies. It is common, nonetheless, for standards thought by management to be near absolute maximum to be substantially surpassed. More importantly, it is not an industrial engineer or planning department that typically discovers how to gain this greater efficiency. It is the worker or the supervisor on the shop floor who finds a better way to do the job and thereby smashes old records for output. Both companies have discovered how to use training and development of their workers to reestablish the worker in his or her role as craftsperson.

Staff support in these two companies is exceedingly lean. Staff experts do not establish and enforce methods as Taylor had envisioned they should. Rather, they are consultants and trainers to the shop floor staff, assisting in problem solutions and counseling those who make them, rather than assuming ultimate responsibility for those solutions.

Management control in both these companies is exact. At Lincoln Electric, every piece, every product is on record for who performed the work. Failure of their equipment in operation can be traced back directly and precisely to the worker responsible. There is no place to hide when it comes to keeping quality high.

Lincoln Electric and Nucor Steel both use a mix of piecework and profit-sharing bonuses as pay incentives to high work output. The technologies of their industries, however, tend to be stable. There is only limited improvement in production technology, which could profitably be introduced as major new capital investment. Output is more often increased through improved methods applied to existing plant and equipment. Most improved methods are developed on the floor. Where capital investment is needed and defensible, it is more often major and dramatic, making obvious the need to revise existing piecework rates and standards.

Changes in rates and standards are seldom viewed by workers in these companies as an attempt to take away their earnings. Long-standing trust characterizes management/employee relationships. Full financial information is shared with workers concerning prices and costs so that workers can assist in the revision of rates when appropriate. Rate changes are rarely undertaken, and only when absolutely necessary. Bonus systems are openly and fairly administered, with bosses and executives sharing scalebacks in bonus earnings along with workers during tough economic times. Status differentials between managers and workers are minimal and responsibility is pushed as far down into the company as possible. Top management, while it is technically knowledgeable of the respective business and industry in great depth, intervenes in operating decisions only when its level of discomfort with current results is high. There are no company planes, no private dining rooms, no lavish perks for top management. Ken Iverson, CEO of Nucor since 1965, is legendary for his frugality on business trips. He flies coach, takes a bus or subway in preference to a limousine, eats in diners. The management offices of Lincoln Electric are described as spartan and functional. There are no high-priced art collections or half-inch-thick pile rugs here. The general managers of both companies are wealthy people, largely because they, too, enjoy hefty bonuses and stock ownership opportunities suited to their level and paid for with exceptionally high plant productivity. But their base pay is modest, less than ten times that of the average worker.

Workers are carefully interviewed and selected for open positions at Lincoln Electric and Nucor Steel to assure the best fit to their high performance systems. Many candidates attracted to the prospect of exceptionally high wages fail to appreciate how high and difficult the standards of these companies truly are. Turnover among new employees is high, as many of those attracted solely by the prospect of high earnings discover that they don't fit into these high-output cultures. Those poorly fitted by temperament to rigorously high work standards drop out or are forced out quickly in their probationary term.

One might be tempted to call the management styles of these companies "participative" to categorize them with the management style so widely advocated in the 1950s and 1960s by academics and management theorists. Standards, though, are set high and strictly enforced by management in every corner of these organizations. Top management is firmly and totally in control. It abdicates no major decisions downward. Consensus decision making is limited to the give-and-take problem solving required between operating functions and supporting technicians. At Lincoln Electric, supervisors rate workers' performance through a system that establishes participation in the profit-sharing bonus pool. Workers may discuss these ratings with their supervisors, but the boss' judgment and rating is absolutely final. There is no toleration of griping or complaint over the final decision. Nucor gives full responsibility for success of the operation to its local plant managers, then backs them up completely. It would be more suitable, given these circumstances, to classify management style as benevolently autocratic. It would probably be most accurate, though, to say that classifications like participative and autocratic don't help much in describing high- or low-quality management in these settings. The closest either gets to active worker participation in policy setting is the practice of assuring that every worker complaint and concern is intensively investigated by a member of top management, usually the COO. Bosses are firm, fair and dedicated, humane but tough. Anyone not willing to live by the same standards had best look for the nearest door.

Tasks and output goals at Lincoln Electric and Nucor Steel are pitched at a high level of challenge and clearly communicated. Performance feedback is clear and frequent. Worker wages are tied to output in at least two ways, one an individual incentive, another a group incentive. These systems fit Taylor's prescriptions for effective management and high output closely. The major departures are in the restoration of worker responsibility for work improvement—a return to worker as responsible craftsperson—accompanied by a corresponding diminishment of the technical expert's role as final decision maker.

The major limitation on this form of high performance system appears to be a natural limitation in the availability of workers suited by temperament and preference to its requirements. Indeed, the work culture created to support these high performance systems seems to force out those unfitted to its demands. This would appear to put a severe upper limit on the expansion potential of high performance systems founded on the principles of scientific management. These two high performance companies, though, stand as useful benchmarks against which to test high performance management principles and compare emerging alternative high performance systems. They will be used liberally here to that purpose.

Chapter Two

Democracy, Unions and the Dignity of Labor

For all its high performance efficiency and wealth-generating capacity, scientific management generated considerable popular backlash. The craftsperson in colonial America was an independent property holder who participated as an equal in the affairs of his or her community. A strong sense of participative equity conferred personal satisfaction with the prevailing division of economic return. The consolidation of industry in major centers through the factory system represented economic progress at the expense of personal social regress. Not the least of the employed craftsperson's discomfort stemmed from loss of the vote franchise as an unpropertied laborer. At its inception, American democracy in the eighteenth century was reserved to white, male freeholders. The industrial revolution undercut the universal democracy of colonial cottage industry. Retention of America's democratic spirit demanded a shift onto the new and revolutionary base of popular democracy. Popular democracy, in turn, became the indispensable foundation of an organized labor movement. The transition to popular democracy spanned the century from 1760 to 1860 (Williamson, 1960). The labor movement grew in approximate parallel over a somewhat longer course of time, culminating with congressional recognition of labor rights in the National Labor Relations Act of 1935.

INDUSTRIAL CONSOLIDATION AND THE LABOR MOVEMENT

The American labor movement appeared just before the turn of the nineteenth century in a few concentrated, high-skilled industries. The crafts of shoemakers and printers first sought to negotiate wages and control conditions of work through unions. The skilled laborer, now employee instead of autonomous craftsperson, lacked face-to-face contact with customers and was dependent on the master's or owner's capital intensive tools to ply his or her trade. The craftsperson supplied only energy and skill. The master/owner centralized financial functions, collecting a price for the product through an agent, purchasing and maintaining production equipment, acquiring and paying for raw materials, then dividing the residual between labor and return on capital.

Historically this was a wholly new pattern of cash flow dominated at the center by the nouveau industrialist/owner. Pressure on ownership to stay competitive by reinvesting earnings in new product ideas, plant and equipment would inevitably create competition between labor's wage rate and the demand for fresh capital. It is a financial structure that naturally engenders distrust and discontent among laborers, especially as the base of wealth expands and owners adopt themselves to the life-style and powers of kings and potentates. The aspirations of labor and capital needs of newly sovereign owners inevitably collided within this novel system.

In the old world of Europe, Karl Marx would raise this competition to the status of class warfare and articulate an economic philosophy that would bloom into international communism. In America, too, there was no lack of class conflict and accompanying labor warfare. The advance of labor's rights in the United States was regularly accompanied by open warfare, often joined by the federal militia, though usually on the side of ownership. Open, predatory competition among owners for shares in growing, dynamic markets was easily financed through restraint on wages. Owners developed private armies and personal espionage systems to fight organized labor. Labor unions bloomed and faded through the nineteenth century in virtually all United States industries, expanding their power during economic booms, watching it recede in times of economic adversity. The labor movement was shaped by the explosive growth of an economy fueled by market growth and technological advance. Labor—deprived of the opportunity to haggle price with the customer, unable to afford the costly new machines of production required by mass-commodity output, powerless to influence the often-rapacious competition between owner competitors—had little option but to bond together in common purpose. Solidarity, cohesiveness and striving for personal dignity were its principal resources and weapons. In two hundred years, little about this scenario has changed.

The devices employed by labor unions to achieve their purposes are little different from those used by any peoples oppressed by force and intimidation. They begin with restriction of effort, sometimes essential to avoid self-injury occasioned by high stress or severe fatigue under forced labor. Clandestine communication to establish mutual defenses follows. Passive resistance dissembled as ignorance or weakness is invoked to frustrate power. As success in defense increases, a threshold is reached where a decision must be made to survive with the devices available or go on the offensive. It is the moment of choice: risk freedom or accept the status quo. Freedom gained by the worker means loss of control and diminished power for the privileged owner. The worker must be ready to fight for freedom if dignity is to be gained. The contest for liberty must be joined.

THE RISE OF ORGANIZED LABOR

The earliest labor unions were primarily concerned with essentially the same issues that concern labor unions today—setting minimum wage standards, limiting hours of work, minimizing competition from immigrant labor and the unapprenticed, allocating work opportunity fairly to all members of the union, establishing seniority rights in reassignment, and improving health or safety on the job were concerns from the outset.

Those early unions were formed around craft skills in newly consolidated industry. Their members could no longer compete as individual artisans against the forces of organized production and commerce in the ever-broadening markets of the age. Organization of unskilled and semi-skilled workers came later, built on the model of union action established by craft unions. Craft unions were established on a preexisting base of common work knowledge and interest that permitted communication needed to recognize a common enemy and create solidarity of purpose. Owner arrogance and power were often evidence enough of the need for collective action. The earliest strike on record, then called a "turnout," was called by the Philadelphia shoemakers in 1799 to resist an attempt by employers to reduce wages. It was followed by criminal legal action against the union for "conspiracy to raise wages," then considered under law to constitute illegal restraint of free trade.

Early unions were likely to be ad hoc associations formed to deal with common concerns, take appropriate action, then dissolve into dormancy. Lacking any formal organization, Philadelphia printers pledged in 1786 to support financially any journeyman printer forced out of work for refusal to accept a wage cut. These were defensive measures designed to prevent loss of wage status. As the labor movement grew, it adopted increasingly more offensive tactics designed to restore worker dignity lost to employer domination.

Though wage cuts will almost certainly guarantee a defensive response from workers, it is not wages alone that explain the militance of organized labor. With the advantages of labor specialization and large-scale capital investment to support them, their wages as workers were no worse than as craftspeople. The greater gall, perhaps, was limitation on personal autonomy from the controls instituted by owners, but that was only little worse than direct dealings with finicky customers. Ultimately it was that sense of progress accompanying technological change, reinforced by the obvious increases in power and wealth enjoyed by owners, offset by craftspersons' own losses in relative status, that fired aspirations and demanded restoration of labor's dignity. Labor could not hold its head in pride unless it effectively joined the competition to participate in the fruits of economic progress and political liberty.

The emergence of scientific management in the late nineteenth century was viewed by organized labor as just another indignity visited on its constituency by greedy owners. The limited control over one's workplace, the heretofore unchallenged right of labor to set its own pace of output to fit its calculus of wage equity, the retention of those limited shreds of a craftsperson's dignity that were previously enjoyed—all these were subject to loss before the onslaught of scientific management's emphasis on engineered efficiency. Labor paid little heed to the increased wealth and wage potential offered by these powerful new methods. There was little or no inclination for workers to trust the grand promises of management in any event. They had been broken before and could be again. Even so, the greatly increased size of economic pie offered by the high performance potential of scientific management methods promised new potential for wage increases, even if sometimes disproportionate to output increases. Had laborers not perceived loss of self-determination and dignity in the imposition of these new devices, the potential for personal gain might have won their adherence to them. Instead, organized labor brought to bear its considerable political clout and successfully put Taylor and his methods on trial before the U.S. Congress in 1911.

As political democracy and the factory system of production are the foundations of the labor movement, so also do distrust of owners fanned by inequity of labor's status in the factory system and the sense of labor's dignity lost become the causes of labor resistance to management implementation of high performance systems. They must be recognized as major barriers to easy, willing acceptance of methods designed to raise output and quality. Despite their indispensability to labor's significant wage progress in the twentieth century, scientific management and the moving, lock-step assembly line were, and are today still, contemptible evils to organized labor. Without struggle to resist their imposition, labor could not maintain and rebuild its sense of dignity.

Indeed, without struggle, there is little value in any prize. The American labor movement, suitably protected by its own hard-won legislative magna cartas that now make the fight a reasonably fair one, has evolved around a set of institutions designed to contain the most vigorous conflict between labor and management without the necessity for or justification of resort to arms and violence. There is often still good reason for distrust between labor and management. There is no less emphasis now on the need to preserve earnings as a source of fresh capital than there was two centuries ago. To preserve equity in the division of the residual there must be a continuing test and revision of the line dividing labor's and capital's reward. The rights and privileges of managers, no less than those of kings before them, have been curtailed and restrained by new custom and law, but the aspirations of labor can never be fully satisfied without the opportunity to test the system.

The struggle goes on. The battle for dignity, indeed, never ends. New generations and self-renewals continually bring new contestants to its arena. Plato's antidemocratic prescription that justice must be found in knowing one's place in a stable social order is no more viable in the twentieth century than the absolute powers of his philosopher kings. Struggle must be entertained and contained in any free, competitive economy if it is to retain its vigor. Devices through which to manage that struggle are the legacy of the American labor movement. The struggle itself is unavoidable. It is inherent in the consolidation of productive capital and the isolation of labor from the markets it serves. The genius of the system is in its successful containment of the struggle. The fruits of scientific management must frequently be earned by management through its own outstanding performance as labor negotiators.

NEGOTIATION: THE TEST OF EQUITY

Humans whose interests are in irreconcilable conflict cannot and will not accept a compromise of those interests until they exhaust their energies in the pursuit of equity. When parties come at one another from distrust they cannot find satisfaction in a contest that leaves an opponent fresh and unbowed. Anything less than reciprocal exhaustion of energy and resources leaves the matter unsettled, unstable and waiting to erupt all over again. Marathon bargaining sessions between labor and management against a firm strike deadline are indispensable as much for the extended and intensive communication opportunity they offer as for demonstration on both sides of willingness to put "everything" they have into the effort to achieve a settlement. When top management removes itself to a distant, expensively plush resort, or spends its weekends on the golf course while the chief negotiator politely but formally fends off the union's demands, it is not surprising to hear union officers angrily denounce management as lacking seriousness about achieving a fair settlement. Energy and commitment held back in the negotiative exchange is representative of agreements and benefits that labor fears are also held back.

With distrust as the foundation of the exchange, the available options are limited to all-out struggle or permanent disengagement. Wives who distrust their husbands must either struggle painfully to reach genuine reconciliation or enter into divorce without looking back. Workers who distrust their employers must establish workable agreements as to wages and working conditions or find new work elsewhere. Anything less is demeaning of self-respect. Accepting lies and dishonesty in the relationship will only increase the frequency and blatancy of lies and dishonesty, further eroding self-respect. A high-risk middle ground is available in the form of all-out warfare to destroy the adversary. In all but the rarest circumstances, though, that is also the path of self-destruction. It is an irrational choice, even though it may offer a chance at retrieved self-respect. Mutual destruction in failure to disengage from a rotten relationship demonstrates with maximum drama the driving power of self-respect regained. It is no surprise, then, that much of the labor-management negotiation process is driven by the need to protect and rebuild self-respect on both sides. The capacity to endure grueling negotiation that achieves a mutually satisfying agreement is itself a major source of renewed self-respect.

BOULWAREISM: IS A FULL, FIRM, FAIR OFFER ENOUGH?

Avoidance of the struggle has been attempted and failed. The most widely publicized departure from nose-to-nose labor contract negotiations was the General Electric Company's experiment with Boulwareism. Named after Lemuel R. Boulware, a marketing executive assigned to resolve GE's chronic work stoppage problems, this approach attempted to bypass the exhaustion and confusion of give-and-take negotiations through putting forth a single "full, firm, fair offer." Historically, GE prided itself on being a "good employer." In the 1930s it sought to co-opt labor confrontation by politely and civilly inviting unions to organize its operations. Deprived of a common enemy in management, union factions fell to battling among themselves over ideological issues. Jurisdictional strikes between communist- and noncommunist-oriented leadership plagued the company. In 1946 the leftist-oriented United Electrical, Radio and Machine Workers of America (UE) sought to establish a more militant course in negotiations than its sister organizations. Out of this conflict, GE reevaluated its labor relations policies and came up with a "one, full, firm, fair offer" policy of negotiations. Lemuel R. Boulware was its architect.

Rather than talk with union representatives from the various GE unions about one issue at a time and face the frustration of reaching no common agreement with them, GE politely sat at the bargaining table through the normal term of negotiations, patiently listening to any and all arguments the unions chose to put forward. The company made no initial offer and no proposals for modification of any union positions.

From time to time technical reports were presented to the union by management's team of technicians, which had been busily engaged behind the scenes analyzing the prevailing cost of living, wage and benefit trends and contract provisions relevant to the industry to determine what would constitute a full, fair and equitable contract agreement for the coming contract term. These analyses served as the foundation for GE's eventual contract offer and reports to the union bargaining committee laid the groundwork for it. Several days before expiration of the old contract, the company would present its only full, firm, fair offer. For a day or two, company representatives would entertain union demands for change in the package. If new facts were presented that had a material bearing on the package, adjustments were made by the company. A few union notions were, indeed, accommodated as evidence of willingness to give and take in negotiations. Union representatives, of course, were outraged by such tactics and resolute in their determination to strike in the face of them. The company, they were convinced, was holding back. It had not put everything possible on the table.

On the morning a strike was to begin, GE would place gigantic display ads in local newspapers of its plant towns to communicate the provisions of its full, firm, fair offer directly to union members. "Come on in to work today" the ads urged. "There's no purpose in losing wages walking the picket line when this is what you'll end up with anyhow." Day by day, the ads would run, and day by day, the picket lines would dwindle. Three to four days were usually enough to break the strike. Angry, surly but chastened union leaders would then come back to the bargaining table and sign the contract designed by GE's bargaining technicians.

General Electric's unions, of course, filed charges of unfair labor practices against the company with the National Labor Relations Board, claiming that the company failed to bargain in good faith. A cadre of highly skilled labor lawyers on corporate staff, fully backed by a management pleased by the success of these tactics, rarely lost their case. A considerable body of new labor law, nearly all favorable to the management position, was created by GE lawyers in the Boulware years. But the contracts thus won, even though they may have been reasonably fair to workers, were galling to union officers and the labor movement generally. The long-term net effect was to force organized labor to get its own house in order. The many unions representing GE workers came together cooperatively with a Coordinated Bargaining Committee that could mount and maintain an effective companywide strike at GE. In the fall of 1969, it succeeded. Corporate negotiators, complacent from a long string of easy wins over the unions, prepared their full, firm, fair offer and blocked out the ads for local papers. The strike held for 104 days. Boulwareism was ended. Labor and company unions triumphantly regained lost self-respect. The cost in lost business and wages to company and union members was astronomical. Had management and their negotiators not ignored the centrality of self-respect to the negotiations process, it might have been otherwise.

If the parties to negotiations do not come out emotionally battered and bloodied, there is no real settlement. Of course, the best and only genuinely peaceful solution would be to rebuild trust before negotiations begin. Where trust truly prevails, however, negotiations are reduced to a simple exchange of communications. Formal negotiation is artificial and unnecessary. The parties need only look at the facts and accept the best, most rational division of rewards. Trust does not require a written contract. It demands only a simple, scrupulously honored understanding between parties. The need to negotiate signals the presence of distrust. A labor union with its own inevitable internal organizational conflicts and dissentions cannot survive the existence of trust between management and workers. Trust cannot exist without dignity and self-respect. The principal and perhaps only real product of a labor union assaulting the management bastion through labor negotiations is restored dignity and self-respect for its members. Negotiation is war. War is costly, risky and grueling. But war builds pride.

The stable state of modern industrial management is a relation of distrust between labor and management subjected to periodic test by tough, competent, warlike negotiations. It is a condition that permits some minimum benefit from the high performance potential of scientific management to be pursued. Clearly, though, major breakthroughs in future high performance systems must go beyond scientific management and the labor movement's historic and chronic resistance to it. Restoration of a relation of trust and a sense of the craftsman's dignity is indispensable to further advance in high performance management systems. Full restoration of trust and dignity, however, will either transform or kill the labor movement.

It is instructive that neither Lincoln Electric nor Nucor Steel is unionized. Trust is the stable state of these operations, not a fragile and transient thing as it typically is elsewhere. Division of the economic pie is open and equitable. Communications are full and honest. Laborers make operating decisions and solve operating problems with the dignity of craftspeople.

Attempts at creation of new high performance systems that fail to restore trust and dignity are probably doomed to failure. Much of the twentieth century has been devoted to naive efforts by academics and political liberals to discover the quick fix for lost trust and dignity. The many failures encountered in the attempts made assure that there is no easy way. High performance systems demand the extraordinary in their invention and implementation. The classic Hawthorne studies were an early, crude attempt to build worker good feeling as the foundation of increased work output. They are an early, largely inept effort to motivate high performance output among workers. They remain, nonetheless, a useful starting point for the subsequent tortuous and often bumbling research odyssey undertaken by social scientists in pursuit of the behavioral well-springs of high performance. We now turn to Hawthorne.

Chapter Three

The Hawthorne Studies

To many, the impasse between those inhumane devices of scientific management and uncivilized militancy of organized labor was entirely unnecessary. The simple solution, they suggested, required only that good feelings be restored among the disputants. In the 1920s and 1930s, academic and industry researchers set forth to demonstrate that proposition as the foundation of high performance output.

The Hawthorne studies began in 1924 with an inquiry by the National Science Academy and Western Electric's engineering staff into the effects of level of illumination on worker output. Inexplicably, output rose as a function of change in level of illumination, whether it went up or down. Subsequently, from 1927 to 1932, the renowned Hawthorne studies followed on the heels of the illumination experiments, overseen by a Harvard Business Administration School team headed by Elton Mayo and implemented by the Hawthorne division's in-house employee relations research staff. This research effort ostensibly sought to find an explanation for the results of the earlier illumination experiments.

From large volumes of correspondence and documentation, it is clear that interpretation of the Hawthorne studies was extensively influenced by the Harvard social scientists. Although the research was carried out by Western Electric staff members, the Harvard group had their own observers on the scene from time to time and extensive correspondence exists between Elton Mayo and Hawthorne plant management concerning the meaning and significance of the research findings. The question, perhaps, is: which came first, the conclusions or the research.

The onset of the great depression in 1929 that spawned the social revolutions of the New Deal under Franklin Roosevelt generated a social climate in which liberal and humane objectives could enjoy priority status. In this historical context, the world was waiting to hear the joyful message: *the happy worker is a productive worker.* In the early 1930s at Western Electric's Hawthorne plant, esteemed scientists from a world-class university hinted that research on real workers performing real production tasks in a world-class business was on the threshold of confirming the truth of that message. The gospel would go forth into all the land; a kind and considerate boss gets the best effort of his people. Be good to your workers, it pays. Congress could then generously move to enact labor legislation which assured that mistreated, unhappy workers could find remedy for their employment miseries in collective bargaining buttressed by the legal right to strike their employers. If bosses wanted to continue to be tough, organized labor could be equally tough. Law and society thereby assured that *an unhappy worker can be as unproductive as he or she chooses to be.* After all, it was now scientifically "established" that when they are unhappy, workers are unproductive anyhow.

More than half a century has passed, and productivity remains a concern of management. Labor conflict continues wherever bosses are not fair or considerate of worker's needs. Design of work tasks continues to be studied, systems of pay incentive continue to be controversial, and boredom on the job continues to be a problem. Job stress, formerly conceived more simply as fatigue, is a widespread concern. Productivity is still an illusive goal for managers everywhere. The gospel of labor humanism was widely and earnestly communicated. So what went wrong?

RESEARCH ON HUMAN RELATIONS IN INDUSTRY

Hawthorne was the Chicago arm of AT&T's Western Electric network of communications electronics manufacturing operations. Hawthorne plant management was, naturally enough, deeply interested in ways to increase worker productivity. The intention of the study at its outset was to examine the effects on work output obtained from redesigning the work task, reducing boredom and fatigue with rest pauses or shorter work hours, revising the incentive pay system and providing pleasant supervision to a selected group of female assembly employees. Within the first twelve months of worker behavior observation, the researchers were "unexpectedly" and suddenly seized by the impelling insight that social satisfaction arising out of human relations in the workplace accounted for the largest part of work behavior. After nearly two years of observation, investigators claimed an increase in output of approximately 30% and confidently identified the one factor of substantial importance in accounting for this change as provision of humane, caring supervision. Reports of this finding immediately began to appear in the management and then the popular literature. The great human relations revolution in management was born.

The definitive report on the Hawthorne experience was seven years in the making and did not come until 1939 with publication of *Management and the Worker*, written by Harvard professor Fritz Roethlisberger and Hawthorne chief of Employee Relations Research, William Dickson. By that time, the ideology of the worker's right to humane treatment was firmly established as mainstream social, political and management doctrine. A limited few reviewers looked at the extensive detail supplied by Roethlisberger and Dickson and critically challenged this conclusion. But early criticisms of Hawthorne were largely from leftist ideologists who paid little heed to the research itself and were easily refuted for their naivete in questioning science-based conclusions from a platform of mere Marxism.

Some of those who have since undertaken to critique Hawthorne have come to radically different conclusions than those offered by Roethlisberger and Dickson as to what happened in that setting. In retrospect, indeed, there is cause to suggest that rather poor science influenced by the political and ideological agenda of the Hawthorne researchers may have distorted their scientific judgment and thereby distracted the best research energy of social scientists from more substantive issues for as long as fifty years. Hawthorne may have introduced an unfortunate detour for management science on its road to increased knowledge.

A HAPPY WORKER IS, IN FACT, NOT NECESSARILY A PRODUCTIVE WORKER

The major disservice to management science done by Hawthorne was perhaps in suggesting the existence of a causal linkage between employee good feelings, usually referred to as *satisfaction*, and the employee's work output, commonly called *productivity*. For those already convinced that happy workers are productive workers, the emphasis shifted directly to the study of ways to increase worker satisfaction. Demonstrating worker dissatisfaction was tantamount to discovering poor productivity in the eyes of those among the ideologically committed. Research on worker satisfaction burgeoned following the Hawthorne reports. E. A. Locke, in his chapter on "The Nature and Causes of Job Satisfaction" for M. D. Dunnette's 1976 edition of the *Handbook of Industrial and Organizational*

Psychology, identified well over 3,000 scholarly research studies that had addressed the issue of worker satisfaction up to that time. Such a prolific scientific effort on a single subject in the nearly forty-five years elapsed since the first reports of Hawthorne's revelations is impressive evidence of the extent to which scientific energy had been channeled into the measurement and study of worker satisfaction. But evidence of higher output among satisfied workers was disappointingly scarce from this mass of evidence.

In those studies of worker satisfaction that had attempted to link satisfaction with worker productivity, Locke confirmed the earlier conclusions of Brayfield and Crockett (1955) and of Vroom (1964) that there is no "simple relationship" between job satisfaction and worker productivity. That is to say, satisfaction and output are essentially independent issues. It is uncommon to find causal linkage between them. Those unusual instances in which any linkage at all could be identified, indeed, were as easily read as situations where high work output resulted in high job satisfaction as they could be interpreted as showing any direct link proceding causally from satisfaction to productivity. Locke concluded that "job satisfaction has no direct effect on productivity" (p. 1334). Brayfield and Crockett concluded their earlier review with the rather blunt prescription to fellow social scientists that "it is time to question the strategic and ethical merits of selling to industrial concerns an assumed relationship between employee attitudes and employee performance" (p. 421).

Vroom observed in his 1964 book *Work and Motivation* that "correlations between [job satisfaction and work output] vary widely within an extremely large range and the median correlation of .14 has little theoretical or practical importance" (p. 186). Vroom's revelation was carefully couched in scientific caveats and preceded by an extensive discussion of research on worker satisfaction, which constituted slightly more than a quarter of his book's total length. His conclusions were furthermore accompanied by an impressive theory of worker motivation—expectancy theory—which seemed to leave the door open for the operation of worker satisfaction in work motivation. While clearly stated, his harsh pronouncement was easy to overlook.

These honest researchers nevertheless paid a price for their candid clarity on the subject. These were scientifically correct pronouncements, but not politically astute nor popular ones. Though scientifically impressive for the wealth of data on which they rested, these were not welcome conclusions among social scientists who had built their careers on attitude measurement focused on worker satisfaction. The investment in job satisfaction as an outcome in its own right was too great to be abandoned. At best, polite, limited attention was given to such analyses and judgments. They were conclusions that challenged too starkly the very foundations of the then prevailing behavioral theories of management. Taken seriously, they would require that the entire edifice be dismantled and rebuilt. Research on worker satisfaction continued, diminished slightly, but unceasing all the same. As late as 1990, the count of scholarly research in *Psychological Abstracts* under the "job satisfaction" heading exceeded 100 papers for the year. The search for high performance based on worker satisfaction continues unabated.

REEVALUATING THE HAWTHORNE EXPERIMENTS

The beginning point for reevaluation of worker satisfaction as the fountainhead of productivity is quite naturally the Hawthorne studies themselves. These studies have not previously passed altogether without challenge. The literature of industrial sociology entertained a lively debate concerning the validity of the Hawthorne findings through the 1950s. In 1967 Alex Carey offered a scathing critique of Hawthorne in the pages of the *American Sociological Review*. In 1978, Franke and Kaul, in the pages of the same journal, reevaluated Hawthorne using a highly sophisticated time-series multiple regression design. They concluded that 90% of the variance in quantity and quality of output could be accounted for in the imposition of industrial discipline, economic adversity and quality of raw materials. Franke and Kaul further asserted that the Hawthorne experience provides no evidence to justify the necessity for introduction of humanitarian procedures in the shop as a device for increasing productivity.

Perhaps because these analyses represented the views of a limited academic community, they were duly noted and ignored. Hawthorne became a minor embarrassment to practitioners of the human relations school of management science, but the fundamental tenets of the original Hawthorne conclusions continued to drive management theory. The true faith persisted that the happy worker is a productive worker.

THE HAWTHORNE RESEARCH DESIGN

The oft-quoted illumination experiments at Hawthorne from 1924 to 1927 were, at best, uncertain science. A final, formal report on them was never prepared or published. The relay room studies that followed the illumination studies are generally judged to be the scientific core of the Hawthorne research. A small group of female assemblers described as "thoroughly experienced" as well as "willing and cooperative" were chosen—apparently by their foreman and certainly not randomly—from among the larger group of operators in the relay assembly department. The five ladies selected were isolated into a separate production room where their work could be observed, controlled and carefully measured.

From the beginning, the work atmosphere in the relay room was permissive and congenial. Workers were told at the outset that they should work the way they felt like working, and research observers were consistently friendly and supportive. The relay room was served by a single material handler/layout person and was under the on-going observation of one or more research observers. The foreman of the department from which the five workers came continued to function as their "real" supervisor for administrative, pay rate and disciplinary purposes.

At the outset, it is clear that some very curious research methodology was employed at Hawthorne. A sample size of five, while it lent to intensive observation of work behavior in this particular goldfish bowl, is treacherously small for statistical purposes. Attempting to measure change in production output averaged across only five operators would too easily be influenced by the special skill or motivation of only one or two people in the sample. Only the operation of the most obvious and powerful variables could possibly be detected with statistical confidence on such a tiny sample base. A sample of this size is better suited to qualitative research where the experienced judgment of the observer is the principal product rather than the conduct of a quantified statistical analysis.

The experimental and temporary nature of the study group, selected from a much larger, on-going production department, set the relay room group off as special. These research subjects were treated differently from their peers. Their hours were reduced without loss of pay, free lunch was provided and higher management regularly dropped in to see how the research was going. Presumably relay room workers could still communicate with other assemblers in the larger group. Indeed, at one point later in the study when a new incentive pay system was introduced for the experimental group, demands from workers in the larger group for the same pay system clearly demonstrated knowledge in the full department of events in the experimental relay room. Relay room assemblers *were* treated differently and specially compared to their peers. No attempt was made to prevent that difference from being obvious to everyone. It is likely that comparisons between the research group and the larger production department from which it was selected influenced many aspects of the study.

Given these methodological peculiarities, indeed, if we are to accept as a valid explanation of the observed rise in work output the notion that these five workers responded positively to benevolent management attention, then severe constraints must be applied to their generalization to other work situations. Those constraints would begin with a five to one, or *smaller*, worker to supervisor ratio, and require special, differential treatment from other workers similar to that enjoyed by the experimental group, which might include shorter work hours at the same pay, free lunches and regular meetings with the plant manager. Enlightened supervision at this level of intensity would more often than not be too expensive to tolerate. To conclude that the happy worker is a productive worker is a bit extreme if it takes this much to make him or her happy.

WAS IT RESEARCH CONTROL OR JUST GOOD OLD-FASHIONED DISCIPLINE?

Were we to stop here with this popular interpretation of the findings, Hawthorne would become little better than a bad scientific joke. It is probable, though, that a simple explanation for increased productivity in the first relay room experiment is available.

During the first three months of this experiment, problems with the "excessive freedom" of the experimental room were becoming apparent. From the earliest stages of this experiment, the tendency of operators to talk freely with one another was strong. This was evaluated as "a lack of attention to work and a preference for conversing for considerable periods of time." Two workers in particular were thought to be out of line in this regard and were ultimately brought before the relay assembly foreman (who still exercised disciplinary control) to be reprimanded for excessive talking. When they would not stop talking on the job, these two were sent back to the larger work group and replaced.

Discipline administered to the offenders was progressive. That in itself was a major step forward in the humane treatment of workers in this early age. First there was threat that free lunches provided would be cut if the talking did not stop. Then continual "almost daily" reprimands were given to the two offenders. Finally the investigators decided that these two ladies lacked the proper mental attitude for the research setting and they were dismissed from the test room for gross insubordination *and for insufficient output*. Throughout this period of discipline enforcement, the work output of all five ladies was static or declining. After removal of the offenders, the foreman of the assembly area picked two replacements, both experienced assemblers and both eager to participate in the study. One of these two new workers had recently become the principal wage earner for her family. Her productivity and that of her companion replacement immediately exceeded that of the original five ladies in the relay assembly room and far surpassed that from any previous time for either of the two dismissed women. Both new workers led the way in output throughout the remainder of this stage of the study.

The matter of insubordinate talking was later rationalized in *Management and the Worker* as a threat to "control" over experimental conditions. In doing so, Roethlisberger and Dickson appear to have confused experimental control with direct, supervisory control over worker actions. Such confusion concerning control of experimental conditions represents a level of scientific naivete that today would be judged downright unprofessional. It is hard at this historical distance to appreciate how such ignorance of scientific error could have occurred. The observing researchers in the test room, however, received paychecks written on Western Electric, just like their research subjects did. They were imbedded in an ongoing work culture that was not likely to accept an overdose of industrial democracy. It also is quite probable that resentment in the larger department toward the greater personal freedom enjoyed in the relay room became too great for supervision to ignore. Such forces in concert with similar reactions from management could well have accounted for so drastic a step as discipline of subjects at this early stage of the project.

The two worst offenders were, perhaps, merely testing the limits of freedom offered by this situation. The research design was not represented to them as a stable, permanent arrangement and the worst that could happen was to be returned to the larger work group. But whatever the personal motivation of workers, whatever the immediate concerns of management and whatever any other direct causes of this disciplinary intervention there may have been, discipline of these two workers represented a major violation of the integrity of the experiment. The subject population was directly changed in a way that could be expected to enhance the experimental outcome. Researchers guilty of such practices today would be charged with fraud. We may be generous with the Hawthorne research staff and chalk it all up to naivete blended with a general feeling that "it probably won't hurt." Indeed, it didn't hurt the research hypothesis; this disciplinary intervention itself seems almost certainly a major cause of increased productivity arising out of the experiment.

In retrospect it would seem more than ordinarily naive for investigators seeking the causes of increased productivity to hold to their hypothesis that free and friendly supervision *caused* the rise in productivity noted in this part of the study. Rather, it would seem obvious that what turned the trick was imposition of discipline with the noncooperators and selection of replacements who were intrinsically motivated to cooperate for both personal and economic reasons. The more appropriate conclusion might be that productivity can be raised by getting rid of the troublemakers and replacing them with people properly skilled and selected for their readiness to cooperate fully.

SOME REINTERPRETATIONS OF RELAY ROOM EVENTS

The situation during the first three months in the relay test room was extraordinary in many ways. Workers, quite naturally, appear to have tested the limits of the newly offered freedom. Their resistance threatened to undermine output increase goals expected by the researchers and perhaps also to destabilize the larger work group through open challenge to management authority. The quid pro quo of this setting was the prospect of greater freedom and privilege in return for increased production output. From the workers' perspective, there had to be some concern over whether these people—researchers and management—really were sincere. Or was this just a device to raise work standards in this special room and then impose the new standards on the entire original work group without transferring the freedom and privilege back too? The researchers report that "the girls (sic) came into the test with a somewhat suspicious and apprehensivé attitude . . . they were never sure that they were not going to be victimized in some fashion or other by the experimenters or by management" (p. 85).

Workers in the relay room were told to work at a natural pace "as they felt" (p. 21). This was an extraordinary instruction in an extraordinary setting, which probably made little sense to them from the context of their work experience. The first imperative of such a bargain is the existence of trust between the parties. Trust in a power relationship is a delicate matter. The party with the greater power can always betray trust for short-term advantage at minimum or no cost. If one cannot retaliate or escape easily, trust may seem a costly risk. Skepticism is the sounder long-term strategy. It should rationally have been assumed that the relay room worker-ladies were both distrustful and skeptical.

In view of these workers' natural distrust of management's objectives and their loss of dignity in the imposition of discipline to maintain supervisory control, there is little basis for expectation of increased output. Mayo and others involved in the Hawthorne project, though, clearly were possessed with the vision of a new era in which humane treatment of workers would liberate vast productive potential. They saw what they most urgently wanted to see. They saw workers as people with social needs, whose on-the-job behavior was often driven by those needs. Under the right circumstances, their kindness and liberality toward workers seemed to work nicely. It is hardly surprising that, in an age of growing affluence and personal freedom, they wanted to believe that freedom and good feelings among workers on the job would raise productivity. It is ironic that they were only demonstrating truths long known to experienced, working supervisors; that distrust of management can hold worker output down, and effective discipline in concert with astute selection of replacements can reconstitute the group to let productivity rise.

THERE WERE POSITIVE OUTCOMES AT HAWTHORNE

Despite the dominance of an ideological agenda on the reported outcomes of Hawthorne research, there were important positive products from this study. Hawthorne served as the impetus for broad new programs of research on work performance and organization design. Implementation of a plantwide experimental program of nondirective worker interviewing at the Hawthorne plant demonstrated the power of good listening for information gathering and morale boosting alike. Measures of output in the relay room revealed that absolute weekly output need not diminish and can increase when total hours of work are cut even as rest periods are added. Observations of an intact production department documented the defensive power of a work group to restrict output to an arbitrary maximum. These were useful and important additions to the literature of management science.

But it was a prejudice for good feelings as the foundation of high performance output that shaped the dominant theme of Hawthorne. The faith in the good feelings as the foundation of high performance output has diminished little in the intervening years. Much management literature continues to preach the power of good worker/supervisor relations. For the ideologically committed, it is an unshakable faith. For the pragmatic, it is a matter of "oh well, it's got to be good practice to elicit good feelings anyhow." From a coalition of the faithful and the pragmatic, the next stage beyond human relations, the Quality of Work Life movement, emerged.

Chapter Four

Quality of Work Life and Worker Satisfaction

As rigorous science whittled away at the foundations of the Hawthorne paradigm, gradually but surely debunking the notion that "a happy worker is a productive worker," a vigorous rearguard defensive action from adherents of labor humanism was mounted in rebuttal. The lines of defense erected were principally two. One thrust would adopt the position that, regardless of any lack of demonstrated direct impact on productivity, high-quality work life is an obligation owed the American worker. Satisfying, meaningful, pleasant work and working conditions, in their own rights, evolved into a desirable, even necessary, workplace objective.

Introducing the Worker Alienation Research and Technical Assistance Act of 1973, Senator Edward Kennedy quoted into the record the comments of an auto worker's union official, describing how an assembly line worker is left with little but the option to "put his warm body on the line . . ." with only "36 seconds to do a . . . dead end job. . . ." Speaking to the issue of worker alienation, Kennedy quoted from the U.S. Department of Health, Education and Welfare Task Force's report on *Work in America* (1973), observing that "significant numbers of American workers are dissatisfied with the quality of their working lives. Dull, repetitive, seemingly meaningless tasks, offering little challenge or autonomy, are causing discontent among workers at all occupational levels" (see Exhibit 4-1). This rhetoric describes the Quality of Work Life (QWL) movement at the political level. It is the political doctrine that "Americans hate their jobs, and they deserve better" writ large and made into government policy. It is the legacy of Henry Ford's driving determination for greater produc-

Exhibit 4-1
Worker Alienation Research and Technical Assistance Act of 1973: Statement of Findings and Purpose

Sec. 2. (a) The Congress Finds that -

(1) alienation of American workers because of the nature of their jobs is a problem of growing seriousness to the national economy and to individual workers;

(2) alienation often results in high rates of absenteeism, high turnover, poor quality work, a decline in craftsmanship and lessened productivity;

(3) alienation often results in high levels of frustration among workers and causes poor mental health, poor motivation, alcoholism, drug abuse, and social dissatisfaction among workers;

(4) it is in the national interest to encourage the humanization of working conditions and the work itself so as to increase worker job satisfaction diminish the negative effects of job dissatisfaction, and to the extent possible, maximize potential for democracy, security, equity and craftsmanship;

(5) it is in the national interest to promote the fullest development of the abilities, creativity, skills and personal growth of all American workers; and

(6) the problem of worker discontent and alienation has for too long been largely ignored by government, management and unions.

Sec. 3. (a) The Secretary of Labor and the Secretary of Health, Education and Welfare are jointly authorized to either directly or by way of grant, contribution or other arrangement–

(1) conduct research, to determine the extent and the severity of job discontent and the problems related to the nature of work in American work sites, included but not limited to

(A) quality of work, level of turnover, absenteeism, sabotage and lost productivity, and the monetary costs of to the economy of such problems; and

(B) the health of workers, including statistics on mental and physical health and emotional stability;

(2) conduct research on methods now being used in the United States and abroad to meet the problems of work alienation, including more flexible hours of work reduced working days, profit sharing, additional responsibility for workers, job rotation, worker participation in the decision making process with regard to the nature and content of his job, redesign of jobs and production patterns, autonomous work groups, and additional opportunity for education, training and advancement;

(3) collect and disseminate research results and recommendations for relieving worker discontent and for improving the quality of work, to workers, to labor organizations, to businesses, to schools of management and industrial engineering, and the general public;

(4) provide technical assistance to workers, labor organizations, businesses, State and local governments for (i) practical experimentation in meeting the problems of alienation in their own places of work, and (ii) the development and conduct of pilot demonstration projects which show promise of making significant contributions to the knowledge in the field of resolving problems related to worker alienation including such projects as job enrichment guaranteed employment, reduced workdays and weeks, autonomous work groups, job restructuring, increased worker participation in decision making on the nature and content of jobs, increased job mobility, job rotation, group productivity, bonuses, compensation on the basis of skills learned, continuing education and training for new careers and new opportunities for increased job satisfaction;

(5) Provide support for the Triennial Working Conditions Survey of the Department of Labor;

(6) assist in the development and evaluation of curriculum and

programs for training and retraining professionals and sub-professionals in work humanization approaches and methods;

(7) conduct pilot projects for a variety of experiments in both blue collar and white collar work redesign in selected Federal agencies to determine the effectiveness of such projects in improving employee job satisfaction.

(b) In carrying out the research and technical assistance program authorized by this section, the Secretary of Labor and the Secretary of Health, Education and Welfare shall consult with the head of the National Institute of Mental Health, the National Science Foundation, The National Institute for Occupational Safety and Health, and representatives of workers, unions, management, academic and medical experts.

(c) The Secretary of Labor and the Secretary of Health, Education and Welfare shall file a report not later than December 31, 1974 and again not later than December 31, 1975 to the Congress, on the administration of this Act together with such recommendations, including recommendations for additional legislation, as they may deem appropriate, and may file such interim reports as they deem advisable.

Sec. 4. (a) The Secretary of Health, Education and Welfare, in consultation with the Chairman of the Civil Service Commission and the Administrator of the General Services Administration, is authorized and directed to assist Federal agencies in maximizing job satisfaction of their employees.

(b) The administrator of the General Services Administration is authorized to consider maximizing job satisfaction in the design of new Federal Facilities.

tion efficiency, Frederick Winslow Taylor's stubborn insistence on a "fair day's work" and Adam Smith's emphasis on narrow specialization as the foundation of high productivity. It is a call for restoration of American workers' status as responsible, autonomous craftspeople.

The other thrust of the QWL movement is reflected in the title of Kennedy's 1973 Worker Alienation *Research . . . Act*. Among social scientists there were still those who, despite the disappointing paucity of evidence for a link between satisfaction and productivity, remained convinced that if only the right conditions were created, a causal link would be convincingly demonstrated. The act specifically authorized the secretaries of Labor and of Health, Education and Welfare (HEW) to offer grants and other assistance in support of research or pilot projects related to job enrichment, guaranteed employment, reduced workdays and -weeks, autonomous work groups, job restructuring, worker participation in decision making, compensation methods, education and training for new careers, and opportunities for increased job satisfaction, among other issues. The immediate aims of organized labor were addressed in a limited way by authorizing and directing the secretary of HEW and the chairman of the Civil Service Commission "to assist Federal Agencies in maximizing job satisfaction of their employees." The core of the act, clearly though, was a research funding bonanza for those convinced that, if only the proper research were designed and carried out, QWL would be shown to support higher productivity.

Early grants for research funded the publication of book-length reviews of issues specified by the act. Two major, government-funded reports quickly appeared in 1975 and 1976. Not unexpectedly, their titles clearly suggest that a causal link between job satisfaction (now sometimes reborn as QWL programs) and worker productivity clearly exists. *Work, Productivity, and Job Satisfaction*, by Raymond Katzell and Daniel Yankelovich (the public opinion pollster) under a grant from the National Science Foundation, suggests such a linkage in its title, even though the authors concede within the book that simultaneous improvement of job attitudes and productivity is not only difficult and complex, but also that "the two outcomes can be successfully linked only if a number of conditions are met." This book is a survey of variables thought to be important in QWL research by leaders of labor and industry. A lengthy set of issues identified through interviews and questionnaires was rated by research panel respondents and evaluated against the existing research literature. Prior critiques of Brayfield and Crockett (1955) and Vroom (1964), which found no relationship between satisfaction and productivity, are neither discussed nor referenced in this document.

In the following year Edward Glaser, working under a grant from the Department of Labor, published *Productivity Gains Through Worklife Improvements*. There is no doubt about the presumption of causal linkage in this title. The book itself focuses principally on an extended set of case histories, employing a qualitative interpretation of case results to identify opportunities for implementing QWL programs and offering guidelines for bringing about successful job redesigns. Under the heading of "Worker Motivation, Satisfaction and Effectiveness," Glaser is content to link work output with job satisfaction by making reference to a Gallup poll that found that "half of all wage earners say they could accomplish more each day if they tried." The causal linkage is simply assumed, and, again, the critical works of Brayfield and Crockett, as well as of Vroom, are missing from the references listed at the end of the book.

The following year, 1977, T. G. Cummings and E. S. Molloy, working under a grant from the National Science Foundation through its Research Applied to National Needs (RANN) division, published *Improving Productivity and the Quality of Work Life*. Quality of Work Life now displaces job satisfaction as the operative lever on output, with job satisfaction relegated to only the merest incidental comment throughout the book. The major programmatic research thrusts associated with QWL are critically surveyed by Cummings and Molloy as prospective foundations for expected future research. They discuss seven of the most accepted approaches to work improvement: autonomous work groups, job restructure, worker participation, organizational restructure, behavior modification, flexible working hours and the Scanlon plan (a major group incentive compensation method). The authors ultimately conclude that "strategies for improving productivity and the quality of work life abound in organizations today," but that "current knowledge . . . points clearly to the authors' inability to predict precisely how a specific program will work in an organization" and, further, that "it seems highly unlikely that we will ever have all the necessary understanding to guarantee success" (p. 291). Brayfield and Crockett get notice in the book's references, but Vroom's more recent and comprehensive treatise on *Work and Motivation* (1964) is wholly overlooked.

These are by no means the only illustrations of government-sponsored research into QWL issues in this term of history, but each is a comprehensive, serious, book-length discussion of these issues. In concert they nicely illustrate the influence of politics on management research and theory. With the entry of politics onto the scene of this research, strange and wonderful things have begun to occur. Job satisfaction has suddenly died and been resurrected as Quality of Work Life. Research that reaffirms previously well established lack of linkage between job satisfaction and work output is generously funded by the government.

In the nearly two decades since enactment of the Worker Alienation Research . . . Act of 1973, the great Northwest Passage from job satisfaction, newly reborn as QWL and expected to open the way to increased worker productivity and high performance management systems, has continued to elude searchers. Many researchers, having exhausted the search, have settled for the position that the evidence for independence of job satisfaction and productivity does not bar simultaneous pursuit of both as proper goals of management. If not related, they are at least not incompatible. Having crossed the congressional rubicon into the realm of political support for the paradigm, simultaneous achievement of both job satisfaction *and* high productivity is no longer an issue for science; it is now an objective to be pursued in its own right. The rhetoric of happy worker as productive worker is transmuted from research hypothesis into prevailing political and management ideology.

Indeed, delivering job satisfaction to workers through QWL programs cannot now and almost certainly never will be justified by its contribution to the bottom line in productivity increases. The research programs proposed in the language of the Worker Alienation Act and in the works of those authors referenced above are as much subject to corruption in their implementation as Taylor's scientific management was in the hands of Henry Ford. They often have little to do with *either* job satisfaction *or* work output. Thus QWL must either represent an emerging norm of enhanced working conditions in American industry, justified on moral and political grounds, or it deserves to be junked as a concept. The extensive foundations of QWL in job satisfaction research must be reevaluated to discover what is expected and what is practical to offer by way of worker satisfaction measures in managing the U.S. work force.

RESEARCH EVIDENCE CONCERNING JOB SATISFACTION

The job satisfaction research literature has been thoroughly reviewed at about decade intervals in the recent past. Brayfield and Crockett in 1955, Vroom in 1964 and Locke in 1976 each summarized the field extensively. After 1975, as job satisfaction research mutated into the QWL movement, concern among serious scientists with job satisfaction as a major research paradigm faded. In his 1984 review of "Organizational Behavior" for the *Annual Review of Psychology*, Barry Staw dismisses attitude surveys and satisfaction measures as "throw-away variables." He characterizes the field as dominantly correlational in method and "rather atheoretical." In scientific terms, this amounts to consigning it to irrelevance.

In 1985, nevertheless, the tradition of once-a-decade revisits to the subject was continued with an update of the job satisfaction literature by M. T.

Iaffaldano and P. M. Muchinsky. These researchers confirmed the limited causal relation between worker satisfaction and work output, lamenting that "empirical support for the satisfaction-performance relation does not approximate the degree to which this relation has been espoused in theories of organizational design" (p. 270). With so much discomfirmation, it would seem that the relation of job satisfaction and work performance should be a dead issue. Were it not for the QWL movement, which assured continuing concern for worker satisfaction, it might have been.

Regardless of the fate of the work performance issue, there are still findings that suggest continuing relevance in the assessment of worker satisfaction. The extensive literature available contains many potentially informative findings concerning job satisfaction that deserve review. It will be useful to summarize the findings this vast body of research has yielded in its stormy, politicized history. The reviews of Vroom (1964) and Locke (1976) survey the relevant research findings concerning job satisfaction rather fully. The discussion of job satisfaction correlates that follows draws heavily on existing review summaries such as those of Locke and Vroom as well as on the experience and observations of the writer. The object is to construct a cohesive whole that offers fresh directions for management theory and practice.

TURNOVER AND ABSENTEEISM AMONG DISSATISFIED WORKERS

The easiest starting point for summarizing the effects of job satisfaction on worker behavior is with those issues that have been *consistently* related to worker expression of satisfaction or dissatisfaction with their jobs: turnover and absenteeism.

Dissatisfaction is consistently associated with higher levels of labor turnover. Those workers who are most dissatisfied also exhibit a higher frequency of absence. The explanation most often offered for this correlation is the tendency of people to withdraw from unpleasant work circumstances. The correlations found, though, are typically moderate and do not explain all of the variability in observed absence or turnover rates. Many other factors are also influential here.

Absences, for instance, often increase around holidays. The tendency is so common, that many employers require either advance permission for absence or actual attendance on the job on those workdays immediately preceding and following the holiday as a condition for holiday pay. Absences are also known to increase with alcoholism, addiction and poor health. The most common basis for separation for cause is excessive absenteeism, and the major cause of these absences is physical inability to be at work. Absences may also be the result of dissatisfactions outside the workplace that have nothing to do with one's job. Thus, while absences and dissatisfaction are sometimes statistically correlated, costly and extensive redesign of work to increase satisfaction with the purpose of reducing absenteeism would be difficult to justify in many if not most instances.

Turnover is similarly the result of many factors other than unhappiness in the job situation. Economic circumstances and the availability or unavailability of alternative employment clearly have an impact on the level of turnover. Intense discomfort in the job situation, however, can drive a worker to separate from employment in the interest of his or her mental and physical well-being. Even high pay cannot always hold a worker who is seriously ill-fitted in skill or temperament for the job. With all the adverse economic circumstances of 1913 in Detroit, Ford experienced a 380% turnover rate. The causes of turnover at this level, however, were not so much dissatisfaction (although certainly a very high level of dissatisfaction must have prevailed) as it was the generally poor organization of the workplace.

Factory workers at the turn of the century were hired largely because they looked healthy and eager. Foremen and gang bosses went to the gate and picked the men who looked good to them. Little attempt was made to ascertain whether individual experience or background suited employment in the auto industry. Workers were assigned to a crew and expected to pitch in and help. There was no training available, no orientation to the company and its policies, no job descriptions or fixed assignments. Prior to the introduction of the moving assembly line after 1913, workers were assigned to a crew and expected to assist in building a car from the chassis up in any way they could. The potential for confusion, inefficiency, task overlap and mistakes in such a process was immense. Many workers were summarily fired for their ignorance, others quit in disgust or anger. Dissatisfaction of workers who hoped for good, steady employment must have been intense. The problem was not one that would improve, though, until order was introduced into the workplace. The price of that order at Ford was narrowly specialized routine work. With the introduction of this routine, a premium wage was necessary to control turnover and stabilize the work force. Many workers who hated their jobs could not now afford to quit them if they wanted to. This seems a more expensive way to reduce absenteeism. Introducing a measure of satisfaction might well be a cost-effective way to reduce extreme levels of absenteeism, but dissatisfaction and opportunity to quit are always more closely related than are dissatisfaction and the act of quitting. Economic factors appear ultimately dominant here.

In looking for answers, there is both a commonsense and a counterintuitive element to absenteeism and turnover as presumed outcomes of worker dissatisfaction. As quickly as a good explanation is uncovered, a contradictory case can appear. There appear to be no universal generalizations about worker dissatisfaction that permit easy management policy solutions to absenteeism and turnover problems. Each situation seems to require highly specific evaluation and action within the particular organizational context.

GRIEVANCES AND WORKER HEALTH

Dissatisfaction is frequently associated with a high level of complaints and grievances in industry. Highly dissatisfied workers may resort to sabotage and passive aggression. These may be workers who would *quit if they could*! Dissatisfied workers may also be those employees who are highly conscientious about work effectiveness and upset by the prevalence of poor management practices. A worker can be a constructive or a destructive complainer, and either position can be founded on dissatisfaction. It is doubtful, for instance, that higher standards will be pursued by those fully satisfied with their present level of accomplishment.

Dissatisfaction has occasionally been linked to poor health or longevity. Workers torn between making maximum piecework rates and observing the informal ceiling on output set by their work group have more ulcers. Work satisfaction was found to be the best single predictor of longevity against actuarial tables of mortality in another study. Take notice that in correlations of this sort the problem of causal directionality becomes critical in setting workplace policy to improve worker attitudes. We may reasonably ask whether workers have poor health because they are dissatisfied, if they are dissatisfied because their health is poor, or if both dissatisfaction and poor health are the result of some other, unmeasured variable. The relationship of health/longevity with work satisfaction can be demonstrated in various circumstances, but it does not necessarily mean that either can be changed by quality of work life or other satisfaction improvement programs in the workplace.

In specific circumstances, such as relationship with one's supervisor, job content wages or hours of work, there are other policy-relevant and interesting, if sometimes equally enigmatic, research findings. Some are worth cataloging for their potential influence on QWL policy. In reviewing these findings, one should not lose sight of their probabilistic qualities. It may be helpful to mentally qualify any probabalistically couched research observation as a statement that "some of the time, some of the workers express more satisfaction when . . ." There will occasionally be situations and circumstances where the exact opposite condition will prevail. The most common description of the influence of worker satisfaction is likely to be that sometimes you see it, sometimes you don't. There are almost never any exact conditions of cause and effect in the realm of human behavior.

DISSATISFACTION WITH SUPERVISION

To begin we may ask: What qualities of a supervisor seem to result in greater worker satisfaction? Some general principles of worker satisfaction and supervisor style can be drawn from available research. Most employ leader task orientation and social sensitivity, or something very similar, as the basic polarities of supervisory style. Small, close-knit work groups, for instance, exhibit greater satisfaction with socially sensitive, nonauthoritarian leaders. Larger groups where the supervisor is socially distant from workers are more satisfied with a formal, task-oriented leadership style. The style of a supervisor, perhaps, should be consonant with the prevailing opportunity for social contact between supervisor and worker. Small work groups with a limited supervisory span are likely to require less formal order and more flexibility of response. Some large work groups with a broader supervisory span may need formality and structure to get the job done effectively. Workers who prefer close-knit work relations seem to be happier in a small work group supervised informally, while those with a preference for predictable, structured work routines may prefer a large, formal work group. Work group size in many instances may be regulated to the level of formality or flexibility required by the task. Individual temperament and work style preference, in like fashion, may be the basis on which people are sorted out among various available work group assignments. If this is the case, we may find that it is necessary to work on several levels of variables in fitting workers to supervisory style or supervisors to task situations to maximize their satisfaction.

On the whole, those supervisors who act considerately toward their workers have the more highly satisfied work groups. Thus, it may be possible to generate high worker satisfaction through kindly, thoughtful leader behavior. But it is sometimes difficult to get workers to attend to real business crises or to raise their output standards through that same kindly, thoughtful style of leadership. The leader assigned to restore productive discipline to a work group whose standards have slipped can't avoid generating some added dissatisfaction in getting the job done. Some increases in dissatisfaction may be inevitable over the course of a specific work group's history if standards are to be maintained.

Dissatisfaction tends to be expressed through criticism toward those associated with it. Dissatisfied workers generally describe their supervisors in unfavorable terms. Criticism of the worker by a supervisor also generates dissatisfaction. The more frequent and severe the criticisms pointed at an employee in a performance appraisal, for instance, the greater the worker's dissatisfaction with his or her supervisor. This reaction of workers should be considered the "norm," the typical, the average. There is another side to the coin of criticism, though. The rare worker who demands tough performance feedback is likely to get on the fast track to promotion, if he or she is not already there. Champions require tough coaches. Clear, timely, blunt feedback is the most effective device for improving complex performance. Dissatisfaction is an almost inevitable concomitant of performance improvement on complex tasks, though it may take the form of dissatisfaction with one's own performance effort or dissatisfaction with the source of feedback. The difference is critical in shaping the work relationship between employee and supervisor. Defensive, thin-skinned workers discourage criticism from their bosses. Open, responsible workers may demand it.

It is observed in some research settings that employees who express more open dissatisfaction may be subject to closer surveillance and control from their supervisors. Closer control of work performance may achieve improved work results from the complainer, though it may be obtained at the cost of increased dissatisfaction. Moving away from close control toward greater worker autonomy of action has also been shown to generate increased work output, as well as to increase satisfaction. The individual supervisor must master the art of choosing when he or she can obtain improved performance through closer supervisory control at the cost of increased dissatisfaction, or can get improved performance through greater delegation of worker autonomy and reap the reward of worker satisfaction too. Given these choices, it should be no surprise to find workers complaining about "bad" supervision that imposes close controls on performance while they praise "good" supervision that permits autonomy. Level of satisfaction alone is enough to shape worker preference for increased personal autonomy. For the supervisor, the result may be roughly equivalent under either approach, though somewhat more reliable or comfortable when close control is the method used.

Other factors may mitigate in favor of control in preference to increased autonomy. Supervisors are generally expected to "stay on top of things."

Turning workers free to work autonomously can appear irresponsible to higher-ups and be risky. The variables and constraints that apply to worker satisfaction with supervision are complex and numerous. There are few easy choices or safe moves for supervisors where increased worker satisfaction is the object. It is seldom enough to be either wholly task-oriented or intensely socially sensitive. Supervisors are frequently caught between subordinates who want more freedom or autonomy and higher management that wants more control over work activity. Some tough calls are required.

JOB DESIGN

Job content—the work itself—is the object of much concern in Quality of Work Life programs. Job redesign, job enlargement, job enrichment or job rotation all receive much attention from QWL program technicians seeking to improve worker quality of work life and, in the process, productivity. Variety of work, autonomy of action and task significance all figure in designs for increasing job satisfaction through job redesign.

But not every worker wants an enriched, more varied, more responsible, more interesting job. Workers are often resistant to and suspicious of change introduced by management. Some workers prefer mindless simplicity in their work. Where job enrichment adds responsibility, workers may feel that their pay should be adjusted upward. Adding responsibility to some jobs may reduce responsibility in others. Extensive job redesign may amount to a substantial redefinition of work roles that requires a major redistribution of power and responsibility. Job redesign can represent anything from a cosmetic refurbishing of old tasks to a major organizational revolution. The extent of change and the newness of the work experience may itself become the source of considerable satisfaction or dissatisfaction.

Interest in job design as a lever on worker satisfaction is not without substantial grounds in research, though. The extensive body of attitude survey research in industry has consistently shown that satisfaction rises as a function of the level of organization at which it is surveyed. Higher managers, professionals and technicians consistently express greater satisfaction in their jobs. This difference is probably related to many factors, including enhanced personal status, higher pay and more pleasant working conditions. In the content of higher level jobs themselves, though, there is also greater autonomy, variety and independence of judgment. These are factors that often enhance job satisfaction.

Perhaps the critical perspective here is that satisfaction is so consistently lower among those at the bottom rungs of the hierarchical ladder, although it must be clearly recognized that satisfaction is not wholly lacking among the lowest level workers in organizations. Again, this is a probabilistic thing. While anywhere from 25% to 33% of typical factory or clerical workers may express dissatisfaction in their jobs, only 5% to 15% of middle managers or professional workers will be in this category. Under normal, stable circumstances, most workers say they are satisfied with their jobs. But it may be worthwhile to ask why such a substantially larger proportion of lower level workers *do not* find satisfaction in their work.

There is evidence that narrow specialization of work tasks leads to boredom and dissatisfaction, especially among better-educated workers. Some employment officers reject better-educated candidates for routine work, knowing that there is high likelihood these people will soon become bored and troublesome in their jobs. The absence of opportunity to work at craft-like tasks, or, alternatively, the dead-endedness of one's narrowly specialized job, may well be the source of increased dissatisfaction to workers who want their working careers to be interesting and meaningful. Absence of opportunity for responsibility may erode self-esteem among workers who aspire to higher social status in their jobs.

Research reveals that dissatisfaction rises when technological change leading to narrower specialization of the work is introduced. Workers who have control over the pace of their work are more satisfied than those who are machine paced. Workers who feel that their jobs make use of their skills and abilities are more satisfied. Workers who find significant personal identity in their job roles are more satisfied when there is opportunity for self-expression in their work. But merely adding variety in the way of new or different tasks to a job does not seem to improve satisfaction unless the added work elements are related to basic tasks and call for application of valued skill or ability. Finding increased satisfaction through job enlargement or enrichment seems to require a comprehensive, logical redesign of each job that improves its fit to the worker's interests and skills.

COMPENSATION AND ADVANCEMENT

There is no indication that high pay alone improves worker satisfaction or reduces dissatisfaction. Indeed, higher-than-market pay for similar work that locks one into a job may become a source of decreased satisfaction among workers who dislike their jobs but feel they cannot afford to enter more satisfying occupations. The pursuit of job satisfaction is sometimes powerful enough to induce a change into lower paid but more desirable work. There seems to be a limit to the amount of dissatisfaction that high wages can buy. All other factors being equal, workers who are paid above average and *know* they are well paid are probably more satisfied.

Wages are most commonly a source of dissatisfaction with those workers who feel they are unfairly paid for their level of effort, skill and experience. Observing that a co-worker with similar skill, ability and work output is paid higher is very likely to elicit dissatisfaction. Identification of a pay equity discrepancy within one's own firm is more distressing than one outside it. It is not necessary that the equity be real or that it be major, only that it be perceived. The motivational aspects of pay equity are of some importance and will be further examined in chapters on motivation (Chapter 6) and pay policy (Chapter 7) that follow.

Getting a promotion is an almost certain source of increased satisfaction to most workers. Failing to get a promotion can increase dissatisfaction, but only if one was expected. Those who have resigned themselves to staying at their current job levels are largely unconcerned about who gets promoted, and they sometimes appear to be more satisfied than those who aspire to and anticipate advancement. Ambition, it would seem, generates or is founded on some degree of dissatisfaction by its mere existence.

PUTTING JOB SATISFACTION INTO PERSPECTIVE

It was noted earlier in examining the Hawthorne experience that worker satisfaction is, at best, related to work productivity at a trivial level of statistical correlation. Vroom's 1964 estimate that an average correlation of 0.14 characterizes the typical quantified research result available in the literature. This magnitude of correlation implies that no more than 2% of the variance in output can be accounted for in worker satisfaction. Various researchers have observed that satisfaction may as readily flow from high productivity to satisfaction as in the opposite direction. The correlational studies that characterize research on worker attitudes do not permit any more exact interpretation of the results than this. Even the limited relationship of satisfaction and work output that is found offers scant comfort to those seeking confirmation of the "happy worker is a productive worker" hypothesis. It certainly leaves much to be desired as a foundation for organizational policy formulation.

Be reminded also that research findings of the kind reviewed here apply only to some workers and there are large individual differences in behavior resulting from variable needs and motives. There are no exact causal links, only significant probabilities that are expressed as a correlation between satisfaction and some significant element of work experience. The closest we might come to clear demonstration of cause and effect between dissatisfaction and work performance might be the discovery that university students who are requested to repeat a meaningless, routine task endlessly, and are offered neither purpose nor reward for its execution, will almost certainly refuse to continue at some point. Work that requires close attention without offering mental stimulation is repugnant to those who value mental stimulation.

QWL PROBABLY MARKS ESCALATING WORKER EXPECTATIONS

Finding coherence in this welter of findings, which could be the foundation of a Quality of Work Life policy in industry, is no simple matter. It is complex and confusing. It is not just a question of measuring worker attitude and then acting to satisfy concerns expressed by workers. Carried to its limits, that might mean a major, costly revolution in the structure of organization generally.

We may duly take note of changes in work content such as those introduced by Frederick Taylor and Henry Ford. The industrial revolution was characterized by tightly enforced work output standards, which eliminated variety and responsibility from the craftsperson's jobs, and narrow specialization, which trivialized some skills, fragmenting much work into insignificant specialties. The worker as robot is denied dignity as a human being, denied meaningful involvement in work decisions, denied opportunity to take responsibility for high quality work but often blamed, nevertheless, for poor work results. That combination of factors would seem almost certain to increase worker dissatisfaction.

At various times in this century it has been fashionable to decry the absence of the craftsperson spirit in American workers. Perhaps it is time to take note that many workers have been stripped of their craftsperson's role in this century by narrow specialization, exact prescription of task design, enforced output standards and engineered work flow. The wonder of it, indeed, may be the frequency with which a majority of workers seem to adapt to these conditions over long periods of time. Many *are* satisfied with their limited work routine as long as their hopes and expectations are not escalated by external events.

It is important to keep in view that satisfaction is usually measured by attitude surveys, which are the touchstone of most worker satisfaction rhetoric. Surveys define and demonstrate the phenomenon of worker satisfaction. But the action of attitude measurement itself changes circumstances in the workplace. It is necessary to examine the effects of attitude measurement and explore what it means for a worker to express satisfaction or dissatisfaction in a survey setting in order to understand what QWL is all about at its foundation.

MEASUREMENT IS INHERENTLY INTRUSIVE

It is an established principle of physical science that the act of measurement will influence or alter the phenomenon under observation. Measurement of attitudes does not occur without consequences for events in the workplace. Indeed, it becomes a part of the very events it is intended to describe and may end up being central to them. In the decades of the 1960s and 1970s, I conducted hundreds of attitude surveys in a variety of manufacturing and service settings with workers, professionals and managers across all levels of organization. I have seen many of the ways that attitude surveys influence the workplace, both for better and for worse. The discussion that follows is based on those experiences.

It is common for higher level managers to impose an attitude survey on subordinate managers who appear to overcontrol or to have lost control of their organizations and then use that survey to evaluate or remove managers who are found to be unpopular with their workers. It should be expected, thus, that supervisors or managers who have a survey arbitrarily imposed on them by higher management will be terrorized by the occasion. It is not unheard of for survey administrators to use results to intimidate managers and supervisors. I have met personnel managers who bullied supervisors and managers by overplaying the negative findings from surveys conducted in their organizations. Even experienced or confident managers who request conduct of a survey with their workers have been known to experience high anxiety waiting for the results. A careful reading of some attitude surveys will reveal that they can easily become a calculated assault on the basic institutions of managerial power and authority, especially when used judgmentally. It is a naive and reckless purpose, counterproductive to the goal of improving the quality of work life. Managers who have no voice in their use have justification to fear them.

An attitude survey is a power-reversal mechanism that permits workers to chasten those in formal positions of power for their poor judgment or insensitivity. Elected politicians face much the same humiliation every time they must stand for reelection by their constituencies. Politicians protect their positions by avoiding clear commitment and appeasing dominant blocs of voters with services and tax-supported projects. Managers who must regularly endure reevaluation through employee attitude surveys are known to appease workers by avoiding tough enforcement of work standards and evading tough decisions. Attitude surveys have considerable power to distort organizational processes.

The subject matter of attitude survey questions can suggest the possibility of impending change and generate employee expectations for that change. Asking employees if their pay should be increased suggests the possibility of an across-the-board pay adjustment. If the intent of management is to pay fairly, it is better to ask if pay is fair compared to jobs requiring comparable skill and experience. A survey that asks each worker if he or she is informed of promotion opportunities and considered for them suggests an open promotion policy where any employee has a right to expect consideration. If the prevailing practice is to set strict qualification standards and consider only those who meet them, it might be better to ask if standards are set reasonably and fairly, or to inquire as to the fairness of a candidate's evaluation against those standards. A survey that asks if one's supervisor administers discipline fairly and consistently suggests a lack of management confidence in supervisory judgment. It would be preferable to ask if causes for discipline are clearly communicated or if the rules are consistently enforced. If, for instance, there is a clear requirement that workdays before and following a holiday must be worked to get holiday pay, don't ask if it is a fair policy. Ask workers to describe one or more circumstances under which overly strict enforcement of that policy might be seen as unjust.

The best foundation for a constructive employee attitude survey is a thorough evaluation of management's policy and practice intentions. If the intention is to have qualified supervisors, the survey may ask if they are properly trained and supported in carrying out their jobs. If the policy is to pay competitively compared to local industry, ask workers how their individual pay compares to that of friends and associates in the community. If management wants to create a work climate where high standards of quality and quantity of output are enthusiastically pursued, it should ask workers to rate the level of meaningfulness and importance of existing standards.

Even when good, sound issues are raised by a survey, interpretation of worker responses may be anything but straightforward. At the occasion of the first attitude survey I administered, there were immediate expressions of severe upset and anxiety from technicians in the operation. One confided to me that if they answered truthfully, their manager would harass them mercilessly. He was a man who could not handle criticism and used his authority to stifle it brutally. The lid was on this organization so tightly that candid survey results could not escape from it. Results from this component were among the most positive in the entire plant.

One of the most negative results from a survey I have known concerned a large production unit temporarily under the supervision of a bright young management trainee. The prior supervisor had allowed standards to erode badly throughout this unit. The job of the trainee was to bring standards back up, take the heat for being the tough guy, then move on. Survey responses in this component were universally bitter and angry. No one, especially the trainee, had expected such an outpouring of hostility from the survey. And no one intended to do anything to change the circumstances. It might have been better to bypass this unit with the attitude survey, although these results did finally give the plant manager opportunity to bring the standards problem out into the open with this work group and express an understanding of their upset while eliciting some new commitment to improvement.

Good survey results can easily be bought with appeasement of workers by the supervisor, or can induce autocratic managers to tyrannize workers to the point where they fear to say the truth. The manager who fears being "bagged" by higher management through a survey can usually find a way to foil the effort. Bad survey results, on the other hand, may represent existence of problems that are being addressed constructively and honestly, however painful that may be. Alternatively, a negative survey may advertise the onset of mutiny against unpopular leadership.

Artifacts of the measurement process itself must be guarded for in the interpretation of survey data. At extremes of survey positives and negatives, change is virtually inevitable. The best prediction of change from an earlier survey to a later one is that exceptionally good attitudes will probably deteriorate, while exceptionally bad attitudes will probably improve the next time around. It is the nature of most measures that extreme outliers move back toward the middle of the distribution on subsequent measurements. With so much complexity bound up in the attitude measurement process, understanding the meaning of job dissatisfaction expressed through a survey will be difficult at best.

It must always be recognized that a paper-and-pencil attitude survey used without interviews or other qualitative data input is an exceedingly limited channel of communication through which to ask workers to communicate their concerns to management. Typically, many of the issues in the instrument are of secondary importance to workers. Often, from their point of view, few or none of the questions are the right ones. That limitation of a survey may simply reflect a real difference between the points of view of management and of workers. Careful development of the questions asked, using worker interviews before the survey to identify what issues are on their minds, and interviews after to find out what they meant by their answers, can greatly improve a survey as an instrument of communication. It should always be assumed, though, that employees will use the survey to get across to supervisors and management those concerns that are foremost on their minds. The structure of the survey communicates to workers what is on management's (or the survey designer's) mind. In turn, the answers of workers communicate what is on their minds. There often is not much common ground between the two perspectives. It should be no wonder that attitude surveys can produce curious and contradictory results, or that job satisfaction is so often hard to define.

WHAT IS SATISFACTION ANYHOW?

If the measurement of job satisfaction is loaded with traps for the unwary, understanding the nature of job satisfaction is at least as troublesome, perhaps more so. We may begin an examination of satisfaction by pointing out that the implicit assumption underlying QWL rhetoric is that worker satisfaction results from external factors in the work situation. That is, we talk about it entirely as if the worker were a passive vessel within which satisfaction is created by forces largely or entirely outside his or her control. Aside from the possibility that satisfaction, to the extent that it is, in fact, externally caused, may be entirely brought about by conditions unrelated to work or the workplace; blaming it all on management or working conditions robs workers of their own choice and self-determination in the matter. It wholly overlooks the possibility that a person may *choose* to be satisfied or dissatisfied and that chronic satisfaction or dissatisfaction can be a life strategy. The meaning of that strategy for high performance may be hard to assess.

Some individuals seem to be satisfied in almost all circumstances, others are perennially dissatisfied regardless of their work roles. Is propensity to satisfaction a quality of personality, specific to each person? Staw, Bell and Clausen (1986) offer evidence that measures of an individual's typical emotional state are predictive of satisfaction level over time and across varying circumstance. The emotionally maladjusted person is more likely to be dissatisfied in all situations. If this is the case, is management justified in screening out the maladjusted, troublemaking faultfinders who find little satisfaction in anything about their jobs? If complainers are screened out, does discrimination against them create complacency in the organization, eliminating the chance for organizational excellence? If satisfied workers are more flexible and better adjusted personally, does that lend to superior organizational performance? Or does the fact that high commitment requires some degree of dissatisfaction with circumstances as they exist argue that malcontents are drivers of progress? Are the best performers typically harder to satisfy? The sources and meanings of work satisfaction turn out to be exceptionally complex and confusing. There are no quick and easy answers.

What about the individual who manipulatively uses the willingness of another to give satisfaction? Can dissatisfaction be employed as a tool of control over the behavior of another? Is dissatisfaction a strategy workers might use to influence management? Or, if management is dissatisfied with present worker performance, can it properly keep pushing the goal out just a little beyond the limit of achievement to drive performance ever forward? Many successful teachers and coaches specialize in just that kind of motivational tactic.

As long as the worker is held to be wholly, passively at-effect and satisfaction is assumed to be the result of external forces in the workplace, then the firm, the employer, the manager, the supervisor, co-workers, working conditions and an endless list of other external factors can be held responsible for one's sense of satisfaction. Those external factors are alone held accountable for making matters right to the satisfaction of the victimized worker. But if each individual is free to accept greater or lesser responsibility for his or her own satisfaction, how is responsibility to be divided? How much of quality of work life is management's responsibility, how much is the individual worker's choice and accountability?

The finding that dissatisfaction may be related to poor health or shortened life span suggests that dissatisfaction can be a physically and emotionally stressful and harmful experience. If so, why does the dissatisfied person not avoid or escape from the circumstances that seem to produce distress? There are, in fact, numerous stories of individuals who have suddenly and unaccountably changed careers, life-styles or spouses at mid-life, thereby becoming "new" people. Did those individuals rediscover their choice in matters of satisfaction and dissatisfaction? Do people calculate trade-offs between one kind of dissatisfaction and another, or between present dissatisfaction and risk of future dissatisfaction, choosing the lesser dissatisfaction or risk? Or is it possible for one to elect to be serene and satisfied, almost on a spiritual plane, even in the face of the worst conditions of life? Can one choose to find or to create satisfaction in his or her life independent of the forces one is up against?

TOWARD A CONSTRUCTIVE QUALITY OF WORK LIFE POLICY

Clearly, there is likelihood that satisfaction-dissatisfaction can be many different things for many different purposes. What, then, are the merits of seeking to effect a higher quality of work life, measured through worker satisfaction and related attitudes, as a national policy or even just as a company goal?

First, let's scope out the extremes of this issue. It would appear that most take-it-or-leave-it job opportunities and do-it-or-else management edicts are no longer acceptable to a very large and growing proportion of workers. There is broad social consensus that limiting individual choice in this fashion has no place in a civilized workplace. Employers or bosses who arrogantly insist on the right to manage by fiat can be countered by formation of a labor union, court action to enforce civil rights or unwillingness of workers to accept their job offers. The labor market, the law and the social climate of our times effectively close off this option in all but the most unusual circumstances. That establishes the lower boundary of QWL. Jack Welch, CEO of the General Electric Company, clearly articulates and defines this boundary for GE managers in the company's 1991 Annual Report. He states that GE practice "is not complicated in theory or even original. Much of the intellectual underpinning . . . consists of ideas like worker involvement, trust and empowerment—shopworn and even platitudinous concepts." In case there is any doubt about the limits, he goes on to specify that "we cannot afford management styles that suppress and intimidate" (p. 4). The basics of QWL are clearly made corporate policy in this world-class company.

At the opposing extreme, it is neither practical nor prudent to assure full satisfaction to every worker. Some percentage of workers must always be dissatisfied and every worker must have some occasion for experience of dissatisfaction. Otherwise, standards will be low and performance mediocre. Worker satisfaction at 100% is both impossible and unhealthy for the firm. Every life should include both satisfaction and dissatisfaction in balanced measure. Everyone should accept some responsibility for his or her own satisfaction.

Between these extremes there are few universal principles to be found. Bosses and authority figures must play out their roles effectively, not necessarily to the pleasure or satisfaction of their subordinates. Bosses who cannot get the job done without forcing choice on workers should be recognized for this weakness by higher management. But supervisors who are not eliciting some expression of dissatisfaction from some workers are probably not supervising. Any program that seeks to achieve excellence of performance and quality of work life in the work setting must grapple with a wide range of complex and significant variables. It must pay and promote fairly; communicate openly and honestly; offer interesting, meaningful work; select, train and place workers skillfully; as well as provide work schedules that fit emerging life-styles and elicit workers' best efforts.

Satisfaction with wages is a market issue. The soundest maxim in setting pay is "neither a scrooge nor a patsy be." But overall, pay structure in emerging high performance systems seems to require a move from paying for mere longevity on the job to compensating for number, breadth and level of work-related skills possessed by each worker. Paying generously over market is always expensive and only sometimes increases worker satisfaction.

Promotion that is fair enough to assure everyone has a chance to rise is likely to be a source of organizational mediocrity. Promotion is always a political matter in the sense that values are central and trade-offs between priorities are inevitable to the ultimate decision. The choice arrived at is a clear measure of the organizational judgment and sensitivity of the promotion decision maker. The best policy for promotion is to communicate the standards for promotion as fully as possible, select competitively from among obvious stand-out candidates and feed back the rationale for the choice made to all the losers. The winner will certainly be elated, the losers disappointed. That's the way it is. The choice is either to build trust with candidness and honesty that may temporarily dissatisfy or create distrust and certain dissatisfaction by skirting the tough issues.

It is primarily in the realm of job design that opportunity appears high for improved QWL measures. Long commodity production runs that (presumably) benefited from narrowly specialized job design are disappearing. The age of the project shop with its emphasis on one-of-a-kind and short-run projects is increasingly replacing lock-step, engineered production flow supported by narrow, specialized jobs. The educational level of workers is rising. QWL would certainly point us toward restoration of craftsperson-styled tasks as the new core around which to design jobs. Greater worker self-direction will be called for in many jobs. More skilled and multiskilled workers will be required to fill those jobs.

QWL will probably never be supported by the evidence of human relations research alone. Research may provide some limited guidance, but it is seldom basis enough on which to set policy. QWL is, finally, a set of policies intended to recognize the evolving values of society and the rising expectations of the labor force. QWL in the present age demands recognition of the dignity of human life, on and off the job, supported by preparation of workers and design of jobs to achieve the best available fit of work to the abilities and aspirations of each individual worker.

QWL programs may or may not be an element of future high performance management systems. Certainly, the expectation that worker satisfaction can be the foundation of such systems is naive and perhaps even dangerous. Worker satisfaction is a complex matter that deserves careful thought and consideration in any management systems design decision. But it cannot and should not be the touchstone of efforts to invent high performance systems. The *happy worker is a productive worker* paradigm doesn't work. It is lot more complicated than that!

Chapter Five

Worker Involvement and Participation

Quality of Work Life and the right of workers to satisfying jobs was the political thrust of the human relations movement. Progressing in parallel, worker involvement and participation was its ideological arm among social scientists. As one community of researchers labored to build an empirical foundation for QWL programs, another pressed forward the argument for a theoretical and moral necessity of worker participation in their task decisions. In the post-World War II fervor of democratic and antiauthoritarian idealism, every variety of autocratic, centralized leadership had suffered portrayal among organization theorists as ineffective and unethical, if not downright evil. It sometimes seemed that demonstrating the superiority of democratic leadership methods was an ethical imperative. Social scientists in particular seemed morally obligated to defend its necessity.

PARTICIPANTS IN THE GREAT IDEOLOGICAL DEBATE

Rensis Likert in his influential 1961 book *New Patterns of Management* proposed development of participative groups as the surest way to improve organizational performance. He argued that "to meet the demands of our more complex technologies and much larger and diverse enterprises, more complex systems of organizing human effort are needed." He counseled that "there is much greater need for cooperation and participation in managing the enterprise than when technologies were simple and the chief possessed all the technical knowledge needed" (p. 3). In the spirit of the times, his advice was read as requiring worker participation in all management decisions.

Douglas McGregor's universally referenced 1960 essay putting forth management styles termed "Theory X" and "Theory Y" has often been employed as argument for increased management reliance on worker judgment and initiative. McGregor framed his argument to illustrate the power of the self-fulfilling expectations concerning worker behavior held by naive managers. In the ideological spirit of his time it became part of the rhetoric of the worker participation and involvement movement.

G. I. Susman in 1976 published *Autonomy at Work: A Sociotechnical Analysis of Participative Management*. In this book he called for redesign of work tasks to achieve the best match between a social and a technical system. Eric Trist, an associate in the widely revered Tavistock Movement, penned the book's forward. In the opening paragraph of the book's first chapter, Susman asserts that "under present socioeconomic conditions the undesirable consequences to the individual, the organization and society, of much work as presently designed and performed is no longer justifiable on economic, psychological or humanist grounds" (p. 3). H. P. Dachler and B. Wilpert, in their 1978 critique of research on participation in organizations, complain that the conservative methodology upon which rigorous research is based serves to perpetuate theories-in-use (i.e., scientific management), thereby failing to offer support in the movement toward greater industrial democracy. That very participatory democracy, they aver, "has functioned as a social value in itself. It therefore serves as an ideal model or moral standard against which social decision-making schemes can be evaluated" (p. 4). M. Sashkin in a 1986 article written for *Organizational Dynamics* rhetorically titled his argument "Participative Management Remains an Ethical Imperative."

The general specification of a need for more worker power and involvement in decision making was, nevertheless, not universally shared among social scientists. Hard research lent little support to the argument for participation on grounds of either worker satisfaction or increased productivity. In the absence of financial and political intervention by the government, the debate between those ideologically committed to worker participation and those persuaded by hard, empirical research findings has remained largely open and intramural in its quality, though the exchange has often been filled with emotional rhetoric. Dachler and Wilpert's argument was persuasively rebutted by Locke, Schweiger and Latham in the pages of *Organizational Dynamics* in 1986. There were earlier objections to the ideological character proponents' arguments. Worker participation was, for instance, critically evaluated by George Strauss, who, in his 1963 essay, "Some Notes on Power Equalization," pointed out the prevailing general bias of academics toward "autonomy, inner direction and the quest for maximum self-development." Strauss commented on the incongruity of such values with the life- and work-styles of many unskilled laborers and the existence of numerous negative findings regarding the utility of worker participation. A trio of European management educators, C. Faucheux, G. Amado and A. Laurent, writing for the 1982 *Annual Review of Psychology*, skeptically observed the cultural insularity of American scientists who seemed to ignore the obvious failure of partici-pation to transfer cross-culturally to European and Third World settings.

The necessity for worker choice in establishing work objectives has been frequently and effectively challenged through research. E. A. Locke and G. P. Latham, arguing the case for effectiveness of hierarchically imposed work goals in their 1990 scientific synthesis and exposition, *A Theory of Goal Setting and Task Performance*, conclude that available evidence offers negligible support for the effects of worker participation on either worker satisfaction or job performance. Vroom (1964), surveying job satisfaction correlates, noted that workers who are satisfied with their jobs tend to say they also have greater influence on decisions that affect them. He noted, however, that the evidence available was not consistent and concluded that the personality of the worker is an important interven-ing variable of worker temperament, citing findings that authoritarian personalities seem to prefer authoritarian, nonparticipative leadership, while autonomy-seeking personalities are happier when given greater independence in their work.

The relationship between worker satisfaction and participation is further complicated by the finding that dissatisfied workers may perceive that they enjoy less opportunity for participation than they desire. Opportunity to participate at the desired level may increase satisfaction among those who need personal autonomy in their work and increased satisfaction may result in greater perceived opportunity for participation.

For Vroom, these were salient observations that led him toward a more intensive examination of the factors that differentiate effective from ineffective participation in the work setting. In association with P. W. Yetton, he would later (1973) develop a comprehensive contingency theory of worker participation in management decisions. The Vroom and Yetton model subsequently offered opportunity for empirical validation of contingency theory in management decision making (Vroom and Jago, 1988). Decision managers naive to their model, it was found, more often made successful decisions when operating within the specifications of the theory than when departing from it. The theory and validation evidence offered by Vroom and Yetton, taken in combination, supply a sound foundation for the conclusion that the managerial decision mode employed must appropriately fit the situation faced. No one decision-making approach works for every situation.

The Vroom and Yetton model and its broader implications for employee involvement and participation will be discussed later in this chapter. To better set the foundation for development of the subject here, we may first examine the 1948 research of L. Coch and J.R.P. French, Jr., carried out in the Harwood Manufacturing Corporation and widely cited in the 1950s and 1960s as a decisive demonstration of productivity increases brought about by worker participation and involvement. Harwood was the anchor point for a quarter century of worker participation research and ideology. Like Hawthorne, it offers a special historical perspective on the roots of this debate and catalogs most of the variables that are relevant to participative management systems.

THE HARWOOD STUDIES: PARTICIPATION LIVES!

As an early field experiment centering on management issues, Coch and French broke significant ground. The study used intact small work groups with distinct work specializations and on-going work cultures. Four experimental groups consisting of thirteen, eight, seven and two workers, and a somewhat larger control group of unspecified size were studied. Harwood manufactured pajamas. Most employees were young women with no more than a grade school education and no prior industrial experience. Harwood used a strict piecework incentive pay system to compensate its production employees. Time standards were set by industrial engineers in the spirit of specifications originally established by Frederick Winslow Taylor. A sixty-unit rate standard was used throughout the plant.

Competition in the mature garment industry was intense. Pressure to reduce cost was continual on all jobs. Most jobs were simple and highly specialized. Every step of the work process was subject to continual time study reanalysis to cut out labor time and cost. Piecework rates, as a result, changed frequently. The typical experienced worker's response to change in her incentive rate was complaint, frustration at having to meet the new rate, failure to come up to standard and often ended with quitting the job. The problem was severe enough to tarnish Harwood's reputation in the local labor market, making recruitment of replacement workers more difficult. Ultimately these problems led to employee plantwide election of union representation. Clearly the situation was out of control and required fresh solutions.

The solutions applied are carefully described in the published research of Coch and French (1948) In the control group, a change in the task sequence and its accompanying job piece rate was announced. Both changes were said to be necessary to meet the competition. The new work routine and rate were explained to workers. These "control group" workers were then put on the new task and rate. Initially they produced about fifty standard units and for a period of more than a month they remained at or below that level. This performance represented about 83% of the engineered standard. Grievances were filed protesting the rate, supervisors were the target of angry comments and 17% of the group terminated their employment in the forty days immediately following implemention of the change. This was characterized in the study report as representative of worker reaction to other previous revisions in tasks and changes in their related piece rates.

The experimental groups were called together but a change in the task and piece rate was not initially announced. Instead, "the need for change was presented as *dramatically* as possible!" (p. 520). The prices of identical garments produced one year apart in the factory were compared and it was shown that the later price was approximately half the former. The pressure of market competition was clearly communicated. Next, the need to remove "frills" and "fancy work" as a cost-cutting measure was sold to the workers. Management proposed to run a check study on the current job, presumably to determine that rates were fair. Next, *with the assistance of workers in the group*, unnecessary work was identified for elimination from the task and representative operators were trained in the new routine. Once trained, time studies were performed with these operators to set new piece rates. Finally, the new task structure and piece rate were announced to all operators, who were now trained briefly in the new method.

Exhibit 5–1 graphically portrays the results. In two of the experimental groups, groups 2 and 3 on the graph, consisting of eight and seven workers, respectively, output exceeded the new sixty-unit standard on the second day of production and remained above that level, ranging upward toward eighty units throughout the observation. It may be significant to note that in these smaller groups, all operators participated in preliminary training and rate setting, and that, in meetings with these groups preparatory to task and rate changes, "suggestions were immediately made in such quantity that the stenographer had difficulty in recording them" (p. 515). We can perhaps assume that, in these groups, exceptional dynamics were at work creating high group cohesion and group norming in support of the changes.

Exhibit 5-1
Harwood Manufacturing Company Output and Worker Participation
Experiment, Control versus Experimental Groups

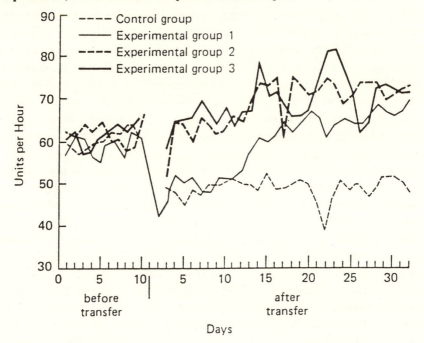

There were no grievances, no angry outbursts at supervisors and no quits while performance of these groups was being measured following introduction of the new methods and rates.

In the largest group, consisting of thirteen workers, designated as group 1 on the graph, output immediately dropped into the fifty-unit range, then steadily and gradually climbed upward until it surpassed the sixty-unit level at the end of fourteen days. Parenthetically, the researchers note that work for this group was "scarce" for the first seven days, which could account for some of the delay in reaching performance standard. A small and noticeable difference between the larger versus the two smaller groups is apparent in the consistency of averages after standard is reached; the thirteen-worker group averaged sixty-one units a day after reaching standard, while the eight- and seven-person groups performed at an average of seventy-four units, slightly more than 20% higher.

A clear difference is indisputably revealed as between performance of the control group and the three experimental groups (the experimental group of two was properly ignored). To underscore that difference, the

Harwood experimenters reassembled thirteen surviving members of the original control group, changed their tasks and rates using the methods earlier applied to the experimental groups and observed the result. The former control group now adapted to change in its work and piece rates very differently. Almost immediately, they exceeded the standard rate and quickly moved into the seventy-unit range of performance.

WAS IT PARTICIPATION OR SOMETHING ELSE?

The major question that must be raised by the study is whether worker participation in management decision making was the sole or even the dominant operant force in bringing about the observed change. Part of the problem with Coch and French, and with most subsequent proponents of the worker participation and involvement idea, is that participation and involvement are poorly defined and are operationalized differently from study to study. A clearer definition was required and, indeed, as will subsequently become apparent, is available in the work of Vroom and Yetton. At Harwood, though, we may reasonably question just how much participation is in evidence.

The changes implemented were clearly desired by management and virtually imposed by it on the workers involved in both the experimental and control groups. The major differences between control and experimental conditions of change might be characterized as the difference between a "here is your system, people, go to it" versus "any way you analyze it, we've got to cut costs and we're happy to hear what you have to say before we decide how to do it." The pressure of price competition in Harwood's market was clearly communicated, time-study engineers ostensibly worked alongside workers, checking the old rate and timing out the new one. Workers appear to have had opportunity to offer suggestions for changes (a stenographer was present at meetings of the experimental groups) that would reduce cost. They may either have offered suggestions that were superior to what time-study engineers would have thought of, or, wittingly or otherwise, anticipated what engineers would propose so that they were already comfortable with what was coming well before the task and rate changes were fixed and announced.

If workers came up with ideas that otherwise would *not* have been included in the new system, we might count this as genuine worker involvement and participation in the decision-making process. If not, it has to have been competent communication of business need that convinced workers that the changes sought were necessary and fair. In their 1981 critique of this research, C. S. Bartlem and E. A. Locke propose that

the main factor in improved performance is the perceived fairness of the
new piecework rate. Belief in fairness, they suggest, is mainly brought
about by increased trust engendered by management's open communication of the problem and willingness to listen to what workers have to say.
In most current-day critiques of incentive pay plans, worker trust of
management's intent in changing rates is presumed central to the success
of an incentive system.

It was later suggested by Locke and Latham (1990) that the result
obtained at Harwood might alternatively be explained as a matter of
increased worker commitment to management-assigned goals. The Harwood study in many ways seems now more a demonstration of the
variables that influence worker acceptance of a revision in piecework rates
and related output goals. Its contribution to an understanding of worker
participation in management decision making otherwise may be incidental
and peripheral.

THE ROLE OF GROUP INTERACTION

There is also the likelihood that dynamics of the internal workings of
these groups played a part. Group size and makeup varied and experimental groups showed variation in response to the change introduced despite
the relative consistency of experimental treatment. Knowledge of group
process and group phenomena in 1948 was in its formative stage. Studies
at Western Electric's Hawthorne plant had documented some of the ways
in which work groups set maximums on work output and enforced them
socially through group normative pressure.

The Harwood researchers took clear note of the importance of group
process they had observed. Coch and French commented that

observations . . . indicate that a strong psychological sub-group with negative
attitudes toward management will display the strongest resistance to change. On
the other hand, changed groups with high we-feeling and positive cooperative
attitudes are the best re-learners. Collections of individuals with little or no
we-feeling display some resistance to change but not so strongly as the groups
with high we-feeling and negative attitudes toward management (p. 529).

Coch and French go on to observe that "this phenomenon of the relationship between we-feeling and resistance to change is so overt that for years
the general policy of management of the plant was never to change a group
as a group, but rather to scatter the individuals in different areas throughout

the factory" (p. 529). In their wrap-up interpretation of the study, they comment that

probably the most important force affecting the (poor) recovery under the control procedure was a group standard, set by the group, restricting the level of production to 50 units per hour. Evidently this explicit agreement to restrict production is related to the group's rejection of the change and of the new job as arbitrary and unreasonable (p. 530).

Here is a general statement of two major phenomena concerning group process, an emerging field of research that would be integrated and described in 1950 by G. C. Homans in his landmark book, *The Human Group*. As concepts explanatory of group dynamics in the domain of sociology and social psychology, they would be generally recognized and referred to as *group cohesion* and *group norming*. At Harwood, those forces of group cohesion and group norming that previously formed around distrust to defeat the new standard were now brought to bear in creating trust and meeting the new standard.

Concluding the study report, Coch and French summarize the major findings with the statement that "it is possible for management to modify greatly or remove completely group resistance to changes . . . by the use of group meetings in which management effectively communicates the need for change and stimulates group participation in planning for changes" (p.530). Group meetings, effective communication and stimulation of group involvement in planning, by their own summary of the study, all contributed significantly to the results achieved.

Certainly important forces were discovered to be at work in this study, even though subsequent commentators chose to deal with them through the rhetoric of participation. The prevailing ideology undoubtedly helped focus attention on this abstract and yet poorly defined issue. But it is more likely that effective management communication that built trust and elicited group commitment to change was the real driving force here.

Groups, unfortunately, are difficult to control and hard to understand. It is more common for American managers to look at high performance management as a matter of individual effort. The prevailing ethic of work in America was and often still is one of isolated, individual effort. Unions are not just dangerously inconvenient, they are patently "un-American" in their substitution of group solidarity for individual initiative. Frederick Taylor battled to defeat worker collusion in his campaign to raise production output levels and obtain a full, fair day's work. Henry Ford created the auto market by applying a blend of personal marketing, operations innovation and engineering genius that needed little or no help in the form of subordinate participation in production decisions.

There is some justification for management prejudice against work groups. Up to the time of the Harwood study, it was more common for group norms to operate defensively against management's purposes than to support them. Nor are groups always an efficient or effective way to get the job done. Research on groups has shown that the group product for simple, noncomplex tasks is often only little better, if not sometimes slightly inferior, to the output of the most capable group member. The same or very similar result that can be produced solo takes longer and requires the labor of multiple participants when assigned to a group. Work group effort takes on the taint of wastefulness, which is sometimes echoed by executives in their real-world complaints about the wastefulness of committee activity.

WORK GROUPS CAN GO OFF THE TRACK

The potential pathology of inappropriate group activity is unmistakable. It has been convincingly demonstrated that a bogus group of an experimenter's confederates posing as a randomly formed group can usually influence a single individual to deny the evidence of his or her own sense and join a false group consensus rather than take a courageous stand and risk being an isolate (Asch, 1956). Irving Janis (1972) has proposed the prevalence of a "groupthink" pathology in decision making that produces a sense of group superiority that prematurely closes off unpopular alternatives and can result in disastrously poor group decisions. He has also suggested, however, that genuinely superior policy decisions may be achieved by a group organized to include roles that demand skeptical challenge and thorough evaluation of all possible ideas pertinent to the problem solution sought.

The implications of a wide range of similar findings from social psychological research into group phenomena are that groups can be strange and unpredictable beasts with potential for great harm, as well as for significant benefit to management purposes. The difficulty inheres in the uncertainty of how to channel the group's end product. In all likelihood, it is absence of clear control that makes participation in decision making by subordinates and workers unacceptable to authoritarian personalities, whether they serve as members or leaders of the group. The path to the group's end product is usually messy and unpredictable. Democracy is a fickle and whimsical instrument through which to formulate policy. We may easily forget that it has often been held in disdain by social philosophers down through history from Plato to Alexander Pope, as well as by a host of past and present-day tyrants and dictators. Taylor's best standard method for performance of a job, like Ford's marvelous and efficient production machine, left no room for participation or involvement by the worker in operations decision making. That was reserved to the superior judgment of management experts. In that special context, Harwood effectively demonstrated the power potential of worker participation in management decision making. What remains is to clarify just what it means for a worker to participate. We must do so without being overly swayed by the still-influential ideological imperative that worker involvement and participation is an ethical imperative that *must* be universally applied to all management decisions. To find the beginnings of that clarity, we may now return to Vroom and Yetton's cogent 1973 analysis of *Leadership and Decision Making*.

TOWARD A CONTINGENCY THEORY OF PARTICIPATIVE DECISION MAKING

Vroom and Yetton began with a comprehensive review of the existing literature and research on management decision making. They concluded that a contingency approach was the sounder one. The function of a conceptual description of leader decision making, they concluded, was not to conform to an ideal mode. Rather, it is to offer a guide that helps leaders choose among decision-making methods appropriately to fit varying decision-making circumstances. They began with the assumption that "no one leadership method is applicable to all situations."

Within this conceptual framework, Vroom and Yetton defined the varying degrees of subordinate participation and involvement that could describe a range of problem-solving decisions. Three general levels were posited: authoritarian or autocratic, designated by the letter "A"; consultative or communicative, signified with a "C"; and group consensus, coded "G." Autocratic and consultative decisions were each characterized on two levels or degrees of participation, but group decisions were described only on a single, group consensus dimension, ignoring, for instance, the potential for deciding by majority vote rather than by pure, jury-styled, consensus.

For purposes of simplifying their research design, Vroom and Yetton assumed that these decisions were all made by a manager working with subordinates in a strict hierarchical organization structure. The soundest presumption in the Harwood-type context is that, under the old system of change, decisions were made by one or more industrial engineers, presented to management for approval and announced to workers. Realistically, many if not most decisions in complex organizations today are made by expert or functional specialists. Increasingly, those decisions may also be the responsibility of project managers and may even be delegated to consultants. For purposes of this discussion, and to account for this range of decision-making agencies, the five stages of participation proposed by Vroom and Yetton are preserved but are translated into more generalized terms. The resulting, modified stages of participation of management decision making with their respective category designations are:

AI: The responsible individual makes the decision based on information already available to him or her.

AII: The responsible individual makes the decision after gathering any needed or missing information from those possessing it. The purpose in gathering information may or may not be revealed to information sources.

CI: The problem is shared individually with those who are likely to have ideas or suggestions for its solution, then the responsible individual makes a decision that need not necessarily reflect the inputs of those consulted.

CII: The problem is shared in an open group meeting with those who are likely to have ideas or suggestions for its solution, then the responsible individual makes a decision that need not necessarily reflect the inputs of those consulted.

GII: The responsible individual convenes a meeting of those persons judged capable of contributing to a solution of the problem. He or she participates with the group in generating and evaluating alternatives, and everyone works toward an agreed-upon solution. The responsible individual accepts and implements the solution reached by group consensus.

It may be noted first that pure participative democracy does not appear among these alternatives except as the final one. At the four preliminary levels of participation, the responsible individual makes and accepts full accountability for the ultimate decision. This is wholly in harmony with classical organization theory. Risking dilution of accountability when the hazards of group consensus are not necessary could be judged irresponsible if the decision were critical or far-reaching. Even inviting the uncertainties of group process through convening a group meeting enters only after utility of the first three levels of decision making participation is exhausted. Participation begins at exact zero of decision-making involvement, progresses to supplying facts or methods and concludes with full delegation of decision-making authority to the group.

Proponents of industrial democracy might readily object that the prejudices of traditional, hierarchical management practice are built into this continuum of participative decision making. It is an objection that reveals a corollary prejudice for the complexity and hazard of group consensus alone. Industrial democracy as ideology tends to fixate on the last and most extreme level of decision-making processes.

As will be demonstrated in the following analysis, though, the benefits and hazards of industrial democracy are fairly and fully entertained by this model. It cannot be faulted for failing to include the option of full industrial democracy. The GII level fully enacts it. Nor can it be criticized for naively overlooking the most obvious and pervasive of decision-making styles—the responsible decision maker alone deciding—level AI. Level CII appears to match the experimental group involvement method introduced at Harwood, certainly not the most extreme group involvement method; and the remaining levels, AII and CI, adequately seem to reflect a realistic range of options for seeking out and sharing pertinent information.

The three principal tests of this participation scale's utility, however, are not necessarily apparent in the scale itself. The first test is in the quality of the decision obtained and the second is its acceptance by those who must implement it. A low-quality decision that will fail must be avoided. A decision that will be blocked, misunderstood or misapplied by those it is imposed on is equally unsatisfactory. The third test is the cost of the decision-making process in time and labor to achieve it, balanced against the payoff from participation in development of decision-making skill and experience among participants.

The first and second tests are expressed by Vroom and Yetton in seven rules for establishing the suitability/viability of a decision-making method. Three are concerned with quality, four with implementer acceptance. The quality rules are:

Q1: If the decision maker lacks information necessary to a high-quality decision, that information *must* be obtained before the decision can be made. AI is ruled out; AII, CI, CII and GII are all potentially acceptable styles.

Q2: If commitment to organization goals and policies of decision-making participants cannot be trusted, the decision *must not* be made by group consensus. AI, AII, CI and CII are feasible styles, depending on how much commitment to implementation is required, but GII is ruled out.

Q3: If the problem is unique and/or complex with no advance definition of what information may be needed or who may have access to it, and decision-making time is limited, group process that allows interaction among members of a broadly representative problem-solving team is necessary for an effective decision. AI, AII and CI are ruled out; CII and GII are potentially acceptable styles.

These three quality rules give full weight to the significance of information unavailable to the responsible decision maker and recognize both
the potential pathology and problem-solving strength of group dynamics
in dealing with messy, unstructured problem-solving situations.

Implementation acceptance rules are:

I1:   If an imposed decision will create resentment among those who must
       implement it, some form of participation is required. AI is ruled out; AII,
       CI, CII and GII are feasible. The level chosen is determined by its effec-
       tiveness in avoiding impaired implementation.

I2:   If commitment to the decision is needed for successful implementation but
       those who must implement it are in disagreement as to the best solution,
       some form of group process to resolve differences and obtain group con-
       sensus is necessary. AI, AII and CI are ruled out; CII and GII are potentially
       acceptable.

I3:   If the quality of the decision is unimportant but commitment is necessary
       to assure full implementation, there is no purpose in risking the decision to
       anything less than full group consensus. AI, AII, CI, and CII are ruled out;
       GII is required.

I4:   If commitment is necessary to full implementation, a high-quality decision
       is required and members can be trusted to test the quality of their solution
       against organization goals and policies, there is no purpose in risking the
       decision to anything less than full group consensus. AI, AII, CI and CII are
       ruled out; GII is required.

Implementation rules, it is apparent, give full weight to those circumstances where industrial democracy can contribute productively to a
high-quality decision, recognizing the mischief that unbridled autocratic
management can introduce into the implementation process. Thereby the
rules award full value to the power of group process to achieve a superior
result under appropriate circumstances.

The advantage of decision rules such as these is that they can be
processed with the logic of sets to test interactions among them, thereby
establishing deductively those decision-making modes that pass the test
of utility. The resulting analysis can be graphically illustrated as a form of
decision tree—guiding a decision about how to make a decision—with
decision nodes for each of the seven or eight factors upon which the rules
are based. Exhibit 5–2 illustrates an abbreviated decision tree model based
on the Vroom and Yetton principles.

Most present-day management texts present the Vroom and Yetton
model to readers in the form of a decision tree similar to though considerably more elaborate than that offered in Exhibit 5–2. Managers through-

Exhibit 5-2

Abbreviated Decision Tree Model (based on the Vroom and Yetton [1973] and Vroom and Jago [1988] Contingency Model of Management Decision Making)

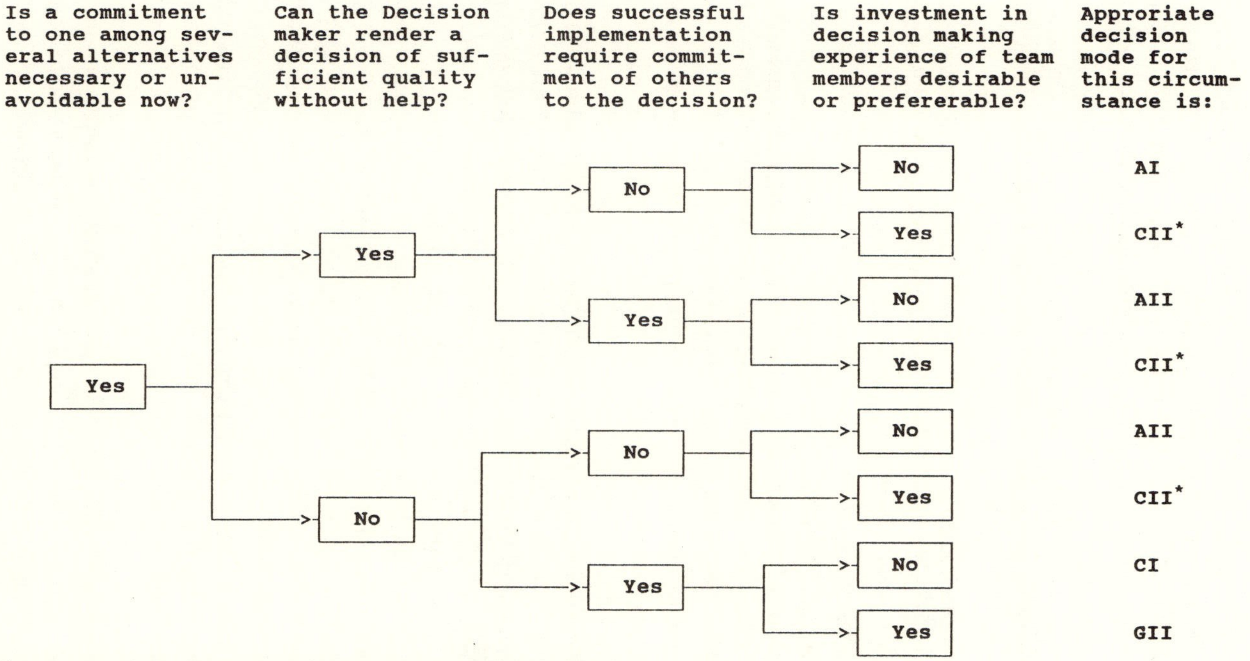

Is a commitment to one among several alternatives necessary or unavoidable now?
Can the Decision maker render a decision of sufficient quality without help?
Does successful implementation require commitment of others to the decision?
Is investment in decision making experience of team members desirable or prefererable?
Approriate decision mode for this circumstance is:
Yes
Yes
No
No
Yes
No
Yes
No
Yes
No
Yes
No
Yes
No
Yes
AI
CII*
AII
CII*
AII
CII*
CI
GII

*Where orgnizational goals are already shared by team members, GII may be appropriate.

out the world carry wallet-sized representations of a graphic model supplied to them by Kepner-Tregoe, the international training organization that is licensed to train managers in the application of the model. In some respects, however, the graphic leadership style decision tree obscures more issues than it illuminates. For absolute maximum simplicity, the Vroom and Yetton decision model can be summarized thus:

- When the decision maker lacks essential information on which to make a minimally sound decision, he or she *must* accept and tolerate some degree of participative help.

- If a high-quality decision is demanded and potential participants do not subscribe to organizational goals and policies, decision by group consensus is never appropriate.

- Messy, unstructured decisions are best handled in a team atmosphere, especially when organization goals are shared.

- Where full implementation of the decision requires trust, understanding and commitment, some appropriate level of participation from those involved in implementing the decision is indispensable.

- Arbitrary choices that must satisfy everyone should always be made by group consensus.

This handful of principles leaves a great deal of latitude in the decision-making style that can successfully be applied in the remaining circumstances, particularly so in situations where almost any degree of participation will suffice. Where judgment and discretion are permitted in choice of a decision-making style, cost and developmental opportunity for participants should guide the ultimate choice. To satisfy cost or developmental opportunity requirements, these rules are followed:

- Where time and budget are limiting, the *least* participative mode applicable should prevail.

- Where development of decision-making ability and problem-solving experience of participants is primary, the *most* participative mode applicable is to be preferred.

Vroom and Yetton provide an especially powerful model in that it is tightly logical, easily explained in commonsense terms and carefully tested through research on all levels. In its original forms, Vroom and Yetton tested the model to determine the extent to which training of decision makers could bring decisions into conformity with the model. The result was demonstration of a stepwise increase in agreement with the outcome of the model as a function of the amount and intensity of training in its application. Managers, thus, can readily learn how to consistently fit their choice of decision mode to the specifications of the model. This offers verification of the logical transparency of the model.

Since introduction of the model, validation tests have been carried out to evaluate the extent of agreement between the mode specified by the model and decisions made by experienced managers. These findings have been consistently supportive of the validity of the model as descriptive of how managers operate from experience alone. Decisions made within the specifications of the model are consistently more successful than those made outside its rules.

Argument for application of the Vroom and Yetton decision-making model, seems so strong that it would appear necessary to require justification for departure from it. Application of the model in the real world, though, is not always a matter of simply checking the specifications for the appropriate decision-making mode. It is not always easy to know when and whether sufficient information is at hand on which to base a decision. The amount of information demanded for a quality decision may be a judgment call. Whether a decision should be made or not may be at question. Good decision makers probably don't make decisions; they let evidence accumulate until the difficult decisions make themselves. Critical decisions are often those that must be made under pressure of time, without full or even sufficient information, knowing that delay will permit opportunity or option to disappear. The extent of participation permissible under such pressure will depend on limitations attending the decision.

Nor is it always feasible to predict the extent to which those who must implement the decision will choose to block it, will misunderstand it or will misapply it. Caution would seem to dictate that the prudent manager anticipates that when anything that can go wrong, it will! But it may be unreasonable to try to foresee *every* potential glitch in an untried plan. The acceptable amount and cost of participation in decision making is likely to depend on the cost and criticality of misimplementation.

Worker tolerance for imposed decisions may be variable. The willingness of workers to go along with imposed implementation may vary from time to time or diminish over time. On the other hand, those prepared by training and/or temperament to accept and follow orders—the so-called autocratic personality—may consistently experience distinct discomfort when called on to participate in decision making at *any* time.

Other major factors may influence the appropriateness of decision-making style. The decision maker's reputation for excellent decisions may justify a much greater range of latitude in making solo decisions. Decisions that can be worked out reliably with highly structured information-gathering processes may become wholly subject to individual or group technical process. These and other variables may deserve consideration in establishing the appropriateness of a given decision-making mode. In their continued pursuit of variables that can influence that style, Vroom and Jago (1988) have developed a computer-based expert system that analyzes a range of variables and recommends an appropriate set of decision-making styles. The soundness of a contingency theory of management decision making seems well established and practical to apply.

Vroom and Yetton have rationalized participation in the workplace in a fashion that accounts for the accepted research findings that bear on worker involvement. They have maintained full respect for the power and hazard of group process, thereby entertaining the best elements of industrial democracy without succumbing to the emotional stridency of its ideological side. They have organized and clearly communicated their theory so that it can be understood and taught. It is a powerful and impressive foundation on which to build further theory of worker participation and involvement.

DOMINATION OF DECISIONS BY TECHNICAL OR FUNCTIONAL SPECIALISTS

What remains for examination once this foundation has been accepted and understood is the peculiar distortion of both decision making *and* worker participation created by long-term accumulation of decision-making power in the hands of narrow technical and functional specialists. We must evaluate the damage done to organizational and operations effectiveness by experts with their powerful but limited decision-making scope.

The joint legacy of Frederick Taylor and Henry Ford in twentieth-century management practice is the concentration of technical decision making into the hands of technical specialists accompanied by the exact, often narrow, structuring of jobs at the production level. Taylor said to the worker, your job has been scientifically analyzed, here is the best way to perform it and these are the expected output standards. Ford went a step further to say, here is your little piece of the work and here are your standards, don't do anything differently unless I tell you to. Taylor recommended against use of the military model of organization, but Ford found Taylor's methods well suited to a strict chain of command flow of orders. His workers might innovate, but Henry Ford as the ultimate expert had to approve any change before it became standard practice. The expert's power to veto or approve became a standard dimension of organization structure.

As organization and technology became increasingly complex, Ford's structure remained, but decision making began to fragment into a variety of specialized technical domains. In the automotive industry, there now were styling engineers, mechanical engineers, electrical engineers, production engineers and quality control engineers. There were cost accountants, receivables accountants, payables accountants, general ledger accountants, and tax accountants. The decisions that were once made entirely by Henry Ford with help from James Couzens are now fragmented into multiple functional domains. Among mechanical engineers, there are now specialists in doors, brake systems, chassis structure and a dozen other structural elements. Payables accountants now divide between payroll and purchasing support. In other functional areas like the personnel department, sales, marketing, legal, computers and the rest, an equivalent fragmentation of technical specialization has evolved. Trained, technical specialties formed around specialties of method and depth of knowledge in their field, sometimes on a foundation of science, dominate an increasing proportion of management decisions. If the technical expert does not directly make the final decision, as increasingly he or she has come to do, mandatory review prior to implementation is likely to be required. Only the politically weakest experts have found it necessary to "sell" their assistance and persuade others to support their objectives. The strange, theoretically unexamined role of technical specialist with narrow decision-making accountability has thus evolved as a standard element of complex organization. The new experts echoed Henry Ford in saying to workers and managers alike, this is your narrowly specialized task; don't do anything differently until I tell you to.

Aside from the unsupportable assumption that experts have all the answers, the error of this role design resides in assuming that all or even most decisions are best made by a functional expert and that experts from different functions with conflicting purposes will consistently resolve their differences productively. Neither assumption is fully tenable. Messy, unstructured problems are *best* handled by a *team* composed around diverse perspectives, as suggested by the Vroom and Yetton model. The insular independence of technical specialists makes no provision for problems outside their technical domain nor the teamwork they demand. Team collaboration among technical experts who neither understand nor respect one another's functional perspectives is difficult at best. It can become impossible where *each* feels accountable for full execution of his or her functional objectives. This is not the formula for high performance.

Often it is the line supervisor or worker who is best positioned to evaluate or find solutions that are compatible with multiple job demands. Imposed technical decisions may rule out input from the best-informed sources.

Modern industrial and business organization structure, shaped by Frederick Taylor and Henry Ford, has evolved into a feudalistic confederation of specialist decision makers whom workers and managers must often appease before change in existing process or organization structure affecting their domain may be implemented. Crises are routinely referred to the appropriate specialist(s). Legal counsel, thus, does not counsel management; rather, it makes legal policy and legal decisions for the organization by recommending without specification of options. Managers are often left only with the most trivial decisions. They spend the largest part of their time mediating the political battles of subordinates and dissenting experts. Political skill and experience now more often shape cross-functional policy decisions and operational effectiveness than do organizational objectives.

The great secret competitive weapon of Japanese industry in its assault on the U.S. auto industry was organization structure that took accountability for problem solutions away from technical experts and pushed it down to the lowest appropriate levels of the line operation. Workers, not quality engineers or inspectors, were made fully accountable for quality. Line managers, not cost accountants or industrial engineers, were made accountable for cost reduction and efficiency. Specialists were put in the roles of teachers and advisors, not decision makers.

The result has been truly spectacular. Better decisions that address problems more broadly, that avoid ego-involved specialists who can't always claim to have all the answers but must often pretend they do to protect their political base, and decisions that are owned by those who must implement them have been the consistent, winning result. In light of the Japanese success, the best explanation of results at Harwood is that task design and piecework decisions formerly made by the industrial engineers, rubber stamped by line management and announced to workers as management's final, fixed decision on the matter were partially delegated to workers. The major barrier to worker acceptance of new tasks and rates had been in the structure of the industrial engineers' "expert" role. When the expert, specialist decision maker's role was sharply circumscribed at Harwood, resistance to change was greatly reduced. One can only wonder what production engineers thought of this new form of worker participation. Engineers' attitudes, unfortunately, were not surveyed at Harwood.

The fundamental problem with greater participation by workers must always be that increases in participation for one individual or group must always be offset by losses in autonomy by another individual or group. The basic instinct of ideologists in pursuit of greater industrial democracy were correct in focusing on power redistribution. Their principal error has been in assuming that power must be taken from *managers* and given to workers. The proper solution more often is to reverse the long-standing prescriptions of Taylorism that demand dominance of decision making by experts and reduce the power of technical and functional specialists to let workers *and* managers take fuller accountability for broad operating results.

THE NEW IDEOLOGY OF TEAMWORK

Participation today is more often approached through the modern ideology of improved teamwork. Americans, it would seem, are not natural team players. They must learn to coordinate their efforts and do so best when faced with some form of competitive threat. The long-standing norm of American industry is excellence of individual effort. Teams as well as groups are not always acceptable in the framework of business organization. Team effort is sometimes suspect. Work groups at Harwood used teamwork to resist changes in work method and piecework rate as well as to embrace them constructively. To a Henry Ford, all forms of teamwork probably looked like collective collusion to defeat his will.

The complexity of modern technology and social/legal constraints on business, though, are increasingly beyond the problem-solving powers of a single individual. As Rensis Likert (1961) pointed out more than a quarter century ago, business decisions are now often too complex to be left to a single expert. The contribution of individuals with different technical and business viewpoints is increasingly more necessary to achievement of a high-quality business decision. The formation of a strong team is increasingly more critical to project or business success. In embracing the imperative of team decision making, though, all of the possible pathologies of group process are also invited.

An effective team must be built on a foundation of mutual trust, which protects the independence of personal, technical judgment. It must perform to high standards of shared purpose. Teamwork is often hard, grueling work for team members. Honest disagreements are frequent and indispensable. Polite agreement is more often a measure of team failure. Without internal conflict that permits full play of disparate perspectives, the team decision will most likely degenerate into a covert contest of will where the strongest, most politically astute prevails. Without a clear, shared mission, there is no standard against which to measure the quality of a tentative decision. A team is the most difficult way to reach or implement a decision. Teamwork should not be called for nor entered into lightly.

At some point, participation mutates into teamwork. All the experience, evidence, theory and practice that applies to participative management has relevance to teamwork. The major difference is that, for a team, every member has an obligation to help choose the best mode for reaching a decision. The shape of the decision-making process itself must be openly debated by team members. The team may delegate a decision to a member or reserve it to the whole. The team must create and manage its internal structure and culture in the service of its mission.

Teamwork, like participation, is no simple matter. Team members who seek out the warm, cozy support of a tight, cohesive team are not necessarily good team contributors. The individual who commits to the team out of rational, personal self-interest may be among the strongest contributors. The conciliatory social director role on a team may impede good decision making. The argumentative and unpopular devil's-advocate role may greatly improve it. Teamwork as the successor to participative democracy shares all the weaknesses of ideologically advocated participation. Teamwork, too, is subject to evaluation in contingency terms; there are occasions to use it and occasions to avoid it.

Emerging high performance management systems often emphasize teamwork. Managing teamwork and working as a team member require social skill and insight that are still rare. Individual, isolated functional experts, still the norm of American industry, are more likely to be barriers to teamwork than aids. Future high performance systems will probably demand major upgrading of teamwork skill that will lead to radical revision of many job roles, especially the role of worker. Increased worker participation, as best we understand the notion, will likely be a major element in the invention of future high performance management systems. Their design will certainly require the best knowledge and understanding of the participative rules and principles outlined here.

Chapter Six

Worker Motivation: Goals and Business Strategy

The obvious, direct route to high performance management systems would seem to be the discovery of those motivational wellsprings that drive human action. Much thought and study have been invested in the search for this key, but little theory of practical use to the invention of high performance systems has been produced until recently. A brief review of the more popular strands of motivational theory will help illuminate the limitations of traditional theories and why the more basic, prosaic practice of goal setting frequently works.

RADICAL BEHAVIORISM AS MOTIVATION THEORY

In its application to the workplace, motivation theory drew heavily on radical behaviorism, especially so as enacted in the role of worker as robot by Ford. Behaviorism as championed by B. F. Skinner simply ignored and denied the influence of internal, intrinsic psychological factors, rejecting with special contempt the notion of "mind" as the cause of behavior. Mental processes for Skinner (1974) are only fanciful metaphors that, in his reality, are better depicted as poorly understood complex contingencies of reinforcement.

In an age of scientific management corrupted by Henry Ford into worker-as-robot it was inevitable that radical behaviorism, with its insistence on externalization of behavioral cause as the exclusive and final source of human behavior, would dominate theories of motivation, especially as applied to the workplace. In Ford's production domain, the mind of the owner-master was supreme. Only those sensitive subordinates whose mind-sets blended unobtrusively with Ford's were permitted to participate in decision making. Everyone else was "motivated" by money or fear to produce at standards acceptable to Ford. That the provision of clear work standards alone was probably sufficient to motivate high output went unnoticed under circumstances where this one, grandiose ego set every purpose.

Human relations, quality of work life, and cognitive volition would, however, ultimately not be denied. Workers have minds too. Reinforcement theory lacks utility and foundation until it can explain why a particular kind of reinforcement works with one individual and not another. As long as it is a matter of hungry pigeons pecking vigorously away at miniature piano keyboards, food release levers or missile guidance consoles, behaviorism enjoys great predictive simplicity. When it comes to explaining why one worker volunteers eagerly for overtime pay, another demands the boss' personal assurance as to the importance of the task before working extra hours and yet another insists on the day off to go fishing, radical behaviorism offers little help. Vague reference to yet poorly understood complex contingencies of reinforcement offers little satisfaction.

Volition cannot be so easily dismissed. People do seem to act on the basis of their personal world-view, and many reinforcers of behavior seem entirely internal and mental in quality and source. If choice and volition do shape simple work behavior, cognition must be called on to explore and explain what is going on. The better supposition for work motivation purposes is that, if permitted to use them, workers have minds that direct choices in behavior. They forego paychecks to strike for restored dignity. They cooperate heartily for the satisfaction of being a member of the team. They choose their own standards of performance.

External reinforcers certainly do have influence. It would be foolhardy to deny the effectiveness of money and threat as reinforcers of desired work performance. But choice is dear to the free, independent human being. Future high performance systems will almost certainly not tolerate any signficant abridgment of individual choice the way those of the past have. Management must be prepared to go beyond radical behaviorism and actively consider how workers *think* about how to respond, even to those undeniably powerful external inputs and events like money and fear.

Exclusive focus on reinforcement as motivator of behavior ignores the cognitive richness and complexity of motivation. An understanding of motivation requires appreciation that it operates in two distinct psychological dimensions: *direction and purpose of action*, and *energy and intensity* with which the action is carried. Reinforcement that is sufficiently dramatic can focus behavior. And, while punishment or physical need like hunger may consistently evoke high intensity of response, much variation in intensity of response to reinforcement, even that which avoids physical discomfort, seems cognitive. A comprehensive grasp of human motivation must explain differences in choice of motivational direction *and* in level of intensity.

DIMENSIONS OF MOTIVATION

Motivation to action starts with awareness of the situation's existence and an understanding of its structure. It moves on to interpret and analyze the situation's implications for personally desired or undesired outcomes, then proceeds to determination of preference for a suitable behavioral response and ends with assessment of what response to choose and the appropriate level of energy with which to apply that response.

Even this complicated summary is an oversimplification that risks misleading. Applying motivation as a practical management concept requires, at a minimum, that the stage of the motivational process to be managed be identified if the application is to be effective. Much prevailing theory fails in this identification, leading to misunderstanding and miscarriage in operational use of the concept. Motivational theory may focus on the manner in which opportunity is grasped or dramatized, or deal with expected outcomes. It may try to explain the manner and choice of responsive action, or it can be concerned with source and intensity of activation. With most contemporary motivational theories, one dimension of motivation always seems prominent while others hide in the shadows. It is not until theories of motivation are refocused around goal-setting methods that significant progress is made at integrating and understanding the directive and energizing aspects of work motivation.

MOTIVATIONAL THEORY BEYOND BEHAVIORISM

Considerable theoretical meandering in the tall grass of motivational theory preceded identification of goal setting as central to effective work motivation. A brief look at several of the more popular theories of motivation is useful as introduction to the nature and power of goal setting.

Midcentury motivational theory focused on *need* with particular emphasis on physiological drives as expression of need. A. H. Maslow's (1954) hierarchy of need theory proposed that work motivation is driven by worker need at successive logical levels and that the soundest approach to motivation is to build satisfaction of need from the foundation up.

Beginning with physical needs for food and water, progressing upward through security, social acceptance, self-esteem and, finally, to the apex of self-actualization, Maslow offered a hierarchy of levels through which the needs of humans progress. It is an intuitively appealing theory that is easy to describe and understand. There are always problems with need-based motivation theory, though, in arriving at clear definitions of need, and there can be major difficulties in reconciling conflicts among needs. It is surprising, for instance, how often young women deny the need for adequate nutrition, a physical base imperative in Maslow's scheme, risking debilitating anorexia in pursuit of self-esteem from enhanced physical appearance. Young males, equally, risk death and life-long injury in pursuit of wealth or fame from a sporting career. The danger to security and health of high-speed driving or overdosing on drugs is daily ignored by legions of people. Social peer pressure encourages risky, dangerous activity among young and old alike.

There are too many instances where Maslow's hierarchy fails to explain behavior. Maslow argues that pursuit of self-esteem needs at the expense of health or safety needs should not be possible where lower level needs for health, security and social acceptance are not earlier satisfied. But individuals who lack self-esteem often seem to be unconcerned with basic physical need, suggesting that self-esteem should be put ahead of security and social needs. The semantic tangle introduced by a hierarchy of needs only complicates the lack of clarity already created by poor definition of need. Human behavior is too complicated to be explained by so simple a concept as need or a need hierarchy. Perhaps most telling, merely specifying a need that must be satisfied does not identify the course that will be followed in satisfying it. And, for practical purposes, it is most likely that we will infer the need from the nature of the goal it is focused on. Need may energize behavior, but goals direct it. Need without a goal goes nowhere except, perhaps, in circles. Need theory attempts futilely to identify the source of energy behind action, and it leaves the question of its focus unanswered.

D. C. McClelland (1961) and J. W. Atkinson (1958) subsequently proposed an alternative structure of motivation, suggesting that motivation is culturally conditioned toward achievement, power or social affiliation. Needs, according to these writers, are learned by the young of a society from existing social models. Motivation thereby becomes a cultural thing. The economic implication of this theory is that work performance is preconditioned by training and social example to be focused on achievement, or on power or on social affiliation. The practical significance of this theory is that if one can determine a worker's or manager's predisposition to achievement, power or social affiliation, his or her actions can be predicted.

This is a theory of subconscious drives more than of motivation, which is not surprising in view of its roots in projective psychological measurement method. As McClelland and Atkinson approach it, achievement, power or social affiliation might more accurately be conceived as subconsciously instilled drives or needs that activate an individual's behavior. Prediction of specific action courses within these categories is difficult at best. To gain power for this theory of motivation, it would be well to seek increased specification of goals within the three general typologies offered.

Stacy Adams (1963) offered still another alternative theory of motivation, proposing that inequity—which is, approximately, unequal treatment of those under equal circumstances—when perceived to exist, can activate an effort to restore equity. The practical prediction deriving from this theory is that those who consider themselves underpaid will likely work less hard than their better paid fellows, while those who feel overpaid will make up the difference with added output. There are other possible outcomes, of course, including asking for higher pay where underpaid, or rationalizing one's value upward where overpaid. It is an interesting finding, though, supported by an ingenious research design. It cannot easily be dismissed. Adams seems to have identified an energizing event that, like need, requires better understanding of how it can become focused in order to function as motivator.

Victor Vroom in his *Work and Motivation* (1964) put forward expectancy theory of motivation that introduces an element of cognitive choice into the behavioristic stimulus-response formulation of motivation. In simplest terms, this theory says that a worker will perform a task *if* reasonably confident he or she can perform it, *when* the reward outcome is valued and *if* the reward can reliably be expected to follow successful performance. Again, we encounter the energizing element of motivation without focus on purpose beyond getting the desired but unspecified payoff. The specification of the direction of performance must be added before the formulation is fully useful.

THE POWER OF GOAL SETTING

Goal setting has emerged as the soundest practical means for providing focal direction and energizing high performance in work settings. A substantial body of research has accumulated rapidly since 1970 in support of goal setting as the best explanation of why workers do or do not perform effectively. Naive approaches to motivating workers typically emphasize *either* goals or energizing mechanisms. But concern with worker motivation must be approached as both a matter of energizing and of focusing performance. Goal setting does both. In their landmark summary of goal planning research, *A Theory of Goal Setting and Task Performance*, E. A. Locke and G. P. Latham (1990) review the findings of almost 500 research studies accomplished with over 40,000 research subjects in eight countries. A wide variety of tasks lasting from minutes to years in duration and representative of both laboratory and field settings are reviewed. The evidence summarized in their analysis convincingly, even overwhelmingly, attests to the efficacy of goals as motivators of high performance. Goals, whether set on an individual level or for an organization, consistently focus performance with greater clarity. Specific, difficult goals consistently energize a level of performance that is superior to that obtained with unspecific, "do your best" goals. Goals clearly direct *and* also energize task performance.

Locke and Latham find that clear goals work equally well to enhance performance whether self-initiated or assigned. Participation in the establishment of goals is not a critical factor to their effectiveness. More than a century ago, Frederick Taylor demonstrated that clear, specific, doable goals could be made to influence performance even in the face of active resistance from workers. Goals may be resented and resisted where workers actively distrust management and supervision but, even so, may still have a positive effect on performance. Existence of a clear, specific goal provides a standard against which to compare performance. The focusing, directive effect of clearly set goals is virtually inescapable.

Assigned goals are almost always as good as participatively chosen goals. Long-standing rhetorical concern for increased participation as a lever to better performance among managers and social scientists sometimes creates reticence to accept the notion that assigned goals are as effective as participatively chosen goals when it comes to increased performance. In a comparison of motivational methods carried out by Locke et al. (1980) the relative absence of effect on level of performance produced by participation alone was convincingly argued. Indeed, it often appears that workers must consciously and actively resist assigned goals to defeat their effectiveness. That usually means that management credibility must be a shambles before assigned goals fail to work.

Therefore, under normal, nonconflicted circumstances, assignment of specific goals to a worker can be at least as effective a means for improving performance as is offering a choice of goals. Assignment may even be *more* effective than offering a choice of goal levels in many circumstances. Assignment of difficult goals to workers suggests confidence in their skills, which, in turn, can raise workers' confidence in their own performance capability. Assignment of even seemingly impossible goals by supervision may constitute a stimulating challenge, deserving of one's best effort. Many, perhaps most, assigned goals are adopted by workers as their own goals with the result that assigned goals become impossible to distinguish from self-set goals. The respected, experienced boss who demonstrates command of the product/service and process is looked to for leadership in setting work standards. His or her legitimacy as a leader is usually sufficient to give force to assigned goals.

Many workers may be inclined to set easy goals when left to make their own choices. Success at meeting goals is a source of satisfaction. Thus, worker-set goals may be set modestly because their ready achievement leads to relatively certain personal satisfaction. Workers who focus on difficult goals are often *less* satisfied with their performance. This appears to be a function of the relative mastery demanded by difficult goals. Easy goals are more readily met and mastered, yielding surer satisfaction with the result as judged relative to a low standard. Challenging, assigned goals seem to motivate workers to forego the surer satisfaction of lesser goals and accept the potential disappointment of not meeting goal objectives.

Specific, difficult goals, assigned or self-set, are shown by Locke and Latham to be consistently effective motivators of high performance output. The robustness of challenging goals as a performance driver is accounted for through research in a variety of ways. Some of these are:

- Specification of goals reduces ambiguity as to what constitutes good versus poor performance. Confusion about performance standards is minimized.

- Persistence toward achievement of the goal is increased. The presence of an objective standard offers opportunity to close the gap between present and potential performance.

- The effort and energy necessary for its achievement is more likely to be applied to the goal.

- Work routine is more clearly focused and directed toward a purpose, rather than merely generating continued repetition of the task.

- If the path to the goal is not obvious, the need and opportunity to seek out alternative strategies and plan for their utilization are clearly present. Preparation and planning for pursuit of the goal is realistically engaged.

- Self-confidence in one's ability to achieve the goal increases.

- The complacency of satisfaction is more difficult to invoke without effort.

- Desired outcomes—rewards—which are independent of goal achievement but potentially available as a result of goal achievement, are easier to estimate as outcomes and have stronger effect on performance. (Linking pay directly to goal success, though, is likely to result in setting low goals that assure receipt of the reward.)

The stages that describe effective motivation through goal setting are straightforward. Goal setting theory proposes that high performance begins with the demand for output created by challenging goals, whether assigned by manager or supervisor, negotiated through discussion with the worker or accomplished through group consensus. It is limited by level of worker task skill, which may restrict maximum performance, by commitment to goals where they are unusually demanding, by availability of feedback when knowledge of performance results is not clear or obvious and by recognition of need for planning or learning when task complexity requires them as a foundation for goal achievement. It is focused on specific achievement by the specificity of those goal performance measures available and applied. It is reinforced and acknowledged by the outcomes that attend high performance in the form of objective rewards, satisfaction, by future opportunity created, by new skill attained and by peer or management recognition. Satisfaction with outcomes enhances confidence in one's performance ability, as well as trust in leadership and organizational purpose. Increased satisfaction can then result in greater readiness to embrace new challenging goals, assigned or self-determined, that follow. Exhibit 6–1 offers a graphic model of these forces.

Acceptance of goals is always shaped in part by the degree of trust and confidence existing between worker and manager. In the absence of trust, clear goals reinforced by consistent, appropriate penalties and rewards is the surest path. As trust is built, the high cost of reinforcement through sanctions against poor performance can diminish. Acceptance of challenging goals is increasingly maintained through fair, consistent provision of desired rewards. An essential supporting dimension of rewards throughout this process is the enhanced skill and self-confidence obtained from increasingly more effective performance obtained from response to challenge. The cycle is self-correcting, self-generating and self-fortifying when competently managed. This cycle is illustrated in Exhibit 6–2.

GOALS AND MANAGEMENT BY OBJECTIVES

The general outline offered here can deal only with the major points of the personal goal-setting process. Specification of organizational mechanisms that can direct and energize performance is still needed. The model as presented can serve as a guide to effective motivational programs, but

Exhibit 6-1
Graphic Model of Factors That Can Influence Work Motivation (based on Locke and Latham [1990])

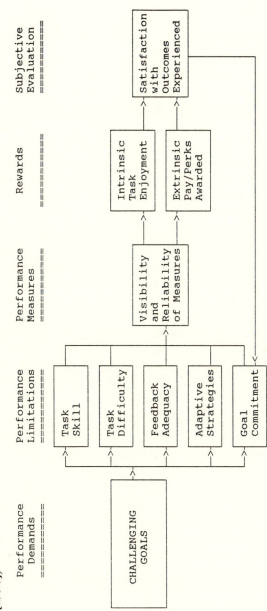

Exhibit 6-2
The Trust-Building Cycle to Support Acceptance of Challenging Goals

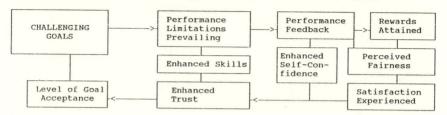

individual goals set without reference to broader business objectives and strategy may even be wrong. Goals must be set and pursued within the broader context of business mission and overarching management purpose.

In practice, an integrated program of business planning and goal setting is the best approach to implementing goal setting on the individual worker level. The consistent and effectual focusing power of goals suggests the desirability of providing a context of companywide goal-planning and goal-setting programs, such as Management by Objectives (MBO).

MBO is not without its problems, of course. Managers and supervisors typically complain about the extra paperwork and administrative effort demanded by MBO. Some workers and supervisors complain of added pressure for high quantity and quality of output. That, obviously, is the point of any motivational program—enhanced performance is the objective. Such complaints are a measure of success.

Workers sometimes complain that goal setting and MBO are clever ways for management to elicit more work for the same pay. This protest is a clear and useful indication of worker concern over pay equity in the sense of Adams' inequity theory of motivation. It cues management either to justify pay in objective market and competitive terms, or adjust pay to restore equity before worker confidence and trust are damaged by perception of inequity in the goal-setting system. Regular, anonymous employee attitude surveys can identify hidden problems that need solution to maintain worker trust. Focusing worker and management attention *on the system* avoids wallowing in personalities when dealing with worker complaints and constructively spotlights system problems that demand repair.

MBO AND BUSINESS STRATEGY

A valuable by-product of goal setting in an MBO context is the communication of clear organizational objectives in the form of mission statement and business strategy on which to focus lower level goal setting and business planning. A major failing of CEO-level leaders in large and small businesses alike continues to be neglect of clear strategy formulation to guide business decisions at all levels. Some CEOs are inevitably opportunistic at the extreme in their strategy courses, avoiding clear commitment to any given goal to preserve flexibility in choice of emerging options. Up to a point, this may lend competitive flexibility to an organization, permitting quick movement to cover niche opportunities or seize unprotected market share. Expecting his or her organization to follow a steady course, while the CEO zigzags among the competitive land mines is both inconsistent and naive. Flexibility too is a strategy. Followers must be given opportunity to support and adapt to it. Goal setting can be adapted in support of flexibility. It needs only to identify a range of options and prepare workers to pursue the best that become viable.

Clear statement of the CEO's business vision in strategic and goal-oriented terms invites relevant and effective goal-setting support. MBO without the umbrella of overarching strategy articulated becomes, at best, a guessing game for functional components. The result will usually be uncoordinated, even internally competitive, goals that serve narrow, politicized, functional purposes of sales, finance, production, engineering or administration divisions.

Goal setting in isolation from organization purpose will likely direct and activate performance effectively toward those goals that have been set, even if wrongly so. In a stable organization and for the new or replacement worker in an existing job role, a supervisor or co-worker may usefully apply isolated goal setting to guide and train the new person in the performance expected from the job. Almost any other circumstance merits organizationwide, coordinated, MBO-styled goal setting carried out within the context of clearly articulated strategic objectives. In some respects, work motivation throughout an organization necessarily begins with communication of a coherent business strategy with attendant organizationwide objectives. Without strategy to guide it, goal setting may too easily go in narrow or wrong directions. Without mission and goals, organization and individuals alike are rendered rudderless in the restless and competitive economic sea. The key to successful goal setting is likely to be aggressive, visionary leadership in setting organizational purpose.

SOUND LEADERSHIP FOCUSES AND ACTIVATES PERFORMANCE

A simple, functional definition of leadership is that it entails the ability to recognize activating need and supply purpose to it. Workers in modern society, expecting the benefits of industrial democracy, need a job, a paycheck to pay their bills, stimulating work, an opportunity to grow and learn as individuals. Management leads by providing integrative purpose to this package of diffuse and unfocused need. Management sets grand strategy, formulates measurable business objectives and sees that specific, individual goals exist for every worker. It makes little difference in strictly motivational terms whether those specific, individual goals are assigned by management or participatively negotiated between workers and management. The rules that establish appropriateness of participation determine which approach is the more useful. It is the setting of clear goals that is indispensable to motivating. Tough goals activate by offering challenge. Good leaders effectively set tough goals.

MOTIVATION TAKES MANY FORMS

The objective of effective work motivation is improved performance. The earlier cited comparisons by Locke et al. (1980) examined research studies that provided data on performance improvement with piecework pay, goal setting, job enrichment and participative decision making. They identified many instances in which attention to motivation *did* improve performance within all four categories. Goal setting for seventeen studies reviewed was a consistent contributor at an estimated average level of 16% with improvement ranging from a low of 2% to a high of 57%. Across ten published research studies, straight piecework pay yielded an average improvement of 30% with a range of 3% to 49%. The power of monetary reward is not to be dismissed. Job enrichment in thirteen studies averaged 17% improvement and fourteen studies of participation offered an average improvement of 0.5%. Clearly, performance improvement can be motivated in a variety of ways. Participation is weakest, though even there one research claimed a 47% improvement in performance.

Depending on circumstances, there are many routes to motivating high performance. All, though, depend on sufficient activation of energy applied to the job and sound focus of effort on goals. Piecework is a powerful method for linking quantity (but not quality) of output directly to effort and pay. It can be very effective as is evidenced by the success of Lincoln Electric and Nucor Steel in obtaining more than twice the usual industry output (100%+ performance improvement) when piecework and group incentives are supported by other motivational processes. Participation is effective when active worker involvement is needed to achieve improvement. This is essentially a matter of gaining acceptance of goals that might otherwise be resisted. Job enrichment that confers flexibility on the worker frees him or her to pursue established goals and strategy without the constraint of a narrow work role or overly specific and narrow goals. It thereby has potential to restore attention to high quality in the job. But in one form or another, goals reappear with effective motivation practices.

Human relations theory and research in the twentieth century have been, at the core, a struggle to rise above efficiency and radical behaviorism as the foundation of motivational practice. But the core of sound motivation that was present in the methods of Taylor and Ford and that gave motivational vitality to their systems must not be overlooked. They set clear goals and kept everyone focused on them. It is a proven way through which to achieve clear focus and high activation of work energy. The cost of motivating with high pay and dire threat have come to be a major burden on the economy as well as ineffective for driving higher performance output. Managers must discover how to get workers to enthusiastically accept and commit to work goals if they are to move up from these old devices. Moving up to motivation through goal setting with modern leadership methods is the major challenge of those who would invent twenty-first century high performance systems.

Chapter Seven

The Pitfalls of Pay for High Performance

High performance management systems typically pay their workers well. Indeed, premium pay often goes with consistent high output. This is *not* because pay motivates high performance—sometimes it does and sometimes it doesn't. Rather, it is because trust in management is an indispensable element of high performance, and trust is the first casualty of perceived inequitable pay. Workers in high performance systems expect to participate proportionately in the economic product of their efforts, but if they have no trust or confidence in their management, they will not risk having their best efforts exploited for someone else's gain. They will settle, instead, for a middling reward at a modest level of effort.

Paying workers generously is fine if it works, but it is just an excess cost when it doesn't. In attempting to use pay as a motivator, there are numerous opportunities to create cost without productive benefit. Pay for performance, so-called, spuriously links work effort to size of a periodic pay increase and convinces many workers that they should work less hard if they don't get the size increase they think they deserve. The only sound basis of pay is the labor market. Pay and performance in high performance systems can and should be independent issues. Pay for output, either incentive or piece-work style, can increase cost or decrease quality if not rigorously administered. Pay for high performance output typically is pegged to the labor market *and* augmented substantially with one or more forms of incentive for clearly extraordinary output. But pay is the least of the motivational drivers on which high performance is founded.

High performance systems of the future will probably avoid pay for performance—other than through strictly administered incentive systems—and pay for range of skill. Incentive systems must be sufficiently transparent to workers to guarantee trust in their application, and should be largely freed from arbitrary preset time cycles that create the Christmas Day phenomenon, when everything stops in anticipation of opening the big present.

Most of all, future high performance systems must emphasize the motivational power of the job itself by creating job designs and selecting workers in ways that maximize the worker-job fit. High performance systems must exploit the fun inherent in work activity *and also* pay equitably for output. But these systems will be built on recognition that pay is not the central motivator, often not even a significant motivator of high output.

Pay clearly is not the only thing that motivates work and productivity. Commonsense observation can reveal that pay is *not* necessary to motivate good work or maximum effort. The defect of pay as a motivator is that it is strictly a token reward, not a real one. To be much more precise about it, pay does not reward; it is the products and services that it can obtain for the worker that reward. It is the personal status and self-esteem that go with the size of the paycheck and the style of life it confers that reward. Motivation to work arises from linking a paying job to specific, rewarding payoffs with a paycheck. A variety of physical and psychological needs can activate a person to seek a job. The focus of that activation is a paying job, and not until goals are set for performance in the job is there direction in that activation. Even then, there is no assurance of high performance output.

Thus, pay is always a step or more removed from the real motivators of human action, which may sometimes have no connection with pay at all. Other things independent of pay can activate and focus work behavior. The need for personally meaningful, interesting task involvement is often sufficient to motivate work without pay. Voluntarism is a major source of labor in religious and community service projects. Service club, church group and Parent-Teacher Association members lend diligent labor to fund-raising projects when they could often as readily afford to give money directly. The opportunity for camaraderie in laboring together blended with the chance to represent the values and objectives of one's organization to others in the community is reward enough. The social purposes of the activity are motivators in their own right.

RESEARCH REFLECTS THE PREVAILING CONFUSION

Research on pay as a motivator is limited, vastly more so for instance, than research on satisfaction, participation or motivation. Typically it is also inconclusive if not baffling. Haire, Ghiselli and Gordon (1967) examined the pay increase history of some 250 salaried-exempt employees in two companies over a twenty-five-year span of time to identify the factors that determined pay. Both companies used formal appraisal systems in support of pay increases, and the researchers clearly expected to find evidence that pay is an incentive reward for outstanding performance. The results from this research are anything but clear, though they strongly indicated that current pay level is the best predictor of future pay level, and that pay increases are more likely to be random in patterning than to reflect any consistent superiority or inferiority of work performance. Early advantage in pay and good luck get most of the credit for future high pay. Pay as a direct performance incentive receives very little support from this study. The surprise and puzzlement of these researchers at their results, indeed, generated considerable speculation in their discussion of the nature of pay factors without firm conclusions. What they might realistically have concluded (but did not) is that pay for performance is an unworkable illusion that distorts the pay structure without adding any motivational effect.

THE ILLUSION OF PAY FOR PERFORMANCE

Under specific and limited conditions, tying pay directly to output can supply incentive for high performance. Piecework, group incentive and commission systems of pay have their place in the arsenal of high performance system devices when administered rigorously. Pay can be used to sustain high performance under conditions such as those offered at Lincoln Electric and Nucor Steel. However, the general notion that the prospect of steadily *rising* pay can be the carrot that drives ever higher performance is seriously flawed and often dangerous. Dressing up periodic pay adjustments as performance rewards is little more than a second-rate swindle when, in fact, increases must largely account for inflationary creep, for normal increases in productivity and for realignment of pay to the labor market. The large element of performance that needs no motivator beyond opportunity to do the work becomes needlessly linked to periodic pay increases. Performance thereupon falls off in the absence of a pay increase when it would otherwise proceed unabated.

So-called pay-for-performance compensation systems begin with poli-cies of systematic underpayment of market wage to motivate newly hired, probationary workers. The hazard of such systems is that if a worker does not get the expected pay increase at the expected time, considerable personal stress and anxiety can result, reducing performance significantly. Indeed, an inequity adjustment by way of consciously or unconsciously lowered output *is often predictable* with workers who miss an expected pay increase. Workers on step-increase pay systems not infrequently make their way up the pay ladder with progressively and incrementally improved performance, most of which would be realized from learning alone if not confounded by a pay step system, then reach maximum for the range and start to complain of lack of incentive while their performance steadily slips in the wrong direction.

Within the narrow range of typical performance variability that charac-terizes most worker performance, a pay increase is likely to be the least efficient and most costly way to motivate improved output. An elaborate pay-for-performance smoke screen raised to obscure underpayment against market for probationary workers can become a counterproductive and costly habit of pay increases that continually must be ratcheted upward just to maintain worker satisfaction and output.

Pay for performance as a system of pay adjustment was widely popular in the 1960s and early 1970s, mostly because rapid inflation annually demanded approximately double-digit percent increases to keep pay even with the market. In the tight labor market of that time for trained techni-cians, it was not uncommon for new employees to be hired at salaries above those of last year's worker intake rates, even after normal raises. Rapid inflation alone permits major adjustment in relative salaries depend-ing on evaluated work performance. It was, in fact, this wide range of potential for adjustment that became the basis of pay-for-performance policy popularity in that era.

But large long-term inequities can easily be created by overaggressive differentiation in pay for perceived level of performance. Corrections for good and, especially, poor skill are easy, but inequities because of person-ality peculiarities and communication style are also more common when annual pay adjustments are in the range of 8% to 15% as they were in the 1960s. Some poor work performance is inevitably the result of unresolved misunderstanding between the boss who withholds an expected raise or the worker who doesn't get the anticipated increase. The better reading of Haire, Ghiselli and Gordon is that the tough negotiator who comes in at a high starting pay, or the ambitiously opportunistic worker who plays the system astutely for larger increases, will be the highest paid over the longer term.

Pay for performance is, unfortunately, largely an illusion with more than trivially troublesome implications. In practice, its intent is defeated because the majority of supervisors working under a pay-for-performance policy will assign the majority of their workers a fixed, across-the-board percent increase. Wide variation in amount of annual pay increase is disruptive of teamwork and good relationships. Under administrative pressure, some supervisors may give small or no increases to those workers they wish to be rid of; and under pressure from the occasional aggressive supervisor who is willing to make a vigorous case, a very large increase may occasionally be approved for a particularly strong performer. But the norm is uniformity in increases. So much for performance-based pay increase increments. They are largely fiction, may be conterproductive to the purpose of high performance and usually are more trouble than they are worth to administer.

WHY NOT APPLY INCENTIVE PAY TO EVERY JOB?

Research studies cited by Locke et al. (1980) offer evidence that performance-based piecework pay does, in fact, motivate increased performance. The stupendously superlative output of Nucor Steel and Lincoln Electric workers who work on a mixed pay incentive system clearly includes piecework *and* group profit-sharing bonuses. Don't these findings and situations demonstrate the inherent power of pay tied to actual output? Certainly they do, but piecework and incentive pay are difficult to administer fairly—impossible, perhaps, when worker trust is absent.

Piecework pay, a practice dating back to the earliest nineteenth-century industrial engineering efforts to measure work performance in factories, has its limitations. Its motivational purposes can be corrupted and defeated. It does not fit every worker's temperament. Exceptional high performance with correspondingly high pay seems limited to a minority of the work force. We must examine the utility of incentive pay more closely before attempting to seize on its motivational power.

Piecework pay ties wages directly to work output. In theory, this should be the cheapest, soundest way to pay for productivity. In practice, it can sometimes be the most costly way to pay and a threat to quality as well. An industry or technology that is either emerging or going through rapid change may exhibit a learning curve steep enough to deserve a change of work standards every few weeks or months. Major capital investment in new tools, equipment or processes can change jobs and work standards profoundly. In response to this kind of change, standards should be expected to improve monthly, weekly, sometimes daily.

Intense price competition can create pressure for rate adjustment. To cut costs and meet the competition, a change in piece rates at Harwood Manufacturing with the introduction of new job processes often entailed only the most superficial revision of work methods—as, for instance, in the sequence of steps used to fold finished pajamas. But unilateral imposition of job changes and rates was consistently still rejected as unfair by workers until they were given opportunity for involvement in the decision-making process.

In the absence of confidence and trust on the part of workers in the revision of piece rates, an aggressive, costly sell-in of the change may be required. Even with so active a campaign, the sale may not always be bought. In the absence of revised standards, though, incentive pay rates can become unrealistically high, preventing competitive prices from being met. A company that implements piece rates, and either cannot change them because of labor resistance or does not try to make changes out of concern for worker protest, can find itself paying much higher per unit labor rates than a competitor who pays a straight hourly rate. The flack and commotion that go with keeping piecework rates competitive can outweigh the benefits of incentive pay.

Where piecework is accepted by workers, it is often accepted only up to a point. Many workers actively fear that too high a rate of production will bring about a cut in the rates. In self-defense, they establish an informal, group-enforced norm as to what constitutes maximum production. Piecework thus limited by workers seldom results in more than a 20% to 30% increase in output over daywork standards.

The exception comes with companies like Nucor Steel or Lincoln Electric where multiple incentives in combination with exceptional trust and a spartan work culture raise productivity two to three times above their competitors' standards. Nucor Steel and Lincoln Electric enjoy a high level of carefully nurtured trust with their workers, which permits them to use piecework rates effectively. In both these instances, existing industry experience and standards with piecework systems give stability and legitimacy to the programs implemented. The relative stability of the industry technology used by both companies requires introduction of few changes in jobs or rates. They enjoy the best of all worlds for application of piecework to their work forces. There are few threats to trust in their systems. In the absence of labor-management trust, rigorous cost control and high output standards, piecework often otherwise yields a minimum increase in output at maximum cost in administrative fuss, bother and confrontation.

The remaining drawback to piecework arises in the opportunity for workers to maximize quantity of output at the expense of quality. With products where poor quality is difficult and expensive to identify or hard to trace to its source, piecework can undercut quality excessively. High quality must be strictly enforceable. A variety of devices exist for exacting penalty when quality is slighted in the product or service. Some products bear the signature of the individual or team that made them. If poor quality found later cannot be traced to a specific offender, it may be reworked by the whole team or by individuals in round-robin sequence who must inspect and fix every problem on their own time or on straight dayrate. Service givers who deliver poor quality may be expected to remedy the complaint without pay on their own time. But these devices require the support of costly administrative processes.

Only when quality can be enforced surely and cheaply is piecework safe from quality deterioration. The sheet steel produced by Nucor Steel is routinely given a visual check and each lot is sampled metallurgically. Quality problems are immediately known and communicated to the responsible production team. Scrap within Nucor's profit-sharing incentive scheme raises cost, which reduces profit-sharing proportionately. Poor quality clearly does not pay. At Lincoln Electric, every part and process is registered for every piece of equipment produced. Later failure of any arc welding system is readily traced to its individual worker source. The cost of poor quality in field service and equipment repair will certainly be reflected in the responsible worker's next profit-sharing allocation. There is nowhere to hide and no way to get away with poor quality work.

Strict, almost oppressive, controls are required to defeat the tendency to sacrifice quality for quantity when piecework introduces the possibility of that transgression. Without trust between labor and management that supports a high performance work culture, the typical worker would more likely view these devices as personally directed, unfair harassment. They could easily become occasion for walk-outs and other job actions, and could bring about election of union representation as happened at Harwood.

Piecework may yield more output, but the struggle to maintain quality in opposition to workers' efforts to make maximum (usually group norm set) rates at minimum expenditure of personal effort can create costs in the form of added administrative routine and bad feelings that are not worth the result. Implementation of piecework is loaded with landmines and pitfalls for the inexperienced and unwary. It is generally best to avoid it until absolutely necessary and until an extended period of relative stability in work processes is attained. Even then, experienced help in planning the piecework system should be sought out and used. There are too many ways, otherwise, for piecework to go wrong.

If pay for performance is unworkable and piecework incentive pay is potentially an administrative nightmare, how does a high performance system invoke the motivational power of pay? To answer that query, it is necessary to radically revise present theories of motivation and pay. It will be helpful to trace today's pay back to its economic roots in a craft and barter economy.

THE TRANSITION FROM COMMUNITY TO ECONOMY

In the relatively isolated rural, colonial community of eighteenth-century America, economic exchange was almost wholly on a one-to-one, face-to-face basis. Food was grown and exchanged, products were created and bartered for food or other products. Cash was largely the representation of economic surplus, set aside by the elders of the community for capital investment in needed tools or equipment. Division of rewards was based on shared standards of value and on equity of exchange. Most capital investment was driven by common agreement as to what constituted the best interests or unmet needs of the community. Whether to build a bridge, dam a mill pond or buy an organ for the new church was a question to be resolved by consensus guided by the counsel of the worldly wise elders of the community.

In colonial America before the Revolutionary War the community was largely self-contained, importing only the materials impossible to attain with local resources and skills. The community for all practical purposes was the economy. It could and did function for long periods of time with little or no outside economic contact. Division of the common economic product was, by consensus, based on the value of skill, knowledge, physical strength and need of each individual. Greed for a larger share, like sloth and waste, was handled as a moral problem rather than an economic one, since these behaviors directly subtracted from the well-being of others in the community. One's place in and contribution to the community was visible to all. Dependence on neighbors for exchange of goods and services, as well as for support in adversity, created a tight-knit community in which the division of economic rewards required maximum balance between equity and prudence. One was either satisfied with his or her lot, or not. Those dissatisfied made isolates and outcasts of themselves. Most people accepted their economic lot gratefully.

This was an era of crafts and barter. Jobs and pay were foreign to this way of life. They did not enter the scene until industry specialized and consolidated, trading at a distance from customers and suppliers. Now, exchange was no longer one-to-one. Goods and services were bought and paid for with money in exchanges between relative strangers. The producers of the goods purchased might be workers in a factory an ocean away. Money flowed through centers of commerce, not through the village bank. The individual worker with his or her paycheck became little more than a conduit from one center of commerce to another under this system. He or she could decide to work or not to work for pay, to buy or not to buy for a price. The communal values that ordered economic life in earlier times were replaced by the invisible, impersonal forces of the economy. In today's economy, a job and a paycheck are necessities for participation in economic exchange. The long hours of labor expected in the early factory—twelve to fourteen a day, usually six and a half days a week—ruled out any other form of economic pursuit. The job no longer contributed needed goods and services that enhanced the lives of one's neighbors. It was simply and imperatively required to "make a living" in an impersonal, faceless mass economy.

The token system of paychecks and money that undergirds modern economics is relatively quite recent in history. Even the double-entry system of accounting, essential to long-distance exchange based on credits and debits of many nations and merchants, dates back only to Luca Pacioli in the fifteenth century and emerged as a necessary support to long-distance commerce. As commerce and economic exchange consolidated to exploit local materials, resources and skills, it was necessary to invent jobs and monetary systems to regulate equity of exchange between distant, unknown parties. Pay for a job is essential for one to participate in this new economic system. In a complex system of economic exchange like this, the need to participate even at the most basic level activates readiness to perform a job. The specific activities that make up that job are whatever the supervisor, the employer, the owner, the customer or the market dictate them to be. Without job goals, there is little way for the worker to know what is needed to collect a paycheck other than to show up daily for work. Provision of that paycheck confers the right to specify what the job entails onto the market, the customer, the owner, the employer or the supervisor. A job is an open-ended bargain between worker and employer for a paycheck in return for commitment of the worker's time, skill and labor. Within this bargain, the specific activities and purposes of the worker are subject to renegotiation every week, every day, every hour.

MASS ECONOMY AND DISTRIBUTION OF ECONOMIC WEALTH

With the consolidation of industry in factories and cities, impersonal forces thus come into play. The value and power of tools and resource ownership increase greatly when they are critical to increased economic product and the common welfare. Concentrations of plant and equipment undergirding mass economies of scale require a special conservatism of temperament that values savings and investment above the immediate rewards of consumption. The so-called protestant ethic of hard work and deferred gratification serves well the demand for an expanded base of capital investment, increases the total base of economic wealth and justifies high reward allocation to the capitalist-owner for his earlier self-denial and frugality. The centralization of cash management in the hands of the capitalist-owner permits a wide range of discretion in allocating cash to the need for new capital, to return on investment (i.e., reward to himself for ownership) and to paychecks for workers. The expectations of workers for their share are formed from the current labor market, and comparison of their relative status with others in the community. As long as living style and economic share improve with continued reinvestment of wealth in plant and equipment, satisfaction will likely prevail among workers. When it does not improve, the ostentatious wealth and regal status affectations of well-paid managers and newly rich owners will likely generate dissatisfaction. In the new age of marketing when "need" is cleverly, powerfully and continually driven to new heights by mass advertising, absence of progress that permits participation in the latest offerings of wealth also directly influence level of satisfaction. Need is no longer limited to adequate food, comfortable clothing, warm housing and social support from a community of peers. It is created by expanding aspirations.

The value of one's economic contribution in a job today is still determined in part by skill and knowledge as it was in colonial times. Strength, once an heroic economic quality, is much diminished as an economic factor by cheap energy and labor-saving machinery. Need takes on new impetus and meaning when expressed in ambition for higher status work, readiness to invest in advanced skill and increased knowledge, or willingness to risk pursuit of a larger economic share through astute venturing as a capitalist-entrepreneur. With the coming of great affluence wherein modest expectations can easily be satisfied by a modest paycheck, the division of the economic pie takes on distinct discretionary dimensions. Those who actively seek out greater monetary reward can probably attain it. Surpassing the ordinary in current-day, affluent economic participation may very well require greater energy in its pursuit, endurance of higher job stress, better judgment, greater skill, wider experience, a talent for opportunism in the exploitation of others' weaknesses, greater capacity for personal commitment, above average vigor and health, exceptional economic vision or just plain good luck and persistence in trial and error. Those who seek riches can probably find them through one or several of these routes. Those who do not can usually enjoy a comfortable, quiet life with the basics well met and even a little extra as reward for flowing with the prevailing economic tide. The motivating power of pay changes considerably within these variations of aspiration against available opportunities and circumstances.

For the ambitious who pursue high economic payoff as their first objective, it pays to have high expectations in all matters of economic exchange. One does well to expect and demand high pay, high quality, exceptional service and high value if a larger share of economic division is one's goal. On the contrary side, if one is economically unassertive and seeks of the economic system only modest reward that can be satisfied with modest pay, modest quality, unexceptional service, and middling value, the result will likely be self-fulfilling. The foundation principle of an impersonal economic system guided by an invisible hand is to seek highest expected value for lowest expected cost in every exchange. With so wide a range in the level of expectation, value and cost must inevitably shift to match variable levels of expectation held by participants in the exchange. The energy expended in maintaining a high level of expectation and in pressing vigorous demands becomes a significant factor in the level of economic reward attained. Social equity is the casualty as opportunistic seekers edge out those less aggressive and modest of expectation.

One's pay is his or her share in an available pool of economic goods and services generated by the system. One is either satisfied with that share or not. It is entirely possible to be satisfied with share but not with the work one performs. On the flip side, one can as readily be satisfied with the work but not the economic share received for its performance. There is no necessary correspondence between them. Exhibit 7–1 illustrates the work performance impact of variation in satisfaction with economic share and satisfaction with the work itself.

Examination of the interaction between pay satisfaction and work satisfaction proposed in Exhibit 7–1 suggests the potential for complex response to being unemployed and without a paycheck altogether. In the absence of work, one may be delighted with opportunity available for leisure activity but dissatisfied with participation in economic exchange. Alternatively, one may be rendered miserable by the absence of satisfying

Exhibit 7-1
Satisfaction Obtained from Pay and Work

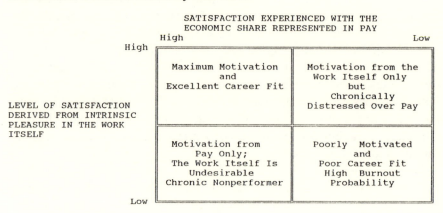

work activities but remain relatively unharried by the immediate lack of a paycheck. There are many varied patterns of satisfaction and motivation to be found in the relation of work to pay. Workers may be alternatively

- motivated to participate in the division of economic returns through earning a paycheck from performance in a job,
- unmotivated to be involved at all, and
- motivated to participate on variable levels of aggressiveness depending on the size of payoff sought.

In any organized economic system it is possible for some to participate on the fringes, living by their wits, off waste or through crime. In an affluent society, it is possible for many to scavenge the garbage of society as passive participants in its benefits or to prey on the affluent weak. Those with property or income entitlement may not need to hold a paid job to participate aggressively. It is clear, then, that the motivational power of a job and paycheck can be quite variable. Passive participant scavengers and criminals may expend high levels of energy in their pursuit of uninvolvement. Those with ample income from sources other than jobs can work at anything they please at any level of energy output they prefer. Wage earners can choose to participate at a very modest level of time and energy demand or at an aggressive level. There is something for every taste and character in this economic barrel. Exhibit 7–2 illustrates workers' payoffs as a function of ambition and engagement in the economic system. Workers at Lincoln Electric and Nucor Steel, as an example, are highly

Exhibit 7-2
Ambition for High Rewards versus Extent of Legitimate Engagement in the Economic System

	Intensely Engaged in the Economic System	Marginally Engaged in the Economic System
Participates at a High Level of Personal Ambition	Highly Paid Workers	Criminals
Participates at a Low Level of Personal Ambition	Modestly Paid Workers	Scavengers

ambitious for economic reward and energetic in its pursuit. But those who do not enjoy the work for its own sake find their jobs too stressful to justify pursuit of high pay. They have high ambition but low engagement in the economic system.

THE MARKET IS THE FINAL AUTHORITY IN PAY AND BENEFITS

Ultimately, the only sound approach to pay is to *meet the labor market.* There may be some limited exceptions. Workers who possess valuable know-how in their employer's product, processes or markets can be paid above market to hold them in their jobs. If that know-how is valuable to a competitor, the market for it is likely to escalate sharply at almost any time. Pay above market in these circumstances is more a matter of anticipating the market's direction so as not to be caught by surprise by a rash of undesired resignations when it suddenly rises.

Pay for job longevity is a bad idea. It buys very little. Awarding increased vacation and sick pay time to workers with long seniority frequently recognizes little more than already existing withdrawal from or uninvolvement in dead-end jobs. Seniority-based pay may extend an employer's hold on experienced workers who barely tolerate their jobs, but it certainly does not guarantee that they will perform any better. Pay variations that exceed plus or minus 20% of market are rare. Pay differential outside this range should always be questioned. Pay that consistently falls outside a range of plus or minus 20% of the going labor market rate is a mistake of it does not support high output.

Variations around the market are permissible to account for amount and quality of experience, exactness of fit or learning needed on the job. A part of that variation will inevitably flow from the negotiative aggressiveness or passivity of the individual candidate, suggesting that cautious, conservative judgment is always prudent in departing from market average for pay. Within the market, some competitors will pay a little higher, some a little lower and there will usually be offsetting working conditions to account for the difference. Many little factors can nudge pay up or down off the market midpoint, but this must not obscure the fact that market median anchors every sound pay decision. Significant departures, however urgently argued, are ill-advised.

Benefits in the form of health and life insurance, paid time off, disability income or retirement annuities must, similarly, meet the market. Changes in costs of benefits and worker preferences must be recognized and responded to. Laws and regulations will influence the shape of benefits packages. The enactment of Employment Retirement Income Security Act (ERISA) legislation designed to protect workers' benefits under retirement plans, for instance, has resulted in a widespread movement away from fixed contribution retirement funds toward profit-sharing plans that can be invested in tax-sheltered retirement accounts on the workers' behalf. Indeed, the dominance of federal social security as the universal retirement income account begs the question of whether an employer-supplied annuity account has any place in a modern benefits package. Profit sharing offers several advantages as a base for supplemental retirement savings. Aside from avoiding the strict regulatory restrictions of ERISA, profit sharing results in an automatic wage cost reduction during poor economic cycles. This flexibility, combined with the implementation of a performance incentive that need not cost any more than the former retirement annuity that it replaces, could add up to a significant net reduction in cost as well as perceived net gain in value to workers.

Discovering ways to raise the value of worker benefits without raising the cost to the employer is a potential source of motivational payoff that has long awaited exploitation. Variable, worker-selected benefits packages—so-called cafeteria benefits—have been discussed for more than thirty years. The complexity of their administration has deterred implementation more often than not. With computers to handle administrative details, though, their time has certainly come. The future of work benefits appears to center on a basic standard package of major medical policy, minimum life insurance and a limited-access savings account for every worker with all the rest selected individually, customized to personal preference at a price that is competitive in the labor market. Future high performance systems must take these market factors into account.

PAY FOR BREADTH OF SKILL

The principal innovation in pay practices in future high performance systems will undoubtedly be the award of pay increase increments strictly for added range and variety of work-related skill. Lockstep work flow that employs narrow work specialties will soon be replaced by short-run and one-of-a-kind project work that demands skill flexibility to permit redeployment of available labor to follow shifting demand. Seniority-based pay, which presumably—if doubtfully—stabilized labor availability on the moving assembly line, must then be replaced with a skill-based pay system that adds pay increments in recognition of a worker's greater flexibility in work assignment.

The package of skills that fits a particular employer's customer needs is likely to be special and unique. There is good reason to try to retain workers who add value to the business through their greater flexibility in assignment. Broadly skilled, flexibly assignable workers are more valuable to their employers and the economy alike. Higher than market pay resulting from skill-based pay increase increments is offset in the larger economy, partly because a broader repertoire of work skill benefits the economy and the worker directly by increasing the range of available opportunity for employment, and partly by reducing the chances of unemployment. It similarly benefits the employer by reducing unapplied (lost) labor hours resulting from unavailability of work that fits a worker's skills. Pay increase increments based on added, business-relevant skill can thus be justified on strictly cost and economic grounds.

Lock-in of an individual's skill package with a high rate of pay is also easy to manage. An increase to above average pay will normally occur only over a span of time. Existence of a career misfit can usually be discovered while pay is still at or near market average. Misfit itself to the industry or career will likely discourage development of added skill, signaling a need for management action.

A variety of advantages can flow from pay for skill. Even so, the variation introduced by skill-justified pay increments must be kept in bounds. Skill-based increases can and must be administered with care. An increase in the market rate for any of a worker's several skills must eventually be matched with an adjustment in current paid rate. The alternative is to risk loss of workers to the competitor or industry that needs more of that skill.

The 20% plus or minus variation permissible with seniority-based pay systems probably carries over to pay for skill. Skill increments that exceed 20% over base of highest paid skill should be challenged. Base skill pay must always be pegged to the most valuable skill: that which is paid best in the labor market. Pay increments added beyond that base should reflect the importance of an added skill to expanded business flexibility and must diminish proportionately with each additional new skill until an approximate 20% maximum above hourly and day rate base is reached. The exception, of course, is with true high performance systems where incentive pay applied with a multiskilled work force may justify 100% over market.

MANAGING PAY ADJUSTMENTS

With any pay system, there must be regular adjustments to reflect changes in market value of skill and inflationary creep. These are the economic forces that have formerly permitted the illusion of pay for performance. It is a mischievous diversion of energy and argument to follow that course, though. Pay at its roots is a market issue. Every worker must be led to understand that reality. New-intake workers paid below market while they prove their merit should be informed they are below market because they are in probationary status. True, their pay will be brought up as performance validates ability, but that is not pay for performance; it is conservative underpayment for unproven performance potential. It is an element of probationary employment policy.

The soundest policy is fair pay for everyone, aggressively and effectively implemented. From time to time, across-the-board adjustments will be needed to meet changes in the economy brought about by inflation or rising productivity. But it is generally best *not* to make such changes on a fixed or predictable schedule. Changes less than 5% are likely to have no effect on workers' purchasing power and will be contemptible if not invisible to most who get them. That diminishes the value of small increases. Of greater significance, though, is the tendency of regular, fixed-interval increases to create anticipatory, Christmas Day anxiety with its various distractive and harmful effects. Annual pay adjustments are more likely to reduce output than increase it, and can become a needless source of emotional stress on workers. A random schedule on anywhere from a six-month to two-year interval generally allows sufficient flexibility. Across-the-board adjustments can be effected either on a percent or a dollar basis, and may sometimes be mixed where that best achieves equity. Strict percent increases, it must be recognized, may amplify built-in inequities of pay. Increases can be announced on the date of implementation, supported by a comprehensive communication of the rationale and supporting labor market data that justify the change. Monitoring the labor market should be continuous so that obvious activity to gather market information is not a cue to a coming increase that spawns needless rumor.

Within a skill-based pay increment system, adjustment for changes in market value of skill are best handled on an individual basis at the point in time when an earned skill increment is to be added. Where base skill rates are openly published—a necessity if trust is to be sustained—workers can calculate the cash benefit of adding a new skill in their repertoire from change in base skill rate. Potential for adjustment to reflect other market factors at the time a skill increment is evaluated can add motivational impetus to skill development that otherwise might not seem worth the effort. But if more than twelve or eighteen months pass without adjustment, or greater than a 10% change is involved, a special individual or group adjustment should probably be applied independent of other pay adjustment action. This circumstance should be sufficiently rare so that no one expects or awaits it.

The anxiety that goes with an expected pay increase can be high, approaching the intensity of a full-blown anxiety neurosis for some employees. Pay increase increments as a motivator *activate* without *directing* behavior. The result can be unpredictable and disruptive. Meyer, Kay and French (1965), noting high levels of defensiveness created by the typical performance appraisal situation, recommended strict separation of pay increase discussions from occasions when performance feedback is required. Their argument centered around the dominant, negative effect of the anticipated pay discussion that can and often does effectively drown out clear discussion of performance issues.

Indeed, the activating power of an anticipated pay increase is potentially so great that it should never be invoked without relating the change in pay closely to clear business goals. There is no other effective way to accomplish pay adjustment other than a full program of pay incentives such as that used by Nucor Steel and Lincoln Electric. But establishment of the necessary supporting high performance work culture is a rare and difficult achievement. In the average organization, the best policy is to openly maintain that pay is market-anchored and acceptable performance is expected. Linking pay increases partially to MBO-set goals may succeed where the MBO process helps engender trust in management's intentions. In the absence of a high performance system that assures high work standards for high pay, the best alternative is to announce periodic general pay adjustments by surprise and bypass the anticipatory anxiety altogether.

PAYING EITHER EXCESSIVELY HIGH OR LOW IS HAZARDOUS FOR AN "AVERAGE" FIRM

Attempts to motivate with money, we may conclude, must somehow be fitted to the level of expectations and preferred life-style and need of each individual. For practical purposes workers must be paid what they expect to be paid within a range of what others of similar skill and experience are, in fact, being paid. Paying below market risks losing their contributions to any firm. In some instances, paying less than expected will yield proportionately reduced work output. On the other hand, paying too much can raise expectations for future pay or raise the expectations of other lesser paid co-workers. Where high pay is not clearly tied to high output by the operating system, it may yield mediocre performance at premium cost. In the absence of measured goals, a worker who cannot afford to change jobs without losing significant earnings can readily slip past the requirement for high-quality performance. There are thus costs to paying too little or too much. Like Goldilocks in search of perfect satisfaction in her tastes, we must usually avoid the extremes in search of sound middle ground.

Pay for a job is dominantly dependent on the labor market. Significant departures for the worth of skill and experience will almost certainly create problems for the average firm. The best calculus for determining fair pay is to work out a compromise between what is expected by workers and what is paid within the firm and across the market, with strong weight given to internal and external equity of pay compared to similar or the same work. Opportunistically hiring below market, especially below internal market, risks dissatisfaction in the longer term unless a careful program of corrective wage equalization is pursued over the near term. For a newly hired employee, of course, pay is sometimes set below market for the required skill and experience because the worker's ability is yet untested. If he or she performs at full expected level after a normal term of orientation and learning, it is safe to raise pay to market, and may even motivate added quantity or quality of output from a worker who gains satisfaction from the experience of early, clear progress in the firm. The newcomer who disappoints compared to established work standards can be discouraged from staying by the withholding of pay progress. The worker underpaid compared to market can probably change jobs easily, either moving laterally to escape supervisory pressure for improved performance, or being attracted away by the prospect of higher pay elsewhere. Carefully programmed, the intake pay policies of a firm for new workers can yield some minor motivational benefits.

One hazard of such a policy can be the exclusion of needed experience available from those fully qualified but who demand full market value. An habitual practice of always bringing people in below market pay can reduce performance potential of the firm and leave it vulnerable to talent raids by other firms. Small firms that lack the time and patience to "develop" newcomers, for instance, may successfully attract the best, dissatisfied talent away from larger competitors by paying full value for their abilities, then demanding high performance.

THE IMPLICATIONS OF HIGH TURNOVER

At Nucor Steel and Lincoln Electric, some new workers, however carefully they were chosen, find that they are made miserable by the strict goals and performance standards imposed and enforced at these companies. Only those prepared by temperament to rise to the challenge of maximum goal achievement within strict standards of performance quality will endure and remain. Cultural misfits may be highly satisfied with the share of economic gains offered by the new job but largely unwilling to meet high work standards and strict working conditions. Turnover is characteristically highest in Nucor Steel and Lincoln Electric among new employees. The existence of high turnover among new employees is cited, indeed, as evidence of excessive demands inherent in these jobs by union officials and other detractors from this style of work culture.

High labor turnover is, of course, commonly viewed in management literature as a sign of poor management or unacceptable working conditions in a firm. High pay in 1913 partially offset the onerousness of Henry Ford's autocratic, driving management style, but not all of it. High pay can reduce some proportion of turnover in almost any firm. But low turnover may also be a sign that pay is too attractive while work standards are too lax in a company. Very high pay and very high performance standards at Nucor Steel and Lincoln Electric discourage all but those most fully suited in skill, experience and temper to the demands of the high output work culture. Turnover among new workers at Nucor Steel and Lincoln Electric is more properly seen as a measure of the ease with which higher than market pay can draw people who appear suited to the careers offered but who cannot adapt to the stress demands of those careers. Indeed, it is a near universal principle that above market pay *without* strict performance standards guarantees that a large proportion of people in the field will be locked into miserably dissatisfying work they cannot later afford to abandon, but which they will make partially tolerable by avoiding stressful or onerous tasks. Even then, the progressive burnout rate will be exceptionally high. High rates of burnout in public education, medicine and engineering, for instance, can be traced directly to the prospect of high pay, which originally attracted many who were temperamentally ill-suited to the demands of these careers.

THE FOLLY OF PAYING HIGH TO ATTRACT THE BEST

It is a poor, sometimes disastrous, operations policy to use high pay in an attempt to attact the "best" into a career field. Extended educational preparation creates a barrier to exit that can be too high to surmount when work satisfaction is later found missing. Selection at the point of entry into extended training may improve the rate of success in training without assuring sound career fit. Indeed, it is probably too much to ask of any selection method to assure a long-term fit for anyone in any career. Only the strictest performance standards will assure that misfits don't stay in the career to deliver a poor quality product. Where standards cannot be set and enforced, high wages must not be set high to "attract the best." High standards and clear goals are not only the most effective motivators of high performance, they are indispensable for policing the fit of workers to the high performance culture.

Common sense and self-interest can contradict this rule. The notion that higher pay will attract better performers is attractive to many. It is the argument made by every public administrator in justification of increased tax budgets, by every corporate middle manager seeking higher pay for his or her workers. It is an argument that contains no small measure of insidious self-interest in that the higher one's subordinate's pay, the higher one's own pay must be to maintain differential pay equity between management and workers.

In the absence of challenging, measured work goals, high performance has little or nothing to do with level of pay. Those who love their work and throw themselves into it enthusiastically do so at high or low pay, sometimes with or without pay. High pay attracts those who are motivated by a larger share of the economic pie. Those so motivated easily convince themselves that they will enjoy any work that is well paid. Having convinced themselves, they are likely to be convincing in their self-pre-sentation as candidates. They seek out coaching, rehearse the "right answers" that will open the door to high pay, get the job, then hate the career. High pay ties them to a misfitted career path. Health problems from the stress of burnout follow, and early retirement is eagerly awaited as the only available escape route. They are locked in by high pay for the duration, miserable, unhappy, mediocre-to-poor performers who would never have considered the career if not for their aggressive pursuit of maximum personal economic payoff in promised high pay.

Where skill or interest are in short supply for existing demand, any approach *other* than increased pay that draws a sufficient pool of likely candidates is preferred. Innovatively redesigned hours of work, increased job responsibility, employer-paid or supplied training in relevant skills, anything *but* above market pay is preferable and probably cheaper. Considerable opportunity appears to exist for invention of high performance systems that recognize the power of these nonpay motivating factors.

CAUTION IN COMPENSATION PRACTICES PAYS OFF

Commonsense notions of pay as a motivator are largely off the mark, sometimes dangerous, usually troublesome. A paycheck represents the share of the economic payout available for division among players in the game that goes to the individual worker. The pursuit of a paycheck is almost always sufficient to assure acceptance of assigned work goals to the worker. Where goals are business relevant, rejection of assigned and appropriate goals is cause for instant and intensive management investigation. Jerking the recalcitrant worker around with promises of high pay or threats of low pay to achieve acceptance of goals is counterproductive if not silly.

Pay increments are useful and appropriate as incentives for workers to acquire added, needed, business-relevant skill. Under exceptional circumstances with appropriate supporting work culture it may be possible to motivate exceptional work output with exceptionally high pay. Piecework pay can sometimes be used to motivate added output up to a worker-established maximum in circumstances where quality will not suffer from tunnel-visioned pursuit of quantity. The anchor point for pay decisions is *always* the prevailing labor market rate for similar skill and experience. Pay for performance is an illusion—a maze in which the trapped may never find exit. High pay to get the best performance can often become only high cost for mediocre performance. These are the basics of sound pay policy for any management system. They are not the end of this discussion, though. There is another, entirely distinct, dimension to pay considerations that is found in the patterning of hours of work to maximize leisure and health while minimizing boredom and fatigue. These issues may have extraordinary potential for invention of future high performance systems that fit new emerging life patterns and styles. The greatest challenge to these systems may be the discovery of devices that retain equitable division of economic rewards within the system. We now turn to those issues.

Chapter Eight

Hours of Work, Leisure and Fatigue

A management system that fails to take worker leisure and life-style preferences into account will probably fail to elicit high performance. Tomorrow's high performance systems will require considerable innovation and flexibility in the design of work schedules to fit new, freer life-styles built around flexible work hours. The eight-hour day, forty-hour week is an anachronism that will be a barrier to high performance management systems of the future. But old customs and work patterns are not likely to give way easily.

The history of industrial working hours begins with very long hours of weary drudgery. Work hours in early eighteenth-century textile factories typically averaged 90 to 100 per week. The industrial work schedule echoed that of the agricultural life, but without the variety of task focus. In the late 1800s, Taylor's experiments with fatigue and rest periods established that hours of work alone were not critical to amount of work output. Opportunity for recovery from muscular fatigue was required if maximum absolute worker output was to be obtained in the workweek. At the turn of the twentieth century, factory managers in Europe and America experimented with reduced workdays and workweeks as a device for increasing total worker output per week. Records available from a variety of industries, accumulated and analyzed by H. Vernon (1921), demonstrated that a reduction in scheduled work hours often did, indeed, *increase* absolute weekly level of output per employee. At worst, under circumstances where machine-paced work offered minimum opportunity for worker variation in level of output, absolute level of weekly output *did not fall* when hours of work were cut. Henry Ford's 1913 decision to cut his standard factory workday from nine to eight hours was relatively risk free in view of the experience with workhour reduction already accumulated at that time.

The eight-hour day, forty-hour week has been the norm throughout the working life of most Americans now employed. It is a standard enshrined in federal law by virtue of a requirement that employees not specifically exempted from coverage under the Federal Fair Labor Standards Act of 1938 must be paid one and one-half times their standard hourly wage for all hours over forty worked in any week. The standard eight-hour day is the outcome of a broad consensus reached among production engineers in the earliest days of scientific management. It was concluded that, for machine-dependent jobs, an eight-hour day was close to optimum for minimization of fatigue and achievement of maximum *weekly* output from every worker. The carefully drawn arguments that founded this consensus are documented by Vernon (1921) in his important and insightful study of work hours and productivity, *Industrial Fatigue and Efficiency.* Long overlooked and ignored, Vernon's work is one of the earliest occasions for blending of scientific management principles with human performance research to establish sound management policy and practice. At the threshold of the twenty-first century, it has potential as a major point of reference for design of new high performance management systems.

The standard eight-hour workday emerged less as a humanitarian gesture than as a pragmatic move to get the highest available output per week from every worker, thereby maximizing output from capital capacity. The conventional five-day, forty-hour workweek, somewhat later in arriving, was a device for building-in labor capacity slack that could be worked overtime to meet exceptional and brief surges in demand. As leisure life-styles have elaborated to fill the Friday night to Monday morning work hiatus fully, the practicality of a productive Saturday workday has diminished to nil for all but the most work-oriented individuals.

Indeed, the productive utility of any form of overtime is often limited or nonexistent. Experienced production managers know that chronic overtime is usually counterproductive in terms of long-term output. In a very brief span of time, output per hour falls to a level where weekly output with overtime equals former weekly output without overtime. Overtime thereby increases cost without necessarily increasing output. If workers *forego* regular Saturday activities for work, Saturday can be a full capacity output day. Partial-day Saturday work that merely competes with preferred weekend activities can suffer the same fault as weekday overtime; output rate per hour drops to a level where absolute weekly output equals the preovertime level. Once accustomed to a five-day, forty-hour week, even Saturday overtime becomes counterproductive.

Problems with overtime are not new. Vernon documented findings concerning overtime with data from various industries under a subheading entitled "The Evils of Overtime." Observing that hourly output rate adjusts upward slowly when regular scheduled hours of work are cut, but drops quickly when they are increased, he offered the principle of "very slow adaptation to a reduction of hours, but quick adaptation to an increase of hours" (p. 55), especially so when extended through overtime. Overtime, even that which is machine-paced, is likely to be noneconomic except where brief and infrequent in response to obvious, major deadline requirements.

Reduced work output from extended work hours follows from a variety of causes. Workers take more and longer personal breaks during long workdays. They are more likely to miss work for all or part of a day. They consciously or unconsciously permit more work stoppages from equipment malfunctions, defective materials and materials shortages. They extend set-up or switch-over time. They slow down more through available self-paced stretches of work when working on machine paced jobs. End-spurts of extra effort prior to a rest period to catch up to standard or meet an output goal are less frequent and less vigorous. Workers appear to manage their energy cycles to fit the length of their accustomed workday. Extending the workday produces rapid adjustment of energy output to fit the longer day. If overtime is not altogether evil as Vernon suggested, it is typically counterproductive and without productive purpose.

Vernon convincingly argued that this phenomenon of spreading or compressing a relatively fixed amount of output over varying lengths of work schedule certainly extends to regularly scheduled working hours in a range of eight to twelve a day and probably operates well below eight hours. Long workdays do not generate more output per week; to the contrary, they can be expected to reduce absolute weekly output. Vernon carefully documented changes in rate of work output and absolute weekly production measured through various natural experiments with workweek length through the first two decades of the twentieth century. In that time, a variety of industries cut hours and days of work from twelve to ten, then to eight hours a day, while working days were reduced from six and a half to six, then to five and a half per week. Vernon tracked changes in output over a sufficient span of time to reliably identify the point where they level off following initial adjustment. Evaluating changes in weekly output, he straightforwardly concluded that "the biggest output may accrue when the hours of work are comparatively short" (p. 32).

Pressure for maximum munitions output during World War I offered opportunity for a particularly telling natural experiment in hours of work. Vernon described it thus:

The great war offered an unrivalled opportunity for obtaining the kind of information required, for vast numbers of men and women were engaged week after week, month after month, and even year after year, in making munitions of certain standardized patterns. Often the character of the articles produced, and the conditions of their production, remained absolutely unchanged over long periods except in one particular, viz., the hours of work. In the first eighteen months of the war it was the general custom to impose very long hours upon workers in order to obtain the biggest possible output, but it was gradually discovered that these long hours did not pay. Owing to the overfatigue induced, output fell off and progressive reductions of hours were instituted (p. 34).

Exhibits 8–1 and 8–2 graphically present the output records of two groups of World War I British munitions workers. Output of experienced females turning fuse bodies for munitions was measured over almost two years, during which hours of work were progressively shortened. When the workday was cut from twelve to ten hours, hourly rate of output increased gradually until it was up 21%. At that point, absolute weekly output was equal to the level available from a twelve hour day. When Sunday work was abolished, the hourly output rate ascended gradually until it topped out at an additional 28% over the ten-hour day rate. At this point, the hourly rate had increased by 56% over the earlier twelve-hour day rate, and absolute weekly output was now up 13% from its earliest measured level. Hours of work were cut by one-fourth but production measured in absolute units per week increased by one-eighth. Munitions worker ladies were more productive on a shorter workweek.

Analysis of similar data for men in the job of fuse body sizing, followed over 22 consecutive months, yielded strikingly similar results, their absolute weekly production rising with progressive cuts in working hours by 19%. Vernon noted that female fuse body turners may have been more limited in potential for output by greater restraints on output from their machinery, thereby conferring advantage on men who were sizing fuse bodies. On the whole, though, the comparison is remarkably similar.

These analyses, carried out on historical data that reflected working conditions that were unchanged for the long period of study, are little less than astonishing. That, indeed, was precisely the word chosen by Vernon to describe his findings in 1921. In other industries, Vernon found similar

Exhibit 8-1
Weekly Output of Women Turning Fuse Bodies

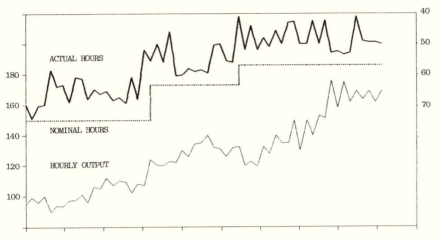

Weekly Measures-Aug 15,1915-May 5,1917

Exhibit 8-2
Weekly Output of Men Sizing Fuse Bodies

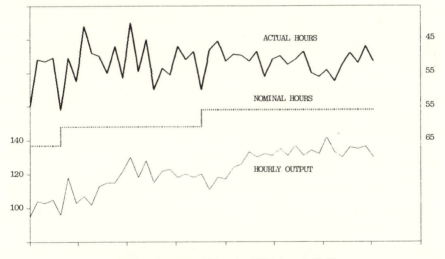

Weekly Measures-Nov 14,1915-Aug 4,1917

patterns. The weekly output of steel melters rose 18% when hours were cut from twelve to eight per day. Tinplate millmen working eight-hour shifts at their heavy, unpleasant task of rolling red-hot tinplate bars into thin plates of steel were subject to reduction to six-hour shifts when equipment broke down or material was short. Vernon analyzed their weekly output for those periods when hours were reduced, then restored to the normal eight-hour length. Hourly rate of output gradually rose on six-hour shifts until it reached a level about 12% above their eight-hour rate. On restoration of the normal eight-hour day, the hourly rate returned almost immediately to its former level.

Where work was *absolutely* limited by machinery, Vernon found that a reduction in work hours quite predictably produced an absolute reduction in weekly work output, though not always equivalent in percent to the proportion of work hours cut. Worker freedom to adjust rate of output is partly but not wholly limited by constraints in equipment used.

The stability of average output rate over time was examined by Vernon and found to be remarkably steady. In a series of analyses of hourly and daily output patterns, he identified distinctive hourly patterns but found a strong tendency for workers to produce at a steady rate from morning to afternoon work periods and from day to day. Even Monday mornings, presumably influenced by the postweekend blahs, as well as difficult evening and week-end shifts, were all more uniform than hourly variations suggested was likely. His conclusion was that workers learn to meter their energies out over the full weekly term of work.

The astonishingly steady output maintained by almost all industrial workers is due . . . to the habit which most manual labourers get into of working at as steady a rate as possible under all circumstances. This steady rate is adopted unconsciously, and it is dependent on a principle which is so important and so widely observed that I venture to term it *the law of maximum production with minimum effort* (p. 26).

Concerning increases in weekly output resulting from reduction of work hours, he concluded that

as a rule, the speeding up of production on the part of workers is adopted quite unconsciously. Owing to the shortened hours of labour they possess a surplus of available physical energy, and, without knowing it, they put a little more vigour than usual into their work. . . . It is possible that they then tire themselves out about as much as they had previously done when working longer hours: i.e., short hours of quick work cause as much drain on physical energy as long hours of slow work (p. 37).

As evidence for unconscious variation in speed of production, Vernon noted that these findings were found to apply equally to both hourly paid and piecework paid workers.

Vernon took note of plans then in the works to experiment with a six-hour day. For the data offered, improvement in hourly rate of output does not appear to have stopped at eight hours. Six hours may have potential for yet more improvement in output. The report of a granite-cutting firm in the United States was cited where more daily output was produced, first on a nine- than on a ten-hour day, then still more was achieved in an eight- than a nine-hour day. The president of this firm was quoted as believing that a good granite cutter could do as much in seven or even six hours as he did in eight.

On the whole, this is an astonishing revelation with wide-ranging implications for the productive efficiency of labor. At the time of its publication in 1921 it was probably revolutionary enough to suggest the superiority of an eight-hour day over longer, traditional workdays. Scientific management was pushing its credibility to the limit arguing for an eight-hour standard. Vernon offered an extended hypothetical argument in his summary of reduced hours of work where he proposed an eight-hour day as the optimally efficient length of a workday for maximum weekly output, particularly so where machine constraints may limit the freedom of workers to adjust their rate of output to fit available energy resources. Whether he was reflecting an existing consensus of production engineering professionals, or catalyzing an emerging consensus among them is hard to judge from this extended distance in time. Conveniently, eight hours divides evenly into a twenty-four-hour day, and that permits scheduling of continuous, round-the-clock operations. So, eight hours it became. Indeed, eight hours it still is. By 1935 the shift to the standard eight-hour workday was largely complete throughout American and European industry. The possibility of a six-hour or shorter workday with equivalent output for eight hours was forgotten. From time to time in isolated circumstances, it briefly raises its head again.

A REPRISE OF SHORTER HOURS AND HIGHER PRODUCTIVITY

In 1979 under contract with General Electric Corporate Employee Relations, I conducted a survey of part-time employment practices in the United States (Bassett, 1980). Tantalizing reports had begun to appear in the Quality of Work Life literature about shorter workdays without reduction in daily or weekly output. Contact with companies experimenting with five-hour "mothers' " and "students' " shifts revealed that some part-timers were, indeed, consistently turning out the equivalent of full-timers' eight hours' output in both assembly and office work. Vernon's law was being rediscovered. Interest in shorter workdays with full productivity waned rapidly, even though part-timers were paid less per hour than were full-timers, were paid several hours less per day and received only the legally required minimum of benefits coverage—FICA, Workman's Compensation and Unemployment. None were covered by medical, life or disability insurance, much less by a retirement annuity plan. Employers were reaping a cost-savings windfall of embarrassing proportions from these part-time workers.

A discrepancy as far out of the norm as this was is almost impossible to reconcile. In the absence of evidence one way or the other, the conservative hypothesis would be that full-timers limited their standard output to a modest level judged fair for the level of economic participation represented by their paychecks. Part-timers were not included in the work limitation agreement and it was not a factor restraining their output. Alternatively, within Vernon's framework of the law of maximum output at minimum effort, the drain of eight hours on the job might have served as a drag on output for these full-timers. A shorter schedule may have exploited the fresher energy of part-timers. Either way, the comparison was too hot to handle. Whatever the explanation, the threat to full-time wage earners in loss of employment to lower wage earners offered clear potential for organization of a labor union where there was none, or of open labor warfare where one existed.

Employers who benefited from this windfall in low-cost output may have preferred to see it as an unexplained anomaly in an otherwise invariant and predictable world. The then long-term expectation in manufacturing and office management was movement toward automation—increased dependence on machine-paced work—that offers minimum potential for increased performance through shorter hours of work. There appeared little purpose in pursuing the potential of a shortened workday for unskilled labor at that time. Thus, nothing enduring came out of this brief flurry of experimentation with shorter workdays.

What was overlooked in this logic of denial is that with an ever greater proportion of mass commodity production performed by machinery, labor is today more likely to be assigned at flexible, project-styled work where opportunity for adjustment of work pace is maximum. Vernon's law of maximum production with minimum effort applies best with work that offers the workers freedom to adapt their rate of output. The greater the flexibility, freedom and responsibility, the greater the potential for gain in output with shorter hours. Indeed, wherever there is opportunity to maintain absolute output against the eight-hour standard while reducing hours to six, obtaining twice the output in two six-hour stints manned by different workers with different schedule preferences would constitute significant opportunity for increased profit from better-utilized plant and equipment. In this new, project-shop-based, global era of economic competition, rediscovery of potential for increased productivity from shortened work hours could be a critical competitive weapon.

SHORTER WORKDAYS COULD ALSO BRING ECONOMIC DISLOCATION

Before concluding that the moment has arrived for implementation of a six-, or five-, or four-hour workday, it would be wise to examine closely the broader economic implications of scheduling and working fewer work hours.

Were a widespread reduction in hours of work effective at raising absolute output of product even 10% or 15%—a modest increment by previous standards—a glut of products could be introduced onto the market that could drive prices and wages down severely. It is difficult enough in an unplanned economy to maintain a balance of capacity and supply to meet demand, even with a standard eight-hour day. Destabilizing an already delicate balance would be risky. Quite possibly it would be necessary to cut hours to a point where any absolute increase would be prevented.

On the side of economic advantage, we might argue that if Vernon's law holds at very short hours, it could offer unparalleled opportunity for capacity flexibility to meet sudden, large shifts in demand. With an exceptionally short workday, it should be possible to adjust quickly and fully respond to large swings in market demand simply by working an hour more or less a day. If Vernon's law of maximum production with minimum effort continues to apply down to an extremely low number of hours per day, that's how it could work. But experimenting with reduced hours of work would still be a bold leap into the unknown of labor economics, which could be wildly unpredictable. If successfully implemented as the basis of a high performance management system, it could be a smashing competitive success.

Wages for reduced hours of work is another problem. Where a reduction in work hours maintains or raises absolute output, it would be necessary to maintain worker income lest reduced pay for the same product would undercut the purchasing power necessary to sustain demand for those products. Part-time workers on five-hour shifts who produce the equivalent of eight hours' work do so because the share of the economic division awarded them is satisfactory for the *time* and *effort* expended. They need not be concerned with the lack of parity between their income and that of full-timers. If, though, their aspiration for greater participation in division of the economic pie were to rise, we might expect them to withhold their labor for the wages offered, organize a union or take other direct action to raise wages. A job and a paycheck represent one's share of economic division under the rules of a complex economic system. If hours are reduced but output is not, the rules for allocation of that share will need to be radically revised. Certainly an hourly rate is no longer a useful reference point. Maintenance of weekly income levels would be the more appropriate concern.

The wage transition from an eight-hour to shorter workday might be managed with some form of piecework pay system. A period of transition, though, is the least desirable time and condition for application of piecework pay. Maintaining adjusted parity for a piecework system would be difficult. A system of daily or weekly output goals set at parity with historical levels for eight-hour output might better be employed with full pay assured for output at those levels. In effect, a worker might work until the goal was met, draw a full paycheck, and end the day's or week's work upon achievement of the output goal. That would be fine as long as quality of output was not sacrificed in cheap satisfaction of the bargain. Another transitionary device might be temporary adjustment of hourly rates. New rates might be conservatively estimated with a temporary parity bonus guaranteeing some minimum former rate until the new arrangement settled down. Achieving a satisfactory division of the economic pie is always a lengthy, tortuous and approximate process. Reestablishing that division with reduced work hours would be difficult.

Greatly increased productivity *per hour* from existing plant and equipment would naturally increase effective plant capacity without increased capital investment. Less demand for capital, if sufficiently widespread, could reduce its cost and its value. Investors would be unhappy with reduced dividend returns. Capital goods industries would suffer from falling demand for their products. Free added capacity thus obtained would require long-term adjustment in capital goods industries that could produce an economic depression. Free added capacity from reduced hours of work that maintain former absolute daily or weekly output levels might tempt owners to compete for added market share by driving output up to the new capacity levels with added workers and shifts. Costly price wars might result. The potential for economic destabilization from so radical a change in work hours—*if* it could be obtained without diminishment of output—is awesome.

Vernon's law might not hold. If shorter work hours reduced absolute output somewhat, but less than proportionately to hours cut, an interim solution might be to reduce wages partially and expect the difference to be offset by the value of increased leisure or discretionary personal time. As advancing automation expands the base of commodity goods at ever lower cost, simultaneously reducing paid hours of labor, it may be socially desirable to permit displaced workers to earn at reduced pay while they develop alternative skills and careers. Some workers may even be satisfied to participate on a smaller scale of share in return for an enlarged personal, family and leisure life. Cafeteria hours that permit an employee to work a personally adjusted schedule have been tried in some industries, and could readily be adapted in support of the transition to a shorter workday.

The shape of an economy reconstructed around the shortened workday is difficult to predict. The risks, uncertainties and adjustments that would go with it are not necessarily welcome events. The standard, eight-hour, five-day workweek, though, has become stale beyond recovery. There are many firms and industries that could immediately profit from adoption of a shortened workday. It might be well to experiment under favorable conditions now rather than wait for the wave of change to overtake them. Eventually, it will certainly come.

ALTERNATIVE, FLEXIBLE WORK SCHEDULES AND WORK FATIGUE

Other work scheduling options exist beyond the shorter workday, of course. Fewer, longer workdays are an alternative. Experiments with four ten-hour days or three twelve-hour days that concentrate productive output have not been widely successful because the buildup of fatigue through the course of the longer workday often does reduce available work energy. It is sometimes as if a ten-hour day for the average individual works out the same as any standard eight-hour shift with two hours of overtime added. Eventually, only four days of work for five days of pay result. The ten-hour day, four-day week sometimes works well temporarily, as during the summer season, but output has the potential to sag when scheduled continuously. Otherwise, an ongoing ten- or twelve-hour-day schedule seems to demand exceptional personal discipline and physical conditioning from those who adopt it.

Exceptions to the ineffectiveness of long workdays are frequently found among professionals. Doctors, lawyers, consultants and self-employed technicians or specialists who *choose* to work longer hours, either *when* the work is available or to consolidate leisure time, can maintain high output in anticipation of future falloff in demand. Long periods of restorative leisure seem sufficient incentive to maintain performance for these workers. But once in this mode, some may find it necessary to support the long workday with a discipline of physical conditioning that supports the higher stress and energy demands of such a concentrated schedule. It is in these circumstances that the reality of fatigue as limitation on work effort reemerges for observation.

FATIGUE CAN STILL BE A BARRIER TO OUTPUT

Fatigue is partly physical, partly a function of life pattern. A vigorous, physically demanding job can condition the worker physically, raising the threshold of fatigue. A passive, sedentary job, especially where the job is alternated with passive, sedentary leisure, can result in significant loss of physical tone and conditioning, thereby lowering the threshold of fatigue. Muscle and body tissue can be strengthened or toughened with a planned program of conditioning. Alternately, it can be injured and weakened if imprudently overstressed. The trained singer develops strength in tiny vocal cords capable of supporting a high "C" that fills a concert hall. The poorly practiced public speaker injures those same unconditioned vocal cords with simple overuse. The active worker bicycles to work and runs up the stairs three at a time. The inactive worker drives when it would be as easy to walk, routinely hyperventilates climbing the stairs and avoids anything more strenuous than lifting a coffee cup.

In the absence of demand for physical exertion to produce the basic necessities of life—food, clothing and shelter—physical conditioning must flow from planned activity and self-discipline. One's threshold of fatigue is a function of one's level of recurrent, noninjurious physical activity. In an affluent age, supported by a multitude of labor-saving tools and fuels, level of activity becomes largely discretionary. Factory and office jobs that keep workers on their feet and moving actively are increasingly more rare, though the adoption of work cell methods that demand flexibility of physical movement may reverse this trend. The opportunity to lose conditioning through lack of activity continues to be widely available. Inactive people go soft. The threshold of fatigue drops. The energy pool available for allocation between work *and* leisure diminishes.

Workers do seem to measure their output energies against the anticipated opportunity for restorative rest and leisure activity. The fatigue of grueling, hard physical labor that once characterized factories has long given way to hoists, cranes, forklifts and air-conditioned control cabs. This does not mean that workers no longer suffer from ordinary physical fatigue. The emotional stress of a demanding job today is capable of bringing on as severe a case of fatigue as carrying iron ingots on the loading dock once did. The threshold of fatigue for each individual worker is a direct function of the level of physical activity engaged in daily. Where there is little or no vigorous activity, the onset of fatigue from overstress will be early. The corollary to Vernon's law of maximum output with minimum effort is that the threshold of fatigue rises or falls to match the level of physical activity characteristic of one's daily and weekly activity pattern. Within a regimen of regular physical conditioning, a worker might easily maintain the usual level for eight hours of output over ten-, twelve- or more- hour work schedules, especially so across fewer working days. Calisthenics for all workers at the opening of the workday makes perfect sense in terms of increased resistance to stress and fatigue on the job.

Much present-day fatigue is physically localized. A limited set of muscles or tissues are chronically overstressed while the rest of the body is wholly sedentary. Constant repetition of particular gripping or grasping motions, common to many assembly jobs, invokes for some the symptoms of carpal tunnel syndrome, a disabling disease of the hands. Flatfeet—fallen arches—were once chronic among those who spent long hours on their feet with insufficient footwear support. These are muscular abnormalities from overfatigue that occur with little or no fatigue or stress effects on other muscle groups. Fatigue from mental or emotional stress can occur solely in response to a particular person, type of personality or work situation—almost as a conditioned response—for individuals otherwise emotionally unresponsive to many events. Stress may show its effects in many small ways, as through high blood pressure, elevated heart rate, increased stomach acidity, or spasms of the small neck and back muscles. Ignored, all of these local fatigues can lead to serious disease and disability. With the appearance of labor-saving equipment, fatigue has not been vanquished; it has merely assumed a new guise.

The experience of fatigue, thus, has not disappeared with diminished hard physical labor on the job. Rather, it has often gone "underground" in the form of stress. It has changed its form, sometimes insidiously. It must be managed differently. In some respects, it is much more subject to programmed control and management than formerly. Twenty minutes every other day devoted to vigorous cardiovascular, aerobic exercise can maintain average physical tone for the average person. One's level of stamina has become more a matter of choice than of response to physical necessity. One can manage his or her threshold of fatigue and stress with the discipline of training.

There is nothing unusual or mysterious about the need to maintain physical conditioning independent of job activities. The physical activity of playing baseball or a round of golf is insufficient to maintain maximum physical tone required for major league and tournament play. Players must condition themselves physically on and off season. Most conditioning effort is applied off the field and away from the links. Attempting to get in condition for wrestling, boxing or the play of football within play of the sport itself would be foolishly dangerous. One could be injured too severely to attempt to continue were that the program. Advance physical conditioning that prepares the player for the anticipated punishment is indispensable to success. Exercise to maintain physical health and tone are commonplace in sports. Physical conditioning to meet the demands of one's job or career is merely less customary. For an increasing number of workers who face high stress in their jobs from the escalating competitiveness of a global economy, regular, systematic physical conditioning for the game is just as necessary. Ulcers, high blood pressure and heart disease have all been linked to job stress that is not offset by exercise and physical conditioning that could raise the threshold. It should be no surprise to discover that productivity and job effectiveness generally may also depend equally on improved physical condition of workers.

Success in raising output with shortened or restructured working hours may depend greatly on the pattern of activities individually chosen by workers in their discretionary and leisure hours. The divorce of work and leisure, formerly common with the eight-hour day, five-day week, may require reconciliation in support of a shorter workweek and shorter working hours. There is potential for diversion of energy into competing activities whenever work does not fully demand all the available energy. "Moonlighting" workers who work two jobs, sometimes with adverse effects on performance in both, are a long-standing concern of managers. Workers who rush from the job to a full schedule of evening activities, then fill their weekend hours with vigorous, continuous personal events, may reserve their best energy for leisure at the expense of achieving high performance in their jobs. Nonjob time can easily compete with job time for limited energy, especially where leisure activities are regularly pursued to excess and sometimes end in exhaustion.

PRODUCTIVITY AND INDIVIDUAL LIFE PATTERNS

The shorter working day introduces potential for yet more competition from leisure activities. The eight-hour day, five-day week changed the pattern of the average worker's week from one in which wage work dominated his or her waking hours, to one where nonworking, waking hours outnumbered those on the job. Eight hours' work per day may be close to optimum for achievement of maximum absolute weekly output because it offers sufficient opportunity to restore energy diminished by work fatigue without introducing enough time for any major alternative activity to become a serious competitor for energy needed on the job. Even so, healthy workers with strong nonwork interests working a normal forty-hour schedule may hold a second job, pursue demanding educational opportunities, engage in vigorous hobbies and participate in a wide variety of unpaid social or community projects that compete for their best energies. Any of these activities may reduce energy or commitment available for work output unless peak energy is focused onto the job. Alternatively, these same activities can be fully supportive and restorative of maximum work output within a discipline of high physical conditioning. The relative harm or benefit is likely to be a function of an individual's overall life pattern of work and leisure activities. That same pattern probably establishes what each individual's optimum daily and weekly work hours will be.

In this respect, Henry Ford's "sociological department," established to identify those workers whose life-style was worthy of Ford's generous incentive bonus, may deserve more credit for increasing productivity than it has heretofore been given. Direct interference on the part of an employer in the personal lives of workers today is, of course, improper. Instructing workers in the proper use of leisure hours would constitute an unwarranted invasion into their personal affairs. But Ford's insistence on evidence of a conventional, sober and moral family life as a condition for deserving his bonus assured that those leisure hours outside an eight-hour working day would be prudently applied to activities that complemented rather than competed with work behavior. Substantial restoration of physical and emotional energy would be assured, and maximum incentive to meet family obligations through consistent performance on the job would be created. Encouraging off-the-job activities that complement the job is less easy now than in Ford's time, but may be equally desirable from the employer's perspective. It must only be approached right.

Ambitious, maximally productive workers today often act out their aspirations through a carefully orchestrated life-style that uses off-the-job activity to enhance on-the-job performance. The experiences, hobbies, friendships, vacations and associations sought out by the career-focused worker all serve the central purpose of maximized performance on the job. The sales representative whose productivity is determined by a handful of brief meetings each month organizes his or her life-style and leisure in support of those limited, peak occasions. Lawyers enter politics for the benefit of those indispensable contacts, experiences and exposures that political involvement confers. A university professor focuses reading, friendships, vacations and hobbies onto the topic of his or her degree specialty, bringing it all to a focus in the few hours each week of classroom contact with students, then summing it up as a book. Ample demonstrations of life-styles centered on career and work are available to illustrate the significance of leisure and nonwork activities as contributors to the productivity of working time. It is easy, thus, to propose as a working hypothesis the centrality of one's life pattern to success in maximizing productive output in shortened work hours.

The problem with bringing life patterns into consonance with output goals on the job is that this cannot and must not be demanded or required as a condition of employment. It is legal and feasible only when offered voluntarily by the worker. The worker who is offended by suggestions or pressures to order his or her life around a job can easily defeat them in any event. Resenting absence of choice will, alone, undermine the commitment required for a disciplined, work-focused life-style. Social pressures off the job work against a job-centered life-style. Friends and family may resent competition of the job with *their* centrality in the worker's life. Moral concerns may intervene. One's children may miss something in their development from lack of parental support because the job has closed them out of the worker's priorities. The pattern if forced and uncomfortable may become counterproductive as a form of "workaholism" that diminishes energy and effectiveness with the passage of time.

These are excesses that generally go with *total* focus on work activities that excludes all else. An excessive work focus narrows and limits the individual, ultimately leading to disappointment or failure in the career. For a full life, more than just a job is needed, even when it offers an intrinsically desirable and significant career. A job that holds no intrinsic fun or interest for its incumbent but demands all a worker's energy is workaholism at its worst. The job that is performed for the inherent satisfaction it offers is less likely to be overdone. When satisfaction or energy runs thin, this worker can turn to diversion and leisure that allow him or her to play, re-creating emotional and physical energy. The opportunity must always be open to the worker's choice for restorative diversion and rest when a complementary life pattern is sought to support peak job performance.

The job that is intrinsically interesting and engaging will not lack for a worker's commitment and full energy. Where tasteful, legal, unobtrusive guidance is offered in ways to support peak performance with off-the-job activity, those ways will be enthusiastically pursued when work excites and activates the worker directly. Those jobs in which optimum output is obtainable in six, five, four or fewer hours per day will be those that would be attractive even at a minimum level of economic—paycheck—participation. Five hundred years ago the poverty of the cloistered scientist and academician in a monastery was no barrier to dedicated pursuit of tasks requiring long, arduous hours, on a work schedule dictated by impulse. Peak performance is forthcoming, regardless, in such jobs. That the quality of performance under these circumstances is likely to be maximum augurs for generosity in calculating a peak performer's paycheck award. Pay is determined largely by value, convention and market comparison in these jobs. The necessity of high pay to support off-the-job activities that permit peak performance is the most likely justification of high pay for them.

Even routine, uninteresting jobs may yield high absolute output in shorter work hours when standards and goals are set by the employer that require discipline of leisure time in their support. There is no longer justification or social tolerance for intrusion into personal affairs by a "sociological department," but there is justification in penalty for inadequate performance that results from misuse of leisure. Alcoholics and drug addicts holding a wage job, for instance, may not be disciplined on grounds alone of alcoholism or drug addiction. Most grievance arbitrators and judges today will strike down discipline imposed on those grounds *unless* clear evidence is offered that performance has suffered. Discipline for drug use is legitimate only in those circumstances like organized sports where drugs may spuriously produce peak performance for competitive advantage in those limited short periods of time when they are used. In both circumstances, contrary as they are, effect on performance is the anchor. Shortened hours of work structured with high standards and difficult goals to optimize output during scheduled working time are naturally supportive of peak performance. The expectation that off-the-job activity will be organized to support peak output is not unreasonable. Requiring it may be improper, but expecting it and using observed performance as the anchor for recognition and pay is feasible.

TASK VARIETY AND REST PERIODS

In most ways, shorter work hours represent only a tighter, more intense concentration of productive activity within the scheduled working time. Intense concentration of energy and intellect onto a limited, difficult goal can be trained and learned. If soundly practiced, it will be balanced against total diversion immediately following so that fatigue or injury can be avoided. The typical span of time over which such concentration can be held by most healthy adults appears to range from two to four hours. This is the length of most sports events, continuous trial work in a court room, concerts and dramatic performances. The preparation, rehearsal, conditioning and general anticipation of these activities takes at least as many added hours. Indeed, without that preparation, without the discipline of supporting life-style, those performances probably could not occur.

We may observe that long, full productive days are experienced by anyone who varies activity to avoid fatigue buildup arising out of over-emphasis on any one activity. The average CEO applies far beyond eight hours a day to his or her job, but the nature of activity that makes up the long day is likely to be quite varied. A series of meeting discussions punctuated by movement from one place to another, unprogrammed phone discussions, reading, inspection of products, video-viewing, and so on, may all occur in a single day. If any one activity begins to fatigue, continuance can be postponed while an alternative, restorative performance is undertaken. Over the course of a day there will be many different activities, invoking many different skills and muscle sets. If the executive is wise enough to schedule a period of vigorous aerobics exercise during the day to offset long periods of sedentary activity, there may be little if any residual fatigue effect at the days' end to demand extra rest before resumption of the schedule. The best rest is often a change in activity. The life pattern organized around that principle could be awesomely productive.

Fatigue in one set of muscles can be restored while activity is shifted onto complementary muscles without requiring a rest period. In the absence of other useful activity that offsets the fatigue, regular rest alternated with vigorous activity can be scheduled in a manner that optimizes output. Taylor successfully used rest periods as a device for raising output with hard labor tasks like heavy longshoremen's work. Had it been feasible, he might have used an alternative task that called other muscle groups into action as a substitute for fatigue restorative rest. Rest periods are still widely employed to overcome worker fatigue, even in light production work. Most jobs are not yet designed to maximize output by alternating tasks systematically to get the fullest range of muscular and mental energy in a day's time, but many, possibly, could be. Assisting individual workers to vary their task focus to spread energy capacity and dispel fatigue could be a more practical and participatively effective approach than simply enlarging or redesigning jobs. One size fits all is no longer a productive approach to most job design. The opportunity awaits exploitation to develop principles of daily activity and exercise that, once communicated, would raise worker productivity significantly.

The issue of overall worker health must, in its own right, finally be addressed by society and by employers. Too much leisure activity, too much rich food, too little physical activity, with stimulation artificially supplied by caffeine, alcohol and passive entertainment, adds up to poor health. Lost productivity resulting from such a destructive life-style and the direct cost of medical care to remedy neglect of health have become costly burdens on the economy. A poor, or, at least, a work-incompatible life-style is already diminishing output in many industries. More leisure hours without supporting discipline to assure good health and raise energy for job performance can only amplify this pathology.

At a minimum, employers must take some steps to encourage better health among workers. A fair and logical approach would be to require an employee contribution to medical insurance, but remit all or part of it to those workers who could pass a periodic physical examination that included a rigorous stress test. Other opportunity for lower cost insurance could go to those who don't use tobacco, who maintain a trim, normal weight level, neither too high nor too low, and who exercise regularly under company supervision. There could be objections, even court tests of such measures from those who insist on their God-given right to poor health. The most direct solution could be to shorten work hours and set exacting performance standards supported by challenging goals and a recommended regimen of healthful nutrition and activity. Promotion, work reassignment and even discipline anchored on consistent conformance to standards is always legal because it is business-related and contributes directly to higher productivity. Those are the foundation tools for encouraging peak performance on the job.

OPPORTUNITY SEEMS TO LIE ALL ABOUT

Somewhere in this package of working hour, fatigue, stress and leisure issues there is probably available a major payoff for the high performance operations manager. The best hopes of those ideologically committed to full-scale industrial democracy, to universal worker satisfaction through high quality of work life, to genuine worker participation in business decisions, and to maximum efficiency from scientific job design may ultimately all be realized from insights available here. Guidance for constructive discipline and implementation of organizationwide goal setting as the dominant motivator of improved performance come to confluence in hours of work, leisure and fatigue. Sound pay practices that recognize and reward peak performance may become feasible under the right configuration of working hours and personal, supporting life-style. The impersonal routine of an eight-hour day, five-day week in fragmented, overspecialized jobs applied to engineered work flow certainly now offers little or no potential for the design of new high performance output systems. There is but limited risk of loss in looking more closely at these new opportunities.

Vernon's work cited in this chapter and in his remarkable 1921 writings had considerable influence in industrial practices in its time. Taylor, Ford and Hawthorne, though, had disproportionately greater and more lasting influence. It is perhaps time to rediscover the many cogent insights offered by Vernon as the jumping off point for new beginnings. His lessons are entirely consonant with the hard-won principles that instruct us how to effectively redirect our efforts to enhance worker satisfaction, increase worker participation and motivate peak performance. Within this revised framework, it is not exercise of authority or lack of good relations with workers in the work place that is the problem. Management authority need not be leashed and sugar coated to the extent that many have proposed. Rather, enlightened, informed authority focused on the goal of peak performance by every worker seems indispensable to the invention of tomorrow's high performance management systems. Management insight and skill will be required to achieve optimum output potential available from new schedules of work hours. Bold leadership will be needed to improve worker health, manage fatigue, reduce boredom and redirect leisure to healthy, productive purposes. Leadership and competent authority will be fundamental in discovering new high peformance systems.

Chapter Nine

Skill and Knowledge: Developing Human Potential in the Workplace

Of the many changes that characterize American life in the twentieth century, none is more dramatic and far reaching than spectacular advances made in offering universal higher education to all who desire it and can benefit from it. At the beginning of this century, a university education was largely limited to those favored few whose parents could afford the price of tuition and did not depend on the labor of their children to augment their meager income. Universities trained the young for entry into the professions—education, law, medicine and religion. A string of new land-grant colleges, dubbed "A&M" to proclaim their expected contribution to careers in agriculture and mining, prepared students in the practical sciences of engineering, chemistry and biology.

The legal, political and technical foundations of the scientific management movement unleashed by Frederick Taylor demanded the increased skill of trained administrators and technicians. High performance has been effectively augmented in operating systems based on principles of scientific management by raising requisite levels of technical skill and education. Taylor's basic system, as modified by Henry Ford, has changed little in this century, but the level of skill and education applied to it has escalated sharply.

Education has thus emerged as a competitive imperative in the twentieth century. In just the fifty years from 1940 to 1990, the level of education in America underwent a major revolution. In that span of time, the proportion of high school graduates in the U.S. population increased from slightly less than one in four to a little over three in four. Those possessing

Exhibit 9-1
Change in Level of Educational Attainment, U.S. Citizens Age 25 and Older, 1940 to 1990

YEAR:	Percent of Population Completing High School	Percent of Population Completing Four Years of College
1940	24.5%	4.6%
1950	34.3%	6.2%
1960	41.1%	7.7%
1970	52.3%	10.7%
1980	66.5%	16.2%
1990*	85.5%	21.1%

* Estimated from 1989 data.

Source: United State Census of Population.

a four year college degree grew from less than one in twenty to just over one in five (see Exhibit 9–1). And, while demand for increased technical skill and education was driven by the needs of high performance systems built on scientific management principles, the imperative of increased labor skill will certainly shape the design of tomorrow's high performance management systems.

The transition is already under way in U.S. industry from a narrowly specialized to a broadly multiskilled work force as the foundation of high performance operating systems. Cursory, low-budget vestibule and on-the-job training are no longer adequate. Those firms that once minimized training cost through narrowly specializing routine production jobs are now faced with a training challenge of major proportions. Training on the job becomes intense and continual. Typically, 5% to 15% of work hours and labor dollars must be reallocated into the training budget to support new, high performance operations methods, especially so those that require multiskilling of workers.

Training may occur during work hours or off. It may be conducted in-house or outside. It may be custom designed to the need of an individual, focused on the specific technical needs of a particular work group, general to an operation or industry, or broadly relevant to the political, economic and competitive forces in which the business operates. The functional department responsible for administration of the training budget must itself be a highly flexible, professional, well-organized operation. It will "make" and it will "buy" educational capacity as need and opportunity dictate. It will diagnose and meet existing or emerging needs. Training and education, whether public or private, have become fundamental resources to business in this new era, responsible for building and honing the competitive cutting edge of workers' and managers' skills.

The objectives of career training in the new age are complex and varied in themselves. Graduates of the public and private educational system can no longer be expected to arrive fully prepared for their jobs. Everyone will require upgraded training at some point in their career. Labor shortages, responsiveness to social need and social legislation require that even those candidates who are inadequately prepared in basic skill must be reclaimed through training to become effective employees. Once routinely rejected for employment, the illiterate and socially malequipped are now more likely to be individually tutored up to their level of capability. Remedial training becomes fundamental to the training mission.

EXPANDED INVESTMENT IN TRAINING IS UNAVOIDABLE

Skill training in the tasks of today's high performance firm must be extensive and continuous. Flexibility of reassignment demands that workers be as broadly trained in relevant skills as possible. Training may proceed in modules that approximate formerly specialized tasks, but worker flexibility in the new work environment is likely to be demanded the first day on the job. With abandonment of the moving, lock-step, task-fragmented assembly process, the new worker will immediately move through various, multiple tasks in the first days and weeks on the job. Co-workers may train the new person, or formal, off-the-work-floor skill indoctrination may be employed. The choice of which to use will probably have to be cost justified. This requires still another variety of trained skill.

The manner in which training is implemented must be reevaluated for its effect on long-term performance and flexibility of skill application. Recent research evidence (Schmidt and Bjork, 1992) offers persuasive argument that tunnel-visioned, "drill" methods of training designed for fast and efficient training of narrow skill reduces flexibility of worker response to variable workplace demand. Training that offers practice in response to random novelty produces better performance in response to variability in the work itself. Too much efficiency in training can be a bad thing.

Exhibit 9-2
Characteristics of a Modern Work Cell

Three to twelve workers are a work team.

The team is assigned a component of
service or product output
as its responsibility.

More than adequate tools and
work facilities are provided.

Workers are extensively cross-trained
in the task skills required.

Clear performance goals are
established for the team.

The team self-allocates its members'
time and skill as needed
to fully achieve its goals.

Work cells such as those characterized in Exhibit 9–2 have become an important element of high performance system flexibility. Built on principles of group cohesiveness and teamwork, work cells necessarily expand the range of skill training required among their worker-members. Practice in responding to novelty and unplanned change is essential to all training offered a work cell member. The power of the work cell method of organization resides in the ability of the work group to reallocate instantly any or all available labor to any critical, bottleneck requirement within the cell work area. The broader the range of skills mastered by the workers in the cell, the greater its flexibility of response. And the broader the range of skills mastered, the greater the need to verify, reverify and track application of the full complement of required work skills. Trainers must be quality sensitive to the level of skill acquired by each worker and to the regularity of its practice and revalidation on the job. There is no more "demonstrate the skill and walk away" that was once standard in vestibule training. Training must assure continuous quality of all skills needed in the operation.

Although there is likely to be nothing new in the content of task skill training over what has been offered to production and service employees in the past, training in task skill must be organized better than previously.

The training requirement is newly complicated by the range and variety of operations methods skills that must be taught. It is at the operations management level of skills training that the truly major revolution in training begins. Workers at all levels must be trained in basic operations methods so they can make sound decisions about work flow and solve operating problems that arise in their work area.

A REVOLUTION IN OPERATIONS MANAGEMENT TRAINING IS COMING

Until about 1975, even most managers were not systematically trained in basic operations methods. Production engineers were sometimes specifically introduced to standard methods of work flow design, but were most likely to be indoctrinated in the standard Henry Ford, mass commodity, lockstep flow theory of production efficiency. The great convenience to capacity planning inherent in Ford's method lay in the assignment of one worker full time to one machine or workstation. Full utilization of labor resulted in full utilization of plant and equipment and vice versa—at least in theory. A breakdown of production flow for any reason—missing material, bad parts, absent workers, broken equipment—left labor, plant and equipment *all* idle. As colorfully documented in Ben Hamper's (1991) personal account of work life at General Motors, *Rivethead: Tales from the Assembly Line*, the automatic response to a stoppage was instant convergence of managers, engineers, cost accountants and supervisors onto the idled line demanding that it "get moving again." The line was restarted, even when restarting it risked producing poor-quality parts and even scrap. Keeping the line moving was imperative because, in most instances, failing to keep it running threatened the loss of labor and equipment capacity—a direct and measurable cost—even though restarting it reduced quality—a hidden and deferrable cost.

Conventional assembly-line operations management principles in the style of Henry Ford were turned upside down by the Japanese. Focusing on the methods in use by Detroit circa 1950, Taichi Ohno (1988), the perceptive and innovative production manager for Toyota, recognized the flaws in lockstep production flow. It may have helped greatly that the Japan of 1950 lacked the capital needed to build massive, Detroit-styled production plants dedicated to long production runs of a standard product. It was imperative that a more flexible, lower cost approach to the manufacture of automobiles be applied by Japan if it were to compete at all. The undesirable effects on quality of any long sequence of tasks with no built-in flexibility for resolution of operating problems was also evident to Ohno. Both of these flaws pointed to much greater involvement of workers on the production line in the identification and solution of work flow problems. Only a comprehensive education in operations methods would support so bold a revision of production workers' roles in operations problem solving. The solution was provision of intensive operations management training in the form of the highly visible but widely misunderstood *quality circle method.*

In America, quality circles were first viewed as some kind of worker participation gimmick that allowed workers to feel better after airing their gripes. Some companies attempted to implement quality circles only to realize that very little payoff was available in having workers talk about work flow problems when they had no active role in their solution on the work floor and no flexibility to move with the task or deal with work flow bottlenecks. Opening the floodgates of worker discontent in group sessions sometimes just made matters worse. These were problems that, in the prevailing Ford style of work flow management, called for decisions and authorities reserved to production engineers, production controllers and supervisors. Workers had no real voice in their solution. Nor did they have the requisite technical operations knowledge with which to solve the complex flow problems they encountered. In many cases, it was knowledge that was still proprietary to the Japanese. American production managers had yet to discover and master it. Early attempts at quality circles in America inevitably produced frail counterfeits of their Japanese originals.

OPERATIONS MANAGEMENT: THE CONTENT OF QUALITY CIRCLE TRAINING

Operations management method is the scientific management taproot of the high performance management evolutionary tree. And, while the basic operations research building blocks of sound operations management have changed little in a century, the Japanese experience has led to a revolutionary reconfiguration in their strategic application. The operations management revolution generated by Japan begins with growth and discovery of a radically different set of operating priorities. The operations methods used were not new, but the context in which they are applied is. In the revised context, planning and management of capacity becomes fundamental. Locating and dissolving bottlenecks is a never-ending task. Realistic priorities must be identified and allowed to dictate action. The implications of learning on past and future performance must be effectively factored into planning.

The old, continuous flow model set maximum capacity utilization as the efficient optimum, ruled out bottlenecks with lockstep work flow, treated every detail as having equal importance and looked upon learning as a costly, inconvenient irregularity from the engineered norm. The new model differentiates machine and plant capacity from labor capacity. It seeks efficiencies at levels of equipment capacity from low to high and keeps labor productively intensively applied through multiskilling. It expects bottlenecks as a normal consequence of the complexity of production systems, and equips line workers to attack and solve them when and where they occur. Priorities are set ruthlessly to achieve the most cost-effective and timely solution of the most significant problems. Learning is expected, measured and exploited for its planning and strategic implications. The first and most fundamental message conveyed by the new training must necessarily be the requirements of this new model.

Henry Ford appreciated the primacy of labor value over machinery value in the early years of Model T production. He spared no expense seeking out better machinery. His great success at raising the efficiency of labor through acquiring the best plant and machinery diminished the relative importance of labor supply, while it increased the contribution of capital to cost reduction. Once fully joined, his strategy of high capital investment to cut labor dependence required massive investment just to compete in the auto industry. The emphasis shifted away from efficient application of labor onto maximized return on capital investment. Assigning a worker full time to each machine or workstation mixed and confused the issue of efficient labor utilization with the goal of high return on investment. For the largest part of the twentieth century, as a result, return on capital investment has dominated management planning and strategy in America. Capacity has long been synonymous with plant and equipment. Labor skill and experience of the worker was overlooked as a capacity resource. Indeed, with the prevailing emphasis on narrow job specialization, it was squeezed out and ignored altogether. In the future high performance systems, labor again is likely to be the primary source of cost and cost control. Plant and equipment are secondary.

CAPACITY ANALYSIS

Flexible response to variations in work flow requires two pools of surplus capacity; one pool is the availability of sufficient equipment to permit quick reassignment of workers to cover an emerging bottleneck without creating an alternative bottleneck. Intensively used equipment is utilized close to its capacity maximum. Queuing theory, also called waiting-line analysis, easily demonstrates the futility of attempting to keep equipment utilization high when work flow must be flexible and responsive to market shifts.

Capacity arguments founded on queuing theory are technical in nature and are treated more fully in *Management Strategies for Today's Project Shop Economy* (Bassett, 1991) as well as in most standard operations management texts. Understanding of the implications of queuing theory to operations strategy is basic to flexible management of operations. These principles must be widely taught to engineers and managers responsible for plant and equipment capacity decisions. Production workers, however, also need an understanding of methods and standards with which to evaluate available equipment capacity. They must be able to recognize those situations where constraints on equipment availability increase cost by impeding effective allocation of available labor capacity. Training in theory and practice of equipment capacity analysis and planning is now indispensable.

The second requisite pool of surplus capacity is found in the newly enlarged range of skills possessed by the work force. Flexible response to a variety of demand and solution of bottlenecks demands despecialization of workers. Each must be capable of and willing to undertake any of a wide variety of tasks at the appropriate level of skill. The cost here is in the training investment. The payoff, even at minimum, is the ease with which workers can be kept busy, either through internal work-team reallocation of effort or through reassignment by supervision. Other significant payoffs in the form of enhanced worker commitment to and ownership of business goals may also flow from multiskilling the work force.

MANAGING BOTTLENECKS

In the old context, a bottleneck was a signal that something was wrong with the engineered flow of work. It was a limited view that assumed the prevalence of the ideal in unpredictable real-world working conditions. The reality, more often, was breakdown in the system creating bottlenecks. The new model of production assumes the inevitability of bottlenecks at any place and at any time in the system. Bottlenecks, thus, must be anticipated if predictable and solved as quickly as possible when unpredictable. A bottleneck is no more than a relative capacity constraint. Capacity planning and bottleneck management are intimately interrelated. The major principles pertaining to bottlenecks that must be communicated in training are that anticipated bottlenecks become instant scheduling priorities and that unexpectedly emerging bottlenecks can be resolved only by increasing capacity at the point of constraint or decreasing output upstream flowing into it. The modern worker must learn how to chase bottlenecks effectively without needlessly creating additional bottlenecks.

SETTING PRIORITIES

Priority setting in operations is a pragmatic matter. It begins with recognition that, in nearly every situation, a small proportion of causes accounts for a very large proportion of the effects. Every manager, supervisor and worker must appreciate the power of what is variously referred to as Pareto's principle, the 80/20 rule or ABC prioritizing categories. It is a ubiquitous phenomenon that occurs in a very wide range of human and business situations.

The discovery of the phenomenon is credited to the nineteenth-century Venetian demographer, Vilfredo Pareto, who determined that 80% of the wealth of Venice was controlled by 20% of its populace. This historical root of the concept offers the basis of its identification as Pareto's principal or the 80/20 rule, and, in addition, provides a simple benchmark illustration of it. Once thus illustrated, it may simply and easily be applied by analogy to a great variety of other circumstances. Of all inventory items, 20% account for 80% of inventory value. Another 20% of inventory is the source of 80% of materials delay, or long lead time or warehousing cost. Also, 20% of workers account for 80% of grievances, or problem-solving innovation or absences; and 20% of the causes of quality defects produce 80% of product or service complaints.

ABC, a widely used categorizing system for inventory control, carries 80/20 a step further. The "A" category encompasses that 20% accounting for 80% of cost, problems, opportunities and so on. "B" category issues are the 30% that account for 15%, while "C" category items constitute the remaining 50% that account for the residual 5% of operational concerns. ABC offers a small refinement over the basic crudeness of the 80/20 rule. Significantly, it suggests that fully half the problems of operations deserve minimum, even incidental, time and attention. This perspective dramatically illustrates the power of priority setting as a cost-cutting tool. Exhibit 9–3 illustrates an ABC break-out of priority issues.

Pareto, alias 80/20 or ABC, is easily applied to almost any situation where priorities must be set. It is *not* an exact specification of percentages that are universally to be expected. Rather, it is an approximation, a rule of thumb or, in technical jargon, a heuristic, useful as a guide but not offering a precise formula. There is no mathematical algorithm or logical

Exhibit 9-3
ABC Breakout of Priority Issues for a Corporate Controller's Position in a Publicly Traded Corporation

Activity:	Percent of Working Time	Criticality of Task	ABC Category
Monitor cash position	5%	High	A
Prepare government required reports	15%	High	A
Coordinate financial analyses	20%	Medium	B
Answer top management's financial questions	5%	Medium	B
Evaluate immediate subordinates' work	5%	Medium	B
Resolve cross-functional questions and problems	25%	Low	C
Coordinate internal procedures	10%	Low	C
Negotiate with banks	10%	Low	C
Self-development and educational activity	5%	Low	C
TOTAL WORKING TIME	100%		

theory that serves as a foundation for Pareto. It is empirical, pragmatic, the product of experienced observation. Once grasped, it is common sense.

Prioritizing is mandatory in high performance operations management. There are too many unknowns, too many variables for all to be dealt with on the same level of importance. Ruthless priority setting, though, is foreign to many staff technicians, engineers and accountants for whom every detail *must* be treated as of equal importance to every other detail. Attention to exact detail is the foundation of their method. Anything less is professional malfeasance. Frederick Taylor introduced to operations the precision and accuracy of modern engineering and cost accounting. For Taylor and his later disciples, like Henry L. Gantt and Frank and Lillian Gilbreth, details were critical. It was their lot to introduce discipline into an existing operations domain that was then often excessively pragmatic and woefully ill-structured. The value of their contribution is in the principles and methods they brought to bear in solving work problems. In the dominant age of management technocracy, it has been overdone. Eventually and finally, though, it is necessary to rediscover the power of priority setting as a central cost-reducing method in operations. Everyone in the modern operation, engineers and accountants especially, must be retrained in the practical art of setting priorities.

MANAGEMENT OF LEARNING PHENOMENA: THE LEARNING CURVE

Scientific management with its anchoring emphasis on the one best method of work went straight to the acme of performance, bypassing most of the learning and development process. In the stable, well-organized, scientifically managed plants of the past, new replacement workers were few in proportion to those experienced in their jobs. Training need was limited through use of narrow, highly specialized task assignments, and communication among workers was often intentionally restricted. Learning happened, if it happened at all, informally and casually. The significance of learning for improved worker performance as well as to start-up business strategy went unnoticed. Start-up operations were expected to encounter problems—that was merely common sense. But it was easier to ascribe those problems to poor performance than to recognize that learning and discovery must always occur before stability can set in.

In commodity production settings, the early stages of output have traditionally been treated as an anomalous run-in and shake-down period that must be endured to achieve stability. Standards in the stable state of operations were assumed to be permanent and fixed. There was no notice of opportunity to manage the learning curve on every occasion when a change of process was introduced. Nor was there appreciation that potential *always* exists for improvement in quality and cost through learning and discovery of new approaches to the job. A tunnel-visioned focus on long production runs led to treatment of start-up delays as just another kind of set-up cost that had to be amortized over the life of the run. It was an inconvenience to be worked around.

Learning and discovery as necessary and natural phenomena of operations management were not recognized for their importance until the age of military systems arrived. In the manufacture of early military aircraft, it was noted that the first product was always noticeably more expensive than the next, and that consistent improvement in cost and scheduling could be expected over the life of the production run. This was of importance in military contracting because the limited production run, exhibiting great variation from unit to unit, was often the *entire* production run. Where the influence of learning was overlooked, dispute was encountered in determining what cost and labor standards should be used in pricing an aircraft given so much potential for variation in cost over its

Exhibit 9-4
Learning Curve for a Sixteen-Stage Heavy Construction Project

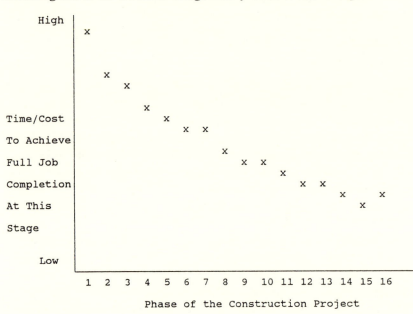

Phase of the Construction Project

short production-run history. Exhibit 9–4 illustrates just such a learning curve.

As market preferences call for increased variation and individuality in products and services, commodity production in the current age increasingly gives way to short and one-of-a-kind runs, similar in operations management requirements to big-ticket military projects. The prevailing project shop economy of present-day America calls for learning, relearning, discovery and rediscovery as a way of work life. Understanding the learning curve and its influence on cost across time is essential to managing operations in this era. Managers and workers must discover the cost and performance implications of learning every new task.

Like Pareto, learning curve theory is a heuristic, though a somewhat more quantitatively structured one. The accepted rule, sanctioned by widespread use in negotiating military and government contracts, is that with every doubling of output for a given product or service, the cost improves by a constant percentage factor. The percent improvement possible typically ranges widely anywhere from 5% to 50%, with a 20%

Exhibit 9-5
Learning Curve for Cutting Hair

Practice Trial #:	Time Required	Rated Quality of Cut
1	55 minutes	Fair
2	50 minutes	Good
3	40 minutes	Fair
4	40 minutes	Good
5	35 minutes	Poor
6	35 minutes	Good
7	35 minutes	Fair
8	30 minutes	Fair
9	25 minutes	Poor
10	25 minutes	Good
11	25 minutes	Fair
12	20 minutes	Good
13	20 minutes	Fair
14	20 minutes	Good
15	20 minutes	Good
16	20 minutes	Good

factor of improvement commonly specified in many contracts. Theoretically there is no limit to the potential for constant improvement in the rule as formulated. After a million repetitions of the performance, however, it takes another million to get the same amount of improvement formerly obtained from the first to the second, or the tenth to the twentieth output. Exhibit 9–5 illustrates how the learning curve might be applied to cutting hair.

In theory, the learning curve applies equally to the skill of learning to solve problems or adapt to change. It implies that a goal of continual improvement can be quantified and specified for any team or individual. It suggests that the boredom of an overspecialized task against fixed output standards can be replaced with the opportunity to learn new skills, discover new methods and contribute added value to the operations process in any job. Learning, growth and discovery can be reintroduced into every job. The worker, the team and the company that learns fastest and best enjoys a competitive advantage in the marketplace. Adaptivity, discovered and mastered in the workplace, will certainly outperform the stagnant stability of engineered long-run, efficient operations. That is the power of the new operations model.

These basic operations methods, capacity analysis, bottleneck management, priority setting and learning curve implications for operations constitute the foundation for a learning revolution in the workplace. They are the proper basics of sound quality circle training in the United States as they were in Japan. Lacking the fundamentals of operations methodology, renewal in the workplace cannot go forward. Competitive flexibility cannot be achieved without them. But they have the power to change the face of industry when used in judicious combination with supporting operations methods to manage inventory, simulate work flow patterns, statistically analyze quality issues and are arranged around sound organization change methodology. Neglecting operations technology resulted in a quarter century of frustration and failure for American organization development technicians who earlier sought to bring about effective, lasting change in American industry through human relations and teamwork training that left out reference to operations methods in its technology.

ORGANIZATION DEVELOPMENT TECHNOLOGY AND CHANGE

Organization development (OD), a disciplined program for managed change in the structure and culture of the workplace, began as part of the human potential movement of the late 1940s. Training designed by leading social scientists to enhance interpersonal (i.e., human relations) skill began with the T-Groups at National Training Labs at the conclusion of World War II (French, 1969). Abhorrence of the totalitarian sentiments that brought about the war blended with widespread disgust for the authoritarian discipline of military life fired fresh sentiment for industrial democracy. T-Groups, sometimes called sensitivity training, were created to bring leaders to awareness of their emotional impact on their followers. Applied early in a cross section of major U.S. corporations, sensitivity training quickly spread throughout industry. Building on a foundation of behavioral science knowledge and experience with industry, Blake and Mouton (1984) adapted the principles of sensitivity training to business and industry through their Managerial Grid training format.

From this beginning experiment at training emotional expressiveness in managers, a range of organization intervention methods designed to introduce major change was developed for use with business organizations. Most early OD training was pointed at middle to upper management on the presumption that attitudes and interpersonal skills of managers was the primary source of autocratic pathologies of organization. The contributions of operations methods and structure were largely ignored other than in recommendations to management for job enrichment and participation in work decision making extended to lowest level job holders.

Not unexpectedly, strong currents of the human relations research and participative management movements found expression in organization development methods and applications. Attitude surveys were widely employed to demonstrate the widespread unpopularity of some managers and management policies with workers. T-Groups, formally "facilitated" but leaderless by design, sometimes produced violent, angry clashes of ego among aggressive, competitive participants. Some fragile personalities crumbled psychotically. Many of the worst potential pathologies of group process were given play in early sensitivity training, creating widespread controversy over their ethical propriety.

When subjected to the crucible of experience, OD ultimately gained realism. The emotional, interpersonal aspects of training were sharply deemphasized and replaced with concern for the structural aspects of organization. Teamwork, it was found, could scarcely improve without careful definition of group (or organizational) goals. Individual contributions and roles required specification, as did procedures for handling common problems. After those elements were in place, whatever residual working friction remained was probably the result of low sensitivity to others brought about by weak interpersonal skills. Basic, sound organization had to be in place, however, before interpersonal sensitivity training could add to fundamental team effectiveness. Overemphasis on interpersonal transactions overlooked the reality that many instances of internal, organizational conflict resulted from simple overlap and incompatibility in adjacent work roles. Some of these conflicts diminished with added interpersonal skill, although improvement in old-fashioned political acumen may have contributed as much as did expanded sensitivity. A change in roles was usually a more direct solution. In some cases, roles designed to clash with one another for their sharper competitive product were assisted by sensitivity training only if it produced an effective (and politically dangerous) coalition between role-players in opposition to higher power. Sensitivity training sometimes introduced change that was unwanted.

Development of skill in emotional expressiveness and even intuitive judgment through interpersonal relationship training undoubtedly brought a new problem-solving dimension to management teams within many organizations. How much of that improvement was accounted for in enhanced political competence is difficult to say. It is sometimes hard to discriminate political from interpersonal sensitivity except on moral grounds. In the longer run, sensitivity training probably made the work of those who participated in it more complex, difficult and interesting. There is little to suggest that it changed any fundamental dimensions of organization structure, that it led to wider participation in decision making by lower level workers, even of those whose jobs were enriched, or that the cause of industrial democracy benefited from it despite the vast energies and costs poured into the effort. Autocracy is a remarkably resilient management style. It has the adaptability to dig in and preserve itself through all but the strongest assaults.

The organization development movement was often patently antiauthoritarian in many of its applications and purposes. It was an onslaught, perhaps well-deserved and long-overdue, on the autocratic bastions of Taylorism and rigid, Ford-styled, top-down organization structure. Many of the elements of early OD, like increased emphasis on goal setting, were sound and have since been shown to be fundamental to improved organizational performance. Power and authority urgently need to be redistributed in organizations to permit responsible role structure in line positions. But in the absence of training in operations technology, little change of substance is supportable in most work settings.

Worker responsibility for quality, efficiency and work flow problem solving works superbly once workers are trained in the technology of operations management and the roles of staff specialists converted from decision making to "facilitating." Power in the new era *must be* redistributed, much as OD practitioners anticipated that it should be, but not so much downward from the autocrats as sideways from technical experts to those directly responsible for delivery of the product or service to the customer.

The organization development movement addressed well the political and interpersonal aspects of organization. There was acute awareness of misfit between traditional organization structure and emerging expectation for wider sharing of performance responsibility in organizations. Ingenious manipulation and awesome political skill were sometimes employed by professional OD consultants in an effort to move modern American organization off its stagnant base. Even so, they accomplished little. The missing ingredient was not commitment nor was it political naivete. It was a grasp of the fundamental influence of operations strategy and method. It was ignorance of the irrepressible influence of operations methods on organizational behavior. Without appreciation of operations philosophy on all aspects of organization, little change can occur even with the most aggressive OD intervention.

OD consultants arrived on the current scene by way of the Hawthorne experience, blended with the science and rhetoric taken from the Quality of Work Life, participative workplace decision making and human relations movements. Operations method and practice came by a different path, from Taylor, Ford, return on capital investment and modern industrial engineering methodology. In the ongoing guerrilla warfare of human relations versus autocracy, they supported warring generals on opposite sides of the battle line. As in many conflicts, each possessed a part of the truth, each part requiring adjustment to fit the other before the objectives of either could be met. The genius of the Japanese was in joining them. The discovery of high performance management systems in American industry must now begin with a reconciliation and joining of these old antagonists. Doctrinaire positions of the past will impede that union. The final thrust of the great human resource revolution must be to overcome those positions through effective training and knowledge.

Once reconciled, the new human resources/operations nexus must be continually supported by growth and discovery at all levels of organization. The traditional goal of the liberal tradition in higher education has been introduction of students into a pattern of life-long, humanizing growth and discovery. The former goal of industry under the influence of the Taylor-Ford tradition was steady performance in a strictly limited, often stultifying job role. University graduates in industry inevitably confronted the discrepancy between these disparate traditions. If there was pursuit of personal, individual growth for them, it was off the job, or in a privileged problem-solving assignment high up in the organization hierarchy. In future high performance systems, virtually everyone must be capable of continuous growth and discovery if the organization is to remain competitively vital. For practical purposes, the twin revolutions of scientific management and human potential development have triumphed in establishing this new imperative for life-long learning. For many who were formerly focused on the human relations side of the struggle, entry is through the strange and unfamiliar door of operations method and philosophy. While their shape is yet only dimly visible, high performance systems of the future will almost certainly merge the best traditions of scientific management and the human potential movements. A practical, humane education of every worker will be an imperative of that merger.

Chapter Ten

From Job Fit to Cultural Compatibility: Evaluating Worker Skill and Temperament

Stability in a high performance management system requires that its workers possess those skills and temperaments that support the demands of the system. Some form of individual evaluative assessment that accurately describes each worker's potential fit to the system is indispensable. Taylor, when he set out to break up the soldiering devices of machinists, sought out the most intelligent prospects he could find in the local labor market. The Hawthorne researchers, faced with resistance to their program by two of the original five relay room workers, selected replacements with solid assembly experience and a cooperative attitude toward the project. Lincoln Electric and Nucor Steel carefully screen candidates to identify those energetic, ambitious individuals who strive for high earnings and can comfortably handle the stress of these high output work cultures.

Systematic evaluation of workers by social scientists to obtain the best fit to the job is a practice that dates from the first decades of the twentieth century. The earliest recorded use of tests to evaluate prospective workers dates from 1910 with Hugo Munsterberg's effort to select trolley motormen. The first large-scale use of tests to classify manpower for task assignment came with application of psychometric measures to military and industrial tasks during World War I. Early screening employed tests that were based on the new Binet tests of intellectual ability—an IQ measure, so-called—used for assessing the mental aptitude of scholars and students. The striking success of the early Binet tests as predictors of academic talent and performance resulted in broad use of similar instruments by educators and managers alike beginning in the decade of the 1920s.

But selection based on intellectual ability has become socially contentious. Indeed, any form of selection may be illegal if not validated when used to reject protected classes from employment. Selecting workers to fit any high performance management system must successfully negotiate the political and legal mine fields of modern Equal Opportunity law and regulation.

IQ: THE UBIQUITOUS MENTAL TEST

Intelligence—IQ testing—is the storm center of antidiscriminatory restraint. IQ has a long scientific history, is easily measured with a wide range of standardized paper and pencil tests and frequently has been shown to predict success on the job.

Applying measures of intellect is consistently most successful for predicting worker success in training. Workers who can grasp ideas, comprehend instructions and communicate their need for an instructor's help can acquire new skills and knowledge quickly and efficiently. The cost of training may otherwise be high. A simple device like a paper and pencil test of mental ability is efficient. It speeds training, puts new workers on the job sooner and saves money. Concern for efficiency and low cost in training, however, is a holdover from the Ford era of narrow specialization and mechanically paced production flow as the foundation of high performance. Absence of training capacity and limited worker flexibility are likely liabilities in tomorrow's high performance operations. Efficiency in learning is not the only measure of success. Slow learners may be exceptionally good learners.

The great merit of fragmented, overspecialized assembly-line jobs was in the ease with which qualifications can be met by almost any worker. Henry Ford could not afford to waste available manpower as demand for his Model T accelerated year by year, placing ever heavier demands on the tight, frontier labor market of Detroit. Narrow specialization simplified selection to the minimum. Foremen looked over the crop of candidates on any given morning, pointed to those who looked clean-cut and healthy, took each to a workplace and had a fellow worker demonstrate the task. Anyone who could not perform the work by morning's end was out the door before lunch. Selection *did* occur. Every worker was tried out on the job and judged for his or her success. The work was simple enough to involve little or no intellectual content. Illiteracy was then widespread among unskilled laborers and may have suited them better to the simplicity of the work Ford offered. The core of selection was in the workers' eagerness to get jobs and their conscientiousness in carrying out assigned duties. Attendance and willingness to follow orders were more important than literacy in Ford's high performance assembly-line system. These were not mental jobs in the sense of requiring depth of language skill. A nod of the head was usually sufficient in response to the barked commands of the boss.

The wide usage that tests of mental ability have enjoyed since World War I has overlooked the absence of need for any but the most basic language ability in many jobs. When the new worker must learn quickly using concepts and ideas to perform the job effectively, when communication with customers and co-workers is critical to job success, language skill *is* fundamental. Under these conditions, a test that measures verbal and numerical skill taps capabilities that can be critical to effective job performance. But those simple jobs that can be trained quickly may be better assigned to those whose best native talents do *not* include language usage. Testing to exclude the less intelligent serves little if any purpose there. Indeed, skill or temperament evaluation outside the mental skill domain is often more relevant. And, in many cases, it is socially desirable only to assure that every candidate has an equal chance at the available work. Slow learners among protected classes must be accommodated to satisfy legal and social constraints. If verbal or any other kind of formal testing is discriminatory, measures must be taken to reintroduce fairness.

AVOIDING ADVERSE IMPACT: OVERCOMING THE DISCRIMINATION OF TESTING AND SELECTION

The uses and abuses of intelligence tests are well-documented and reported. As bases for assigning candidates to training programs they can be useful, but, just as often, tests are also potentially discriminatory. Present-day legal constraints on their use may require validation of the tests used, and this can be straightforward with the classes of jobs that require mental ability for effective performance as long as the worker population in each job is large enough. The major departure from past usage is in the requirement to validate such tests specifically for U.S. minority populations, principally black and Spanish-speaking job candidates. The practical thrust of the Civil Rights Act of 1964 and its supporting interpretive directives is to require that disproportionate rejection of protected minorities, technically referred to as "adverse impact," resulting through any means including the use of tests, must be wholly and convincingly justified through competent validation of the instruments or methods used. But as long as minorities are selected in numbers proportionate to their presence in the labor market, use of tests, even without validation, is not necessarily a violation of the law.

It is important to know that this constraint on selection and evaluation exists, because it applies to *all* instruments and methods of selection used by those firms subject to the law. There are other, perhaps more important, bases for candidate evaluation that are equally subject to the requirement of validation, such as a personal interview. Validation may not always be practical. Avoiding adverse impact by directly assuring proportionate acceptance of protected classes is the only alternative to full-scale validation in these situations.

DIFFERENTIAL PREDICTION OF TRAINING AND JOB SUCCESS WITH TESTS

Selection methods are overdue for revolutionary restructuring as a support of high performance output. Part of that restructuring will likely be a significant deemphasis on the intellectual dimension of work and concern for how to better use all varieties of available talent. Research evidence suggests that just such a redirection may be possible and desirable.

Ghiselli (1973) calculated average test validity coefficients from the literature of industrial psychology for managers, clerks, sales personnel, security officers, drivers, tradespeople and general service personnel. For nearly all classes of jobs, mental ability was an important predictor of success in training.

But high mental ability was substantially more predictive of training success than it was to success on the job. Beyond the training stage, Ghiselli found that mental ability dropped notably as an important predictor of work performance for all classifications except managers. Other tested abilities became significantly more important for other classifications. The more effective clerks, inspectors and electricians, for instance, had demonstrated high perceptual speed in testing prior to employment. Manual workers had greater arm motor dexterity. Salesmen were more personable. Foremen were more accurate with numbers. Ghiselli established that job-related tests of skill are more accurate predictors of success in these jobs.

Sometimes high mental ability is inversely related to job success. Occasional *negative* correlations of mental ability with training success noted by Ghiselli and others for machine- and materials-oriented jobs suggest that training should be structured for those with limited verbal skill as a more hands-on experience directly with the work to be done, with less dependence on talking about the work. The power of mental ability as a predictor of training success may be partly a function of overemphasis on verbal training at the expense of experiential training.

The power of intelligence appears to be in facilitating adaptation to complex problems. Schmidt and Hunter (1992) propose from their extensive analysis of employment selection literature that the major impact of superior mental ability is not on immediate work performance. Asked to perform a sample of work from the job, the bright, inexperienced person will typically lose out to the less mentally quick but experienced candidate. But high mental ability permits quicker acquisition of job knowledge. Job knowledge then enhances the worker's performance capability. Between two workers starting even in experience but with differential mental ability, the brighter will soon outpace the one of lesser mental ability—most of the time, and, when job knowledge acquisition is difficult.

Mental ability sometimes gains an undeserved advantage on the job by permitting the more articulate, verbal worker to explain him- or herself when misunderstood, or to answer the boss' questions more impressively. Supervisors may be swayed more by a worker's answers about performance than by the actual quality of performance itself. If judged primarily on job knowledge rather than job results, the worker with greater mental power will almost certainly come out ahead of others who are less intelligent. A major difficulty with reliance on tests of mental ability in selecting new employees resides in the tendency of supervisors and managers to continue to judge competence on the basis of workers' known and demonstrated superior intelligence rather than through close observation of job performance. It is a sufficiently chronic problem to suggest the desirability of training supervisors and managers to skeptically observe real job performance, uninfluenced by creative excuses and facile explanations.

PERSONALITY ASSESSMENTS: JOB PERFORMANCE AND CHARACTER

Personality traits and characteristics have long been intuitively appealing as the basis on which to pick effective performers and, in their own way, have often been as controversial as intelligence testing. They are, of course, subject to the same legal constraints as are other selection tools, and they must either be validated or shown to have no adverse impact on protected classes or minorities.

Considerable evidence is accumulating that favors the use of personality or character measures such as these in the description of worker fit to particular jobs. In a major study within the U.S. military it was found that, though mental ability predicted general task proficiency in better soldiering, ratings of leadership, personal discipline and physical fitness were better predicted by personality measures. Schmidt and Hunter (1992) make reference to substantial evidence in support of the validity of "integrity tests" as predictors of excessive absences, sabotage, substance abuse and theft. They also cite an analysis by Goldberg, et al. (1991), which determined that "conscientiousness," a widely accepted major personality trait sometimes also labeled "dependability" or "will to achievement," correlates substantially with some kinds of job performance.

Selection for temperament is a difficult and chancy process. It must be approached with a healthy skepticism under any circumstances. Doubt as to its complete accuracy is well founded in most cases. Nucor Steel and Lincoln Electric, for instance, invest considerable time and effort to identify the best candidates. Still, a significant proportion of new hires in both companies quit their jobs within the first months of their tenure, stressed and distressed by pressures, not just of their job, but of the vigorous and pervasive high performance work culture that prevails in those companies. It is difficult, perhaps impossible, to predict a worker's job performance until he or she is trained and working in the job, especially so in the context of a strong, high performance work culture. Direct experience with the culture itself may be the best and most accurate test of fit. The next best thing is likely to be an intensive preemployment interview done by representatives of the culture.

REDISCOVERING THE PREEMPLOYMENT INTERVIEW

The preemployment interview has an uneven history of acceptance among selection professionals. Social scientists have customarily dismissed the interview as unreliable and highly subject to interviewer prejudice. Interviews have, nonetheless, persisted in the preemployment domain and it is rare for a hire to be effected without some form of face-to-face interview contact in advance of employment. For the past quarter century the preferred selection approach among professionals in the field of industrial and organizational psychology has been the assessment center method, a complex series of evaluations that includes tests, role play, situational problem solving, group interaction and evaluative interviews, among other techniques. Indeed, even this approach relies heavily on interviews as a source of evaluative data. The interview remains ubiquitous in selection.

Interviewing has come under considerable criticism in the past. This may have been because it was not properly studied or because it is complex in ways that make it difficult to control and measure. In recent years, though, the repute of interviewing as a major and effective selection method has been rehabilitated. Schmidt, Ones and Hunter (1992), summarizing current research on personnel selection for the *Annual Review of Psychology*, cite a pair of meta-analyses on interview research that establish the mean validity for selection interviews at a surprisingly high level—between .40 and .45 as measured by Pearson correlation. Considerable variability among interviewers is noted, some interviewers demonstrating much greater effectiveness than others, suggesting the importance of sound, thorough training and experience. Overall, the average result is strong and encouraging. Indeed, interviewing alone appears to yield better selection validities than does the greater complexity of an assessment center approach. Correlational meta-validities for assessment center studies cited by Schmidt et al. were found to range from .14 to .37.

The reader need not grasp the technical meaning of these numbers. The measured coefficients are cited only because they offer quantitative contrast between the mundane, often-disparaged and widely used interview method of selection versus the complex, sophisticated design of assessment center technology supported by the best research science and methodology. It is an astonishing result that begs better understanding.

With little evidence of science to fall back on but much confidence from past experience as an interviewer, I would like to suggest that the difference between interviewing and scientific assessment results largely from the opportunity offered by an in-depth, preemployment interview to look at the individual candidate against the shape of the prevailing work culture. Multiple interviews can easily include likely co-workers in the interviewing loop. They typically use several levels of management assisted by experienced personnel office evaluators to assess fit. In some work groups, it is desirable to achieve a specific and comfortable fit of candidate to the uniqueness of the group itself. Companies like Nucor Steel, Lincoln Electric, IBM or Procter and Gamble have distinctive cultures that demand ready adaptation from the newcomer. Those imbedded within the culture who are trained or experienced in effective interview methods can serve as brokers between candidate and culture, working to achieve maximum effective fit of available candidates and their abilities. Prejudice may still operate to exclude certain backgrounds and attitudes when selecting with interviews, but monitoring selection to assure *at least* proportionate representation of protected minorities can assure that interviewing to find fit to culture is legally defensible. In the absence of a technically sound

Exhibit 10-1
A Representative Listing of Measurable Human Abilities and Traits

GENERAL MENTAL ABILITIES	MOTOR CAPABILITY
Comprehension of Speech	Target Pursuit
Comprehension of Writing	Reaction Speed
Spoken Expression	Control Precision
Clarity of Written Expression	Multi-limb Coordination
Logical Reasoning	Arm-Hand Steadiness
General Problem-Solving Ability	Finger Dexterity
Rote Memory	Tapping Speed
Speed of Recognition	
Arithmetical Facility	PERSONALITY TRAITS
Creativity with Ideas	Extraversion/Introversion
Visual Imagination	Friendly/Hostile
Memory for Patterns	Conscientiousness
	Emotional Stability
	Cultural Conventionality

method for measuring culture—a major void of organizational psychology that should be a greater embarrassment to organizational scientists than it seems to be—multiple selection interviews by people trained and supervised in the skills of interviewing constitutes the soundest available present-day selection method.

Tests may be used as supports to the interview process where it is useful to evaluate specific job-related skill or temperament. Specific, job-relevant measures can be helpful to the experienced interviewer and are wholly proper to use as long as they do not result in adverse impact on protected minority classes. A representative listing of measurable human abilities and traits is offered in Exhibit 10-1. Literally tens of thousands of published tests exist with which to measure the abilities and qualities suggested here. It is a variety that suggests high likelihood of finding useful measures with sufficient search. Experienced, professional assistance can be helpful in sifting through what is available to find the right tests or measures for any given company and job. For high performance systems of the future, this may be a desirable investment.

GETTING A GRASP ON CULTURE AS THE FOUNDATION OF HIGH PERFORMANCE

Much discussion about work and organizational culture of a theoretical quality is available in the literature of management, though a large part is characterized by distinct ideological rhetoric reminiscent of the human relations, Quality of Work Life and participative management movements. Work culture as an objectively measured set of dimensions, contingent for their utility and appropriateness on business, technology and competitive constraints, languishes for lack of study. Yet more significantly, work culture as a resource to be created and managed for competitive purposes remains an obscure and mysterious managerial art. Nucor Steel, Lincoln Electric and a few other select companies seem to have succeeded in its application. For most, it is a dominant and enigmatic force, the subject of rumor, myth, complaint, but far beyond any conscious managerial choice and control. It is a door that today's manangers must open to achieve a high performance output.

The Japanese, perhaps, have enjoyed advantage in world competition as much because of their strong social culture as anything. Japanese workers appear to be conscientious in the extreme, voluntarily working extra hours to meet goals or solve bottlenecks. Acceptance of traditional, legitimate authority is easier and quicker among the Japanese. Acquiescence to superior status is comfortably habitual. The prevailing tight industrial order with its high standards is easily imposed and maintained among Japanese workers. Delegation of responsibility to the individual worker is also more natural. The culture of Japan supports personal qualities through a work culture that enjoys a distinct competitive advantage in the world arena. The Japanese culture is the product of centuries of cultural isolation and development of social cohesion to cope with adverse environmental conditions and limited resources.

The Japanese are living testimony that history and economic circumstance create the customs of a national culture. Business organizations are sometimes evidence that a culture can be built, either by happenstance or by design, to support a particular business purpose. Schein (1985) proposes that the central function of leadership is to design, build, repair and redesign organization culture. That, indeed, may define an effective leader. He or she is one who purposefully influences the structure of the organization's culture. A leader creates or recreates an organization's culture. An administrator accepts and acts within the bounds of an existing, inherited culture. A leader can improve or destroy an acquired culture. An administrator can serve and preserve a vital or a rotten one. Culture and leadership as defined in these terms are inseparable. Culture is a tool for improving operations effectiveness when used skillfully. It becomes an iron constraint if accepted uncritically or ignored.

CAN BUSINESS CULTURE BE MEASURED AND MODIFIED?

The great varieties of cultures possible in human affairs are well-documented in the literatures of cultural and historical anthropology. The widely read cultural adventures of Margaret Mead, Ruth Benedict, Colin Turnbull and others representative of this discipline suggest otherwise unimaginable possibilities. Outside such exposure, the range of conceivable culture is typically limited by experience with one's own culture. Lacking exposure to alternative cultures, managerial focus is likely to be administrative. But new, more powerful and productive cultures are every bit as feasible as genetic engineering has become in this age. Systematic study of culture design is largely lacking. Experiment is limited. Like genetic engineering, cultural design probably entails a large amount of trial-and-error experimentation in socially sensitive circumstances, which makes it expensive and difficult. Present-day business culture could, nonetheless, be more effectively studied, measures could be developed and studies carried out to ascertain which factors discriminate effective from ineffective work culture. For purposes of illustration, it can be observed that most work cultures can be classified as either highly politicized—market-oriented is an equally good term—or bureaucratic, which is to say that due process and rule of principle dominate them. Exhibit 10–2 contrasts some empirically validated qualities of a political versus a bureaucratic work culture.

Some functional components within an organization may be more politicized, others more bureaucratic in character. Accounting and engineering functions, for instance, emphasize attention to detail and are disposed toward bureaucratic character. Marketing and production operations, on the other hand, are priority oriented and generally more politicized. Organizations may adopt a marketing, an R&D, a financial or an operating strategy as the centerpiece of competitive, strategic response or can use some blend of them. Differences in choice of these strategies appear to imply different cultural structures within the businesses that use them. Culture and strategy should, perhaps, more properly be designed with clarity of intent for their purpose in mind and then measured for success in their execution. High performance organizations do seem to have cultures that support their strategies and strategies that fit the competitive markets served. Improved design and measurement of culture that supports business strategy is a potentially powerful strategic asset.

New worker selection, from sourcing to evaluation of skill and personality, to orientation for the assigned work role, influences the prevailing work culture and is shaped by it as well. The shape of the organization's culture may limit or expand the range of human capability required, determining quality of adaptation to a tight labor market or ability to capitalize on an abundant supply of labor. Culture may determine who fits a particular job and who doesn't. Culture, in all likelihood, can be

Exhibit 10-2
Benchmarks of Work Culture Politics versus Due Process: The Primacy of Results versus the Inviolability of Rules

Characteristics of a Political, Results-Focused Work Culture	Characteristics of a Due Process, Rules-Oriented Work Culture
Devise the best approach for the job at hand.	Follow customary and accepted work practices.
Be willing to experiment and make mistakes.	Get good advice before trying anything new.
Work independently as much as possible.	Fit into the team smoothly.
Invent new solutions to old problems.	Apply the best existing solutions to problems.
Take any steps needed to overcome obstacles.	Stay within existing limits to solve problems.
Use trial and error to discover what works.	Plan everything out in detail in advance.
Keep all goals general and flexible.	Set precise goals that can't be misunderstood.
Set difficult, challenging goals.	Set realistic, achievable goals.
Look for insights into problem situations.	Use the best knowledge concerning problems.
Use sound common sense on the job.	Use methodical inquiry and analysis at work.
Rely heavily on sound practical experience.	Rely heavily on thorough, formal education.

redesigned to improve performance and competitiveness. Culture determines business strategy or is determined by business strategy. Culture emerges by accident or design in every new and growing entrepreneurial firm.

As far as the success of selection efforts is concerned, a vigorous culture is the culminating stage in a successful selection process, selecting out those poorly suited who have slipped past the formal preemployment evaluation. A weak, vacillating culture, in contrast, may defeat all attempts at improved performance through selection, even those aimed at keeping out dishonesty, sloth and mental illness. The soundest selection strategy would be to create and maintain a vigorous, high performance culture that is self-policing of the skills and attitudes needed for its success.

These are only the most tentative and preliminary comments concerning the role and power of business culture. Until systematic study and measurement of business culture is developed as a discipline in its own right, selection methods remain isolated and detached from this vital point of reference. The best remaining approach to filling open jobs is application of experienced, trained interviewing skills under vigorous leadership, which has established a clear, effective business strategy. For now, the specifics of how to build culture remain difficult to define. They are an important new frontier in the management and development of high performance management systems that deserve much increased attention.

Chapter Eleven

Communication, Trust and Business Ethics

High performance management systems require the establishment of trust as an imperative of their success. Trust requires clear, credible communication from management and consistent ethical behavior in support of it. This may seem a simple prescription. In fact, it may be the most difficult of all requirements to implement.

The wonder of human communication is not so much that there is such frequent misunderstanding as that it is possible to communicate reliably at all. Major management constructs like satisfaction, participation and organization culture are sufficiently complex and abstract to require extended examination for a minimum of understanding. A community of scholars subjecting them to the test of rigorous research design often still has trouble arriving at a common, shared definition of these basic terms. The ordinary manager or worker, lacking collegial involvement in their debate and definition, uses them in ordinary, colloquial ways that fit his or her limited experience. It should come as no surprise that confusion attends their use in ordinary communication. But even when widely misused among average nonprofessionals, there is more consistency of meaning than among social scientists and scholars. It is the job of scientists and scholars to test and redefine the major constructs of their fields. Considerable independence of mind often carries them in novel and unconventional directions.

The conventional meaning of words is mostly a matter of simple majority rule. As with many social domains, leaders work far out on the periphery of the issue seeking the best route to enlightenment while an advancing populace maintains a steady direction oriented only by a loose consensus formulated in their on-going, day-to-day association. The meaning of common words is established by common usage, not by scientists. The dictionary of a living language is anchored by the literature of that language. The way words are used by working, published, widely read writers determines their accepted meaning. The literature of a language is the well-spring of common meaning for its vocabulary.

Communication is complex but common. It is difficult to analyze but easy to accept naively. Computers, those mysteriously powerful logic machines, cannot yet be programmed to translate accurately from one language into another; it is a skill yet monopolized by learned humans. Language is a discipline dominated by vague abstractions and uncertain principles. We can send a person to the moon but cannot make language an exact science.

Much humor centers on crossovers and confusions of meaning inherent in common words. Puns and jokes often owe their power to an unexpected turn of meaning in a simple, ordinary phrase. Television sitcoms use simple confusion of word meaning as a staple element of plot construction. One long-running series, "The Beverly Hillbillies," exploits a rich vein of humor in the differences of conventional word meaning found between that of a simple, nouveau-riche rural Appalachian family and the language of sophisticated speech of affluent big-city folk. Thereby our most common entertainment media daily illustrates the richness, complexity and potential for confusion that resides in language. It is a lesson to be seriously pondered.

ERROR IN COMMUNICATION IS SO EASY

Opportunity for misunderstanding and confusion of communication is widely available. There are so many dimensions to language that it would be prohibitive to attempt measurement of the full potential for breakdown in communication. Previously, though, in discussing managerial communication as an art and practice in its own right, I proposed as a safe estimate that at least half of all communication attempted fails its mark (Bassett, 1976). We misunderstand one another 50% of the time on average. Some simple, highly conventional communications may be near 100% reliability among those who regularly practice them. "Wear your safety glasses at all times around machinery" or "prepare the letter single spaced" are easily understood and acted on by those attuned to the conventional business work culture. More general and abstract instructions may be misinterpreted and miscarried. "Show the customer every courtesy" and "strive

Exhibit 11-1
Experiment in Communication

GEOMETRIC EXERCISE: Instructions

Each group consists of a talker, a listener, and a referee. The talker is given a blueprint which he describes to the listener. The talker tells the listener what to draw, and on the basis of the instructions the listener attempts to reproduce the blueprint precisely. The referee's task is to enforce the rules of the exercise. Each listener is supplied with a pencil and ruler.

GEOMETRIC EXERCISE: BLUEPRINT

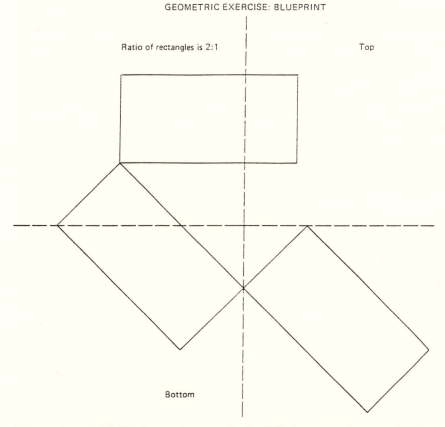

Ratio of rectangles is 2:1   Top

Bottom

for maximum quality" may have entirely different meanings to different people. Until specifics and common experience offer anchor points for meaning, the behavior resultant from instructions like these may be wholly unpredictable.

An elementary experiment in communication is offered as Exhibit 11-1. A simple geometric design must be reproduced exclusively through spoken words so that it can be accurately executed by another who lacks the advantage of visual inspection. To carry out this experiment, roles of communicator and task executor are assigned to a naive pair of individuals and the resulting product is observed. The experimental pair must first work back to back without the benefit of questions and feedback from the executor of the design, simulating one-way communication, manager to worker. Then questions and feedback to demonstrate the effect of interactive feedback may be added. Performance may improve with an exchange of communication between actors, but when communication is limited to the spoken word alone, the principal lesson will be the prevalence of confusion and inefficiency in performance.

The characteristic approximateness of novelty experienced in unconventional communication circumstances becomes quickly apparent from this experiment. Practice and experience with failure may greatly improve the skill of the instructor, but an existing, unpredictable presumption of word meaning by a naive subject (the executing worker) can still block full success. There are too many ways in which untried, unconventional, complex communication can go awry. If simple, conventional communication gets close to 100% reliability, untested, unconventional complex communication can come close to 0% reliability. In these terms, 50% is a simple average over a representative range of possibilities.

LOSS OF COMMUNICATION CREDIBILITY IS EASY TOO

If the risks of miscommunicating are major, the opportunity to destroy communication credibility by communicating badly adds measurably to its failure. Lack of sensitivity to nuances of communication, failure to obtain feedback from one's audience and communicating to manipulate response are old, bad habits that virtually guarantee eventual breakdown or breakoff of all forms of communication. The communicator who assumes that anyone not otherwise stupid must surely comprehend his or her meaning arrogantly ignores both the complexity of communication and the recipient's point of reference for understanding it.

An effective communicator is constantly on the watch for signs of misunderstanding and confusion. Communication that is all one-way, as if it were a failure-proof process, creates its own barriers to acceptance. Similarly, casting about for the magic words that move one's audience to action is likely to be transparent and is certainly manipulative. The cheapest, fastest route to simple action is to play on the hopes and desperations of the reader and listener. Power concepts like "winner," "rich," "sexy," or "hot" are overused to activate the listener without concern for the ethics of pushing the emotional buttons of others for near-term gain. The style itself becomes a measure of the communicator's dishonesty. Politicians especially have relied on the emotional appeal of power words too much, too long, and now widely suffer from lack of credibility in their political roles. Promises without action must eventually generate cynicism.

SHARE VERSUS SNARE

The communication process is shaped at its core by the presence or absence of trust between the communicating parties. Trusting communication is characterized by open sharing and awareness of the many opportunities for misunderstanding. Nontrusting, defensive communication obfuscates and exploits existing potential for misunderstanding. The fundamental strategies of communication are founded on either sharing experience or snaring the unwitting victim. Managers can strive to communicate experience and understanding so that the intimacy of shared awareness can become a more powerful platform for further sharing and understanding. This is communication as an investment in clarity and cooperation. Alternatively, managers can attempt to trap the target of communication into enacting the behavioral result wanted. This is communication to move or motivate another in the directions desired without their cooperation. It is plainly manipulative and assumes the absence of agreed-on, common purpose.

The mere notion of motivating invokes suggestion of control and manipulation over another to obtain a desired or preferred behavior. In the popular sense, motivation includes a clever array of rewards and penalties that are irresistible in their driving power, blended with selective application of vague promises and intimidations to keep behavior focused. It may include a hint of wizardry deemed necessary to force the intended action outcome against the will of the person being motivated. Among co-equals who are striving mutually to snare one another with their communications, motivation quickly degenerates into a competitive game of dominate and counterdominate. The opportunity to share through communicating is sacrificed to the triviality of a snare communications game.

The game of snare is widely played, understood by and transparent to those it is played upon. It should, therefore, be easy to recognize and circumvent when encountered. The game, though, becomes a pastime, an old, bad habit of relating to others primarily by means of an ongoing verbal fencing match. Introduced early to the game in families and schools, many know no other way to communicate. Those who find themselves faced with a power relationship, either as superior or subordinate in a work relationship, for instance, are likely to play along with it merely because it is familiar and predictable.

Sharing is the maximum desirable and highest payoff outcome of all communication. Many aspire to sharing but fear they will fail or make fools of themselves in its pursuit. It is presumed naive, hokey, less than sophisticated, the object of silly idealists. These are the excuses, the mocking defenses that are most often raised to block an attempt to discover sharing in communications. The dominant maxim, the urbane, worldly wise view is that the game of snaring must be played if one is not to risk loss of pride through counterexploitation. Fearing loss of already limited self-esteem, the average employee timidly learns to dance the minuet of mutual manipulation.

Crossing the threshold into high performance culture based on shared communication and trustfulness is greatly impeded by these pervasive, old bad habits. The habit of manipulation through communication snares is deeply set in this competitive American business culture. The expectation of maximum competition between firms, especially those in the same markets, is enacted in the form of federal antitrust laws. Businesses that coordinate or cooperate are presumed likely to cheat the public with poor quality or excessive price. Nineteenth-century industrial trusts in rail transport, oil and steel seemed to demonstrate the natural tendency of an industry to either collude to maximize profits or consolidate into monopolies that then extract extortionate profits. Business that does not compete vigorously was and still is presumed to be either badly managed or guilty of competitive collusion.

Competitors seek advantage through mutual obfuscation and intimidation. It is assumed that one must avoid the straight, clear truth that might offer business intelligence to a competitor in favor of messages that mislead or confuse. If anything must be said, it must be expressed in the most unspecific of terms. The highest form of political skill is an appeal to universal values that promises no specifics. The best politician avoids the convenient lie by couching his or her words cleverly to conceal any clarity of position. The opportunistic politician shapes answers to the audience that asks them. The use of language to fend off those who would seek clarity and commitment is a highly practiced art in American culture, business and politics alike. It is an art, though, that creates cynicism in the hearts of ordinary workers and citizens. Politicians and businesspeople labor under the burdensome stereotype of self-interested opportunism. Honesty is seldom expected of them except among the naive.

TRUST IS THE CASUALTY OF THE SNARE GAME

The depth of this chronic problem can be measured daily in mail ads, newspaper display ads and TV commercials. Auto dealers place an attractive young woman on television to cheerlead slumping sales by trumpeting "let's hear it for American quality," when the truth is that American quality still lags the Japanese. A bank suggests that "we say 'yes' when others say 'no' " but fails to mention the higher interest rate charged to offset added risk. The grocery chain offers "double savings with double coupons" and raises prices on all couponed items.

Workers on the job get endless double-talk and obfuscation from managers and supervisors. The low-paying employer announces that a salary survey is under way for selected, key positions in the firm, and nothing further happens. The boss insists that it is impossible to increase a critical worker's pay because of difficult competitive conditions, then matches the offer made by a competitor to that worker. Prices are raised for product or service on the premise that additional capital is needed for new plant investment, but most workers still must work with old, antiquated equipment, and the rumor is that purchase of a foreign factory is planned. A drop in profit is announced, then a week later, the entire top management team gets a large percentage raise. The CEO cries poverty to the union and buys a new corporate jet.

Sometimes the arguments offered are valid. It costs less to keep an experienced worker by meeting the market for pay, and it is therefore a rational management action to retain the worker offered higher pay by the competition. The business may be besieged with competition and unable to pay higher wages until the alternative cost calculus is clear. These actions appear cynical, nonetheless, to the individual worker and it would be preferable to stay aware of changes occurring in the labor market to remain ahead of the competition in pay. Bad timing is as much the enemy of trust as are hollow words.

The most common source of distrust in the work environment is a chronic discrepancy between pronouncements and actions of managers and supervisors. The executive who wears $700 suits and takes vacations in the company lodge, but lectures clerks on wasting paper or taking pencils home with them, is viewed as a hypocrite. So is the hotel manager who throws lavish parties for friends on the premise that it is necessary public relations, then fires the bartender who occasionally fails to charge high tipping customers for their drinks. The board of directors that forgives the company president for embezzling $100,000 to pay gambling bills, but vigorously prosecutes the bookkeeper who steals $1,000 to pay her son's hospital bills is no better. Where is the equity for the engineer who is disciplined for making personal long-distance phone calls to his elderly and ailing parents while the executive who regularly concocts an expense-account business trip to visit his own family is simply ignored? Worker cynicism should be expected when the technician who breaks a safety rule to save time and money is disciplined with a one-week layoff without pay while the executive who covers up a massive bypass of safety regulations is defended by company counsel at company expense. These are simple discrepancies that proclaim to workers the absence of consistency in action and word more loudly than the front pages of a newspaper could ever do. They are discrepancies that render words hollow and undermine worker trust in management communications.

In the context of continuing competitive give and take, it is easy to let words lose their meaning except as a defense against loss or opportunity to seize advantage. To make the big sale, to get the major account, to get the desired job, to avoid the expensive traffic ticket, to get the desired grade from the professor, it is only necessary, seemingly, to come up with a convincing argument. When one is quick with the dulcet words, it may seem as though nothing else is needed to enter the winner's circle. As in politics, it is best to avoid outright lies, but if deceit is what it takes, it is justified by the game as long as one can avoid getting caught or paying too high a price for the transgression. Plain honesty of the Abe Lincoln, frontier morality style is lost and forgotten in the race for fame, wealth and ego gratification.

HONESTY, RULES VIOLATION AND WHISTLE-BLOWERS

The antidote to dishonest communication may sometimes be whistle-blowing by workers. Whistle-blowers are workers who turn their bosses and companies in for alleged illegal or unethical actions. Some whistle-blowers dwell in a shadow world of paranoid suspicion, looking for the worst and finding it even where it is not. Paranoid whistle-blowing is common enough to lend it credence as a defense against charges, even honest ones. It is hard to discern who is a neurotic crazy and who is a moral giant. On the surface they can appear the same. Some whistle-blowers are just fanatics for exact detail, intolerant of the smallest violation of written rules. Their supervisors may know or believe that the rule is written conservatively, and that there is no harm in stretching the limit when circumstances are otherwise favorable. These whistle-blowers know only that a rule has been violated. Some whistle-blowers come onto evidence of a clear and flagrant crime that has been covered up by the guilty to avoid prosecution. The Watergate and Iran-Contra cover-ups by highly placed, presumably responsible government officials typifies the style. These widely publicized events are useful benchmarks for the regrettably common bad judgment of overly competitive executives who overaggressively seek a win for their firm (or team) and accept major risk to achieve it.

THE AGE OF THE COVER-UP

The cover-up pattern is justified by the rationale that when others can gain advantage to defeat you by breaking the rules, it is necessary to respond in kind to keep the competition equitable. Most Americans accept this principle in practice. The Twentieth Century Fox movie *M.A.S.H.* and the TV series that followed it illustrate the pervasiveness of rule-breaking acceptance in U.S. culture. The central characters of the story line assume as an imperative the need to break rules and cheat the system to be effective in their jobs and take the edge off the misery of human suffering in war. The central mission of a Mobile Army Surgical Hospital, located a short distance behind the battle lines of war, is to apply the best medical skill to mending the torn bodies of wounded soldiers. Rules and regulations must be circumvented and broken that stand in the way of sound surgical medicine or prevent the rejuvenation of weary doctors through their bawdy relaxation. The rules, everyone knows, were written by stupid bureaucrats more interested in political imperatives and paperwork than in saving human lives. These M.A.S.H. heroes and heroines know in their hearts that they *must not* let bureaucrats *or* rules interfere with their job effectiveness. Officious inspectors and senior officers who discover some flagrant breach of regulations are treated as meddlesome competitors who must either be hoodwinked with a clever cover-up or blackmailed into acceptance of the rule-breaking imperative.

A football game in the original *M.A.S.H.* movie depicts a team of bullies who routinely foul the M.A.S.H. heroes. The M.A.S.H. team retaliates by covertly injecting an offending opponent with disabling medication. The lesson is that when one is up against rule-breakers, one must be prepared to break the rules in self-defense. The nature of the rule violation, hilariously funny in the movie, is nevertheless morally and legally grave. Were someone to blow the whistle on ordinary competitors using covert medication of their opponents to win a ball game, public outrage would be maximum. It is an offense that could merit imprisonment. This movie presents the same level of rule-breaking as a harmless form of fun that echoes the rule violations common to the bureaucratic context in which these healers must operate.

It is easy for those engaged in stiff, stressful competition to rationalize their situation as one where either the rules are stupid and will prevent them from winning, or that one's competitors are themselves chronic rule-breakers who must be countered with an equivalent breach of the rules. Reversing these attitudes is fundamental to building high performance systems. The rules and laws of the game must be sound and equitable for all, consistently and even-handedly enforced.

In recent years, whistle-blowers have come under increasing protection of the law. That makes the expedient of cover-up more risky. But old habits of response that treat any whistle-blowing as betrayal of the team are still deeply entrenched. The better policy for a company to follow in its pursuit of a high performance culture is to vigorously encourage and reward whistle-blowers for their willingness to tell the truth and expose rule-breakers even when the charges may occasionally be trivial.

Rule-breakers are typically weak but opportunistic players. Rule-breakers in industry are often only weak or inexperienced competitors desperate to hold position in a competitive market. They are sometimes naive ideologists genuinely convinced their cause puts them above the law. But rule-breakers are never good competitors. They employ self-awarded handicaps to achieve their purposes. Where a handicap is deserved, it should be written into the law. Where it is not, its presumption must be rooted out and punished. Misguided loyalty to the firm that seeks to illegally enhance profit or market share must never be protected or rewarded. A high performance firm must be self-policing to assure that all the rules are respected. The potential cost in moral corruption and failed trust in contempt for the rules is too great to tolerate.

ETHICAL MANAGEMENT DECISION MAKING

Managers must recognize and appreciate the inherent conflict between the rule of law and the rule of the marketplace. It is a clash of purposes that can be discovered in the classical ethics of philosophy. As between the greater good for the greater number of a Jeremy Bentham and the absolute rule of law conceived by Immanuel Kant there is little common ground but much historical point of reference. Business managers, within these contradictory ethical traditions, can either play by the rules or they can strive for the best market result in their effort to win. Rules derive from our historical tradition of rule of law. Results arise from creative pursuit of goals and maximum economic utility. The conflict between bureaucrats and dedicated healers portrayed in *M.A.S.H.* nicely anchors these two ethical positions.

Confusion of judgment can arise out of conflict of rule of law and principle, lending stability and consistency to society, as it clashes with free pursuit of the greatest good for the greatest number, yielding the maximum collective economic benefit to society. Business and political institutions are, naturally, utility-maximizing. They seek to satisfy the largest number of customers or citizens with solutions that yield the highest payoff in profits and votes. Rule of law or guidance of principle is a secondary priority. When this order of priorities prevails, the utility of results is the supreme and final measure of simple success. As long as every possible life is saved by the practices used, M.A.S.H. personnel enjoyed maximum moral justification in their contempt for the Army's regulations. As long as criminals are deterred from assaulting honest citizens, methods used by police are proper and acceptable. If communists are prevented from taking over in Latin America, any source of weapons to arm their opponents is proper. When no one is coming the other way, it is okay to run the red light to get to work on time. These are the arguments of utilitarians.

Moral absolutists, on the other hand, are just as narrow in their arguments for preservation of law and principle. They unwittingly encourage special business and political interests to lobby enactment of laws that lend unearned advantage to those interests or give force to narrow ideology. Moral absolutism demands adherence to the rules without concern for the results. When the spirit of moral absolutism prevails, the interests of endangered animal species under the law stand above human need for expanded recreational space in a society overstressed by crowding. Police must strictly conform to the law even when human life may be lost for doing so. Lawbreakers are punished at the maximum even when rendered desperate and confused by a complex, contradictory society. In the absolute strictness of specific law there is no room for experienced, humane judgment to operate.

Law must not be too precise. The best laws are statements of principle rather than exact specifications for action. There is always occasion for exception to every rule. Room for that exception must be built into the law for justice to be preserved. Poor law must be challenged. Good law must be upheld vigorously. Rules and laws that are overly strict to permit selective enforcement by authority invite breach and are categorically unfair. In equity, if any one person is permitted to break a rule without penalty, then every person must be accorded the same right. Otherwise it is only reasonable to assume that the strictness of law as written is designed to permit harassment of the disloyal or culturally nonconforming.

The high performance operation requires simple, clearly communicated, consistently enforced rules and regulations. Any custom or rule considered proper but that is not consistently enforced should better be explicitly categorized as preferred but optional. Any custom or rule contrary to civil law must be clearly prohibited by management. But it is not enough merely to obey the rules. High performance operations must also be clearly focused on the utility of high goals and exceptional operating results. Mission and strategy must be communicated as living guides to organizational purpose. Every member of the team must know the rules and the results by which performance is judged. Anything less opens the door to abuse and dilutes performance.

Trust is generated out of knowing what the rules are, knowing they have business meaning and purpose, and knowing what results one is to deliver within total observance of and respect for those rules. When management changes an incentive pay system without communicating full understanding as to why the change is needed, the cynical assumption of chronically manipulated workers must be that "we are being cheated out of our hard-earned premium pay." Management that does not establish rules for such changes, stick to them and communicate fully the need for revision of rates, foolishly invites distrust. Realistically viewed, the research findings at Harwood represented the only way things could work in a society of manipulators. A naive, profit-focused management changed the piecework pay system without explaining its goals and purposes to workers. It should have recognized in advance that workers would distrust management's purposes and offer resistance. In similar fashion, the Hawthorne research team, urgently looking for the key to worker productivity, should have known that the appearance of a group of high-paid, high-status researchers coming into the plant to sow democratic enlightenment would be met with distrust and cynicism by workers accustomed to being controlled and manipulated. There could be no trust in these circumstances. Trust requires simplicity in communication, absence of pretense, sharing of purpose and values.

The trusted manager or supervisor is one who tells the truth in all circumstances. Workers, subject to hierarchical power and whimsical judgment of their performance, know the truth when they see it and hear it. A latter-day problem-solving researcher coming on a scene like Harwood or Hawthorne would do well to acknowledge the truth at the outset of the research project. A stranger who comes to them saying "I'm going to make things better for you in your jobs" must realistically be judged as either stupid or a liar. It would be better to admit that "I don't know whether anything can be done to improve your working conditions or not, but I'm willing to try if you're willing to let me." The supervisor who disciplines the wrong worker for misbehavior and then won't admit the error and apologize becomes known as a cover-up artist who cannot be trusted. The manager who promises a pay raise to get performance that satisfies a deadline, then encounters disapproval of the decision by higher management, may pretend that no promise was made only if he wants to be known as a liar. It is often okay to break a promise made in earnest desperation, but never to deny it was made. Trust is destroyed by the denial of a promise given, not by the broken promise itself.

Trust can be built, on the other hand, by always admitting error and failure. "I promised and broke my promise; I will try to make it up to you if I can" is the mark of supervisory honesty. Indeed, in circumstances of desperation it may be preferable to promise reward and own up to its unavailability than to suggest the possibility of reward and claim later that it was never a firm commitment. That is cover-up and manipulation. Managerial error is inevitable *and* is *always* a potential asset. The natural, unavoidable occurrence of an unintended error is potential foundation for enhanced trust. It must be recognized and seized for the opportunity to own the truth that it offers. Even small mistakes should be unabashedly admitted. The widely prevailing habit of hiding behind a mantle of authority in the pretense that nothing has happened undermines trust and destroys confidence in management's word. Workers know that a boss who will not admit error is a phony who will cheat them whenever the occasion permits.

Good managers take risks and make mistakes. The key to trust is admitting misjudgment. Trust demands scrupulous honesty in little matters; intended honesty is not enough. Many highly successful managers intend honesty but avoid clear commitment. Often on advice of cynical, overcautious legal counsel, they offer hollow assurances with strings attached. After a time they simply become unaware of any discrepancy between word and action. Words become a barrier to communicating with workers instead of a conduit to shared understanding. Management's word must always be its bond. Slipping out from under an agreement because it wasn't put into writing is maximum evidence of manipulative dishonesty to workers.

WHY NOT A COMMUNICATIONS AUDITOR TO RESTORE HONESTY?

Old habits of manipulative and ambiguous communication are so deeply set among Americans that many will find it difficult to change them without intensive coaching and surveillance. To assure honesty in financial matters, an accounting audit is conducted on a regular basis in many firms. Much as it is resented by some who would seek better business results at the expense of accounting rules, it introduces an indispensable discipline that enhances the quality of financial records.

In similar fashion, a communications audit function should be implemented in those firms aspiring to high performance. The purpose of this function should be to root out old bad habits of manipulative communications and train constructive, trust-enhancing management communications skills. Such a function would be resented at first but could raise the quality of communications and create a climate in which workers can trust their managers again.

The talent to staff a communications audit function should not be hard to find. Not all businesses communicate badly. The business of communication itself through radio, television, magazines and newspapers competes for public support on the basis of its credibility with the general public. The best and most widely trusted news reporters are those most listened to by the public. They know what it takes to build trust with their audience.

There is a fund of talent in the communications industry to staff a business communications audit function and to raise the trustworthiness of management. A communications audit function can effectively use the talents of experienced news reporters and editors. Someone is needed for this job who has learned to spot inaccuracy, ambiguity and to recognize factually unsupported assertion in memos, policy statements, public relations releases, performance appraisals and any other form of written internal communication. Interviews and surveys of employees conducted by experienced investigative reporters would permit evaluation of verbal, unwritten communications and measure the level of worker trust prevailing in an organization.

This is a radical proposal that calls for a wholly new department in business firms. But communication that lacks credibility is a major source of worker distrust and restricted production output. Audit of management communication to restore clarity and honesty need not be onerous. It can add new dimensions to managerial skill. Mastery of communication skill is fundamental and cannot be left to chance in this competitive economy. A high performance system cannot afford to leave the quality of its communication to chance. A communications audit function goes straight to the need for trust in high performance management systems.

Ethical action and honesty in communication are inseparable. One cannot exist and prosper without the other. Reconciling the arbitrary strictness of rules or principles with the pragmatic flexibility of a business-results orientation is critically essential and never easy. Recognizing and changing old, bad habits of communication can be hard. These are, nevertheless, the essential beginnings for restored trust. Without trust there is little chance of creating a high performance culture.

Chapter Twelve

Inventing Tomorrow's High Performance Systems

The evolution of high performance management offers an instructive review of management history and useful suggestions for the invention of future high performance systems. Taylor's scientific management was a smashing technological success and a major political failure. Ford used the technology of scientific management as a foundation for the efficiency of a mechanized, lockstep flow of work through a series of narrowly specialized workstations. He created the role of worker as unthinking robot. His model was the competitive imperative of industry for more than a half century.

Hawthorne was the humanistic backlash to both labor militancy and inhumane working conditions of the factory system based on scientific management. Hawthorne established the tradition of social science research into the behavioral and motivational roots of high performance output, but, for a half century or more, diverted that research onto the sidetrack of worker satisfaction as the presumed foundation of high performance. The clash between Ford's version of scientific management and ideological advocates of increased worker satisfaction stalled the progress of high performance systems invention for most of the twentieth century.

On the threshold of the twenty-first century, competitive revitalization of American as well as of much world industry depends on discovery of new high performance systems that break the old impasse of scientific management under siege by advocates of labor humanism. The history of past high performance systems and experience with emerging high performance output in global competition may offer useful clues as to the elements of those new systems.

SOCIAL INVENTION IS DEMANDED

High performance systems of the past are associated with the names of their inventors, Taylor and Ford especially. High performance systems dominantly based on efficiency and principles of industrial engineering still seem to require a charismatic core of committed, visionary leadership like that of J. F. Lincoln or Ken Iverson. Increasingly, though, emerging high performance systems of the present day are the invention of a diverse team or the product of a unique business culture. Some of the inventiveness demanded may be contributed by highly trained specialists in strategy development, compensation systems, skill/temperament assessment, training, MBO implementation, statistical analysis or operations methodology. Much inventiveness also seems to arise out of the practical experience of workers in a setting that supports productive innovation. The major job of tomorrow's leadership is likely to be creation of the culture that lets these varied elements of high performance come together in a cohesive, productive whole. While some of these elements may be common to high performance systems across different businesses or industries, the total system configuration is increasingly likely to be unique to its business setting. A uniform, broadly applicable system like scientific management or the moving assembly line that becomes a competitive standard for industry is largely a thing of the past. The coming age will be the age of the customized high performance system. Likert's (1961) expectation of more complex systems of organizing human effort to meet the demands of more complex technologies seems on the threshold of widespread realization. It is not just complexity to match complexity, though. It is superior design of management and organizational systems to achieve consistently high performance.

MORE COMPLEXITY MEANS MORE EXPERTS

The importance of staff expertise and knowledge will undoubtedly increase, not diminish, in most future high performance systems. The major emerging social technologies of worker involvement, goal setting, compensation systems for multiskilled workers, output-based pay, work culture design, legally defensible culture-based worker selection, alternative work schedule development, worker health support and high performance communications sharing will all demand trained consultants and expert specialists. Not all these technical elements will be required in every high performance situation, but some, inevitably, will. Consultants who can competently identify and implement the needed technical foundations of high performance will be indispensable to many emerging high performance designs. Staffers will be required to sustain technically strong performance in these domains in the on-going organizations. The escalation in complexity of organizational design will be on the order of moving up from a mechanical typewriter to a computerized word processing system. The opportunity for conflict and confusion arising out of the new organizational complexity demanded will be great.

Staffers as expert problem solvers with authority to impose their solutions have always been a potential source of poor system performance; inevitably, one staffer's solutions interfere with another's. More staffers with more technical solutions means more opportunity for chronic poor performance. Prevailing assumptions about how staffers should apply their skills in support of high performance will need considerable revision and retrofitting. The most likely direction of change will be toward abandonment of the expert role in favor of the teacher/facilitator role. The staffer's decision will no longer be reviewed by management and directly implemented. The staffer's objectives will, rather, be communicated to supervisors and line workers, possible fixes will be suggested, and the final procedure or policy will be tested and validated by those who must live and work with all the complexity of high performance.

The most dramatic change will occur in the form of widespread overhaul of worker, supervisor and technical staff roles. In tomorrow's high performance systems there will necessarily be *more*, not fewer, staff and consulting experts. There will not just be industrial or production engineers and cost accountants to maintain discipline of work and material flow. There will also be experts in marketing, R&D, finance and operations strategies, experts in legal, social and environmental constraints, experts in assessment of human skill and temperament, experts in learning/training methods, experts in communications. The independent solution devised by any one of these experts will likely be at odds with problem-solving priorities and systems goals of some other expert. The probability of an *untested* solution unilaterally implemented being counterproductive will be excessively high. Conflicts between the goals and purposes of expert staffers will be frequent. Solving those conflicts by reference to an established political pecking order will certainly impair organization performance and defeat the goal of high performance. Conflicts must be constructively and fully resolved. Old-fashioned staff or functional politics will not do the job.

WORKERS BECOME THE JUDGES OF SYSTEM DESIGN EFFECTIVENESS

The logically most defensible approach to resolution of complex system conflict between expert staffers is to designate operating personnel as the court of final appeals in evaluation of problem solutions. This means that workers at the point of production or service delivery must be accountable for high performance goals, experienced in the basic processes required for their achievement, skilled or multiskilled as necessary, and trained in operations basics. Staffers will be their trainers and mentors, not surrogate bosses as at present. Failure to develop the direct labor force to a level where it can be the final court of problem-solving appeals means that every solution offered must be approved by every other staffer before it can be implemented. The hazard of conflict in purpose is too high to tolerate anything less. The political and communications snarls likely from extending veto power to every staff expert before implementation of any expert solution would themselves impair organization performance. There is little question as to which is the superior alternative. Appointing workers as the jury is much the simpler and surer device. For validation of this logic, we need only look to the superior manufacturing systems of present-day Japanese industry where this system is used.

FLEXIBILITY IS A CENTRAL, GUIDING PRINCIPLE

Traditional high performance systems centered on scientific management, worker specialization, and engineered work flow had numerous, obvious, glaring weaknesses. Tomorrow's systems must avoid those flaws. Former systems were typically designed for lowest cost at a preset, optimum level where costs increase with either surges or falloffs in demand. Excess capacity was a major cost burden that was nonetheless often necessary to protect market share. Changes of any kind—in product design, in work process flow, in job design, or in demand—all introduced high cost that had to be amortized over a sufficiently long product run to be tolerable. Corporations often succeeded and failed according to the quality and timing of their physical plant capacity investment decisions.

Variations in worker ability in these same systems were an inconvenience that required setting standards low enough to be met by the largest part of the labor force. Diurnal or weekly variations in worker energy level were poorly accommodated, again requiring that moderate standards be set that would permit reliable work flow at relatively modest energy input.

Flexibility is lacking in the efficient, tightly engineered system to smoothly accommodate the ups and downs of people and markets. In the current era, short product runs, frequent change in work systems and flows, volatile markets and high human labor costs render these old weaknesses intolerable. Tomorrow's high performance systems will fully accommodate change, variety and flexibility.

Individual worker differences in skill, temperament, physical makeup and life-style preference will be fitted with care into tomorrow's product, process and market requirements. The "one worker fits all jobs" approach of the engineered assembly line has long been under assault for its failure to recognize and respect human difference. Tomorrow's high performance systems will be fitted to the individualities of diverse peoples. Assessment of individual ability and temperament supported by business-relevant training will be required at a high level of technical skill and systems sophistication. Worker flexibility will be increased by expanding the worker's range of skill and knowledge. Assessment of skill or knowledge in combination with training to augment missing skill or knowledge seems indispensable to emerging high performance systems.

The rigidly invariant rhythm of the forty-hour, five-day workweek will likely give way to customer- and market-driven schedules that permit much or most work to meet variable market demand without resort to large inventories and warehouses. Plant capacity itself will become inherently more flexible. Tomorrow's high performance systems will likely exhibit a wide variety of work schedules fitted to worker life-style and physical stamina within the characteristic cycles of the business or industry. As productivity rises, hours can be shortened and fewer days can be worked on average to reach the net output result demanded. Normal schedules will routinely accommodate the needs of one-parent families as well as of dual-career couples who must coordinate schedules for care of children and leisure time together. High performance systems will exploit opportunities for greater harmony between on-the-job and off-the-job activities. They will experiment to discover potential for maximum productivity in optimum bursts of high quantity and quality of work output. In work schedules, there will be flexibility in all things, but that flexibility always will be tested against efficient use of labor and achievement of the highest quality of output.

Tomorrow's high performance systems will scrupulously avoid the trap of trying to buy loyalty or effort. They will invest heavily in new or enhanced skills, and will pay fairly against market for high worker productivity. Designers of those systems will discover, as I have detailed elsewhere (Bassett, 1992), that high skill yields the lowest labor cost in product or service. They will recognize that the strongest performers don't need a carrot dangling from the stick to lure them onward; excellence in performance is already fundamental to their self-image and self-esteem. Linking variations in level of pay to variations in effort or result may be useful performance feedback where quality will not suffer from all-out pursuit of maximum pay. But performance excellence is its own reward in a high performance system. High performance systems are *un*likely to be successful if designed on a premise that pay is the primary motivator of high performance.

THE WORK CULTURE BECOMES CENTRAL

High performance systems are usually manifest as unique work cultures. The features that constitute the core of a system are coordinated around a set of central objectives. Taylor's scientific management was devoted to increasing gross wealth generated by available plant and equipment capacity. Ford focused on efficiency of plant and equipment utilization to overcome labor shortages and meet burgeoning market demand. Modern-day Japanese production systems emphasize production flexibility within tight cost control and high quality standards. Tomorrow's systems are likely to serve the customer's expectation for low-cost, high-quality customized product and service delivery within an operations context of work as significant personal self-expression. Some systems may support maximum customization at reasonable cost, others may deliver limited customization at rock bottom cost. Some may emphasize the importance of the worker as skilled artist, others may dictate the imperative of worker as master technician. Some may be built around work as the expressive core of the worker's life-style. Others may offer opportunity to maximize earnings in the short term through intensive application of valued skills. Different systems will be recognizable in their uniqueness as work cultures that support these variable objectives.

Cultures are characterized by the existence of the broad agreement of their members around shared central values. The roles and personalities of members will be selected to fit the culture, and the culture in return will shape the roles and personalities of members. The broad industry and macroenvironment in which the business operates will validate or disconfirm the culture. The interplay between members, customers and broader environment will reshape and revise the culture. Inventing tomorrow's high performance systems will be something of an exercise by their leadership in applied cultural anthropology.

Business plans for entrepreneurial start-ups will likely include specifications of the organization's values and dominant cultural dimensions. They will specify those human qualities that are expected to make a difference. They will estimate which is of greater importance—individuality or teamwork, cooperation or competition, trained skill or acquired experience, social conventionality or personal idiosyncracy, adherence to the rules or achievement of results—to the building of a robust culture. Some of tomorrow's high performance cultures will be temporary and ad hoc, others stable and enduring. In most, but especially in start-up or temporary cultures, values and objectives must be defined early. Worker roles and characteristics must be clearly delineated before the culture has developed too far. Cultures that, in the past, have been allowed simply to evolve willy-nilly will be replaced by cultures that are predesigned, purposefully constructed and tested early for their viability to assess their market, industry and macroenvironmental fit. Culture is already a major asset or liability to many businesses. As the foundation of tomorrow's high performance systems, culture's evolution and impact must not be left to chance.

THE LABOR MOVEMENT MUST TRANSFORM ITSELF

In its relationship to traditional, scientific-management-based systems, organized labor has stood as the antidote to the excesses of management's full control over productive capital and its arm's length treatment of labor as an adversary. Most managers would judge labor unions to be certain obstacles to high performance rather than supports to it. Indeed, the flexibility demanded of tomorrow's high performance systems would seem impossible under even the simplest present-day union contract. As long as labor-management relationships are dominantly characterized by an adversarial mode, the competitive flexibility required in today's marketplace is likely to be impeded by a union.

Historically, the labor movement has not always shown appreciation for the benefits of high performance systems. The methods and designs of scientific management were disparaged and resisted despite their power to increase the wage base and, thereby, the long-term well-being of workers. Even an enlightened management from the age of Hawthorne was suspect by unions as a ploy to undercut laborers' rights and dignities. Organized labor has more often taken a conservative stance in the face of change, demanding assurances that laborers would not be asked to carry any substantial burden of pain or cost entailed by that change. But that has not prevented the eventuality of ultimate change in the disappearance of firms and all their jobs with them. Ultimately, the cost of change must be shared by all.

If it is to survive, the labor movement must reform itself around the principles of high performance systems. Its highest service, that of building and sustaining worker dignity and self-respect, should guide organized labor's objectives for the future. Those objectives must recognize the many major changes that will occur in the workplace. The disappearance of life-long single-firm employment and the security expected from long, loyal service, for instance, requires reformulation of what security really is to the typical present-day worker. As the significance of capital as the source of wealth recedes in favor of human skill, intensity of the struggle between the capitalist and the common man must also diminish. The rising importance of human skill supports the traditional political power position of labor unions, but the reduced intensity of contention between those traditional interests of capital and labor undercuts it. The challenge to organized labor will be to restructure its central values and methods to best fit the demands of a new high performance age.

High performance systems are inevitably limited by the industry and macroenvironment within which they must operate. Labor unions arose as a limitation on the freedom of owners and managers to expand their capital bases without concern for the needs or expectations of workers. Unions were founded on the need to bring balance into those equations that calculate the relative interests of workers, consumers and investors. Their methods and tactics were fitted to a time when most commodities were in perpetual short supply and demand was largely predictable. In an age of widespread economic affluence and abundance of commodities produced with automation, the objectives and methods of labor unions need major overhaul.

Laborers of the twenty-first century will progress through a series of "careers," retrofitting or replacing skills as they move from one job opportunity to another. Massive factories or capital accumulations as the basis of production will be far less important as a source of employment. Small, entrepreneurial firms emerge today as the dominant source of new jobs. These will be harder for unions to organize, much more subject to rapid change in size or technology and far less secure as suppliers of long-term income. Workers of tomorrow will need protection from the natural variations in market demand and sudden failure or transformation of the small firm. Access to relevant training and retraining, insurance against opportunistic exploitation by a predatory owner and sound advice that can be relied on to enhance worker self-interest without unduly threatening the supplier of jobs will be needed. Labor organizations of tomorrow may offer insurance at a fee to individual workers, to groups of workers and to firms that guarantee training to help workers adjust to technological change or competitive adversity. They may thereby insure workers or groups of workers against loss of jobs that result from change in mission, strategy or structure of the work culture. They will offer training or income maintenance as necessary. If loss of job results from dishonesty or misrepresentation, unions may offer legal insurance that permits the wronged workers to attach the firm's real assets or be compensated from an insurance fund specifically established to protect them from fraud. The worker of tomorrow may need to be protected from the owner who absconds with the major assets of the firm or who hides behind bankruptcy after rapaciously raiding them. Unions can appropriately become the insurers of losses from and the licensed bounty hunters of such scalawags.

Providing services of this kind would directly address real worker concerns about the honesty and integrity of the new owner class to which they, themselves, may sometimes belong. As unions today confer on workers the sense of dignity that goes with fighting back when exploited, unions of tomorrow may guard self-confidence by protecting against reverses of fortune to which individual workers are vulnerable. That will increase worker confidence when they are asked to commit fully to the values and purposes of their culture. Willingness and opportunity to extend trust would be the winner.

TRUST IS THE FOUNDATION

Trust in one's bosses and co-workers is indispensable to teamwork, and teamwork is the requisite foundation of high performance systems that must cope with complex markets, technologies and business environments. Flexibility of response may mean variable work and income schedules as the market cycles through its inevitable ups and downs. It may mean variable work assignment and frequent upgrades of skill or knowledge. In the past, these have been sources of uneasiness and generators of distrust among workers. High performance systems of the future must overcome the emotional jeopardy of such uncertainty whenever it is experienced by workers. Better, fuller, earlier information about markets and opportunities will help by attuning workers to the realities of business. Trust is impossible when communication is lacking or is patently manipulative. Clear, truthful communication from management to workers is essential in every high performance system.

There is little hope for breakthroughs in high performance systems where trust between management and workers is not maintained and enhanced. The factory system with its fundamental division of economic interest between owners and workers, the inevitable rise of unions with their long history of antagonism toward scientific management all serve to create a lingering division of interests that impedes creation of trust. Poor communication skill and pragmatic management pursuit of results at the expense of principles amplify worker distrust. These are liabilities of the prevailing systems that must be transcended.

When realistically reviewed and applied in a context of trust, the literature of management social science research offers many guideposts for improved worker management relations in support of high output. Worker satisfaction need not necessarily be ignored. Neither must it be venerated as an ideological icon. Realism in participation can be employed to achieve a balance between simple, efficient decision making and effective, developmental worker involvement in decisions. The potential contributions of practical pay systems can be made an effective support of high performance output. Innovative work schedules and managed life-styles may be made to yield high output at a level previously unimagined. Training and selection can contribute to vital, robust, productive new high performance cultures. Communications skills and systems of audit checks on accuracy and clarity can be greatly improved. The potential in applying these devices to tomorrow's high performance systems seems immense.

The management challenge of the twenty-first century is to sort out the best experience of the past, the best ideas of the present and the best opportunities of the future to invent tomorrow's high performance systems. The opportunity exists to rise above the narrow efficiencies of scientific management and the shallow ideologies of human relations. In its potential for creation of tomorrow's competitive edge it is the most significant opportunity that could be offered to management on this threshold of a new millennium.

References

Adams, J. S. 1963. "Toward an Understanding of Inequity." *Journal of Abnormal and Social Psychology*, 67: 422–436.

Asch, S. E. 1956. "Studies of Independence and Conformity: A Minority of One Against a Unanimous Majority." *Psychological Monographs*, 70(416).

Atkinson, J. W. (Ed.). 1958. *Motives in Fantasy, Action and Society*. Princeton, NJ: Van Nostrand.

Bartlem, C. S. and Locke, E. A. 1981. "The Coch and French Study: A Critique and Reinterpretation." *Human Relations*, 34(7): 555–586.

Bassett, G. A. 1976. *Managerial Communication: How To Master It*. An AMA Tape Cassette Book. New York: American Management Association.

Bassett, G. A. 1980. *Part Time Work in Manufacturing*. Fairfield, CT: Consulting Report to General Electric Corporate Relations.

_____. 1991. *Management Strategies for Today's Project Shop Economy*. Westport, CT: Quorum.

_____. 1992, *Operations Management for Service Industries*. Westport, CT: Quorum.

Blake, R. and Mouton, J. 1984. *The Managerial Grid*, 3rd ed. Houston: Gulf.

Brayfield, A. H. and Crockett, W. H. 1955. "Employee Attitudes and Employee Performance," *Psychological Bulletin*, 55(5): 396–424.

Carey, A. 1967. "The Hawthorne Studies: A Radical Criticism." *The American Sociological Review*, 32: 403–416.

Coch, L. and French, J.R.P. Jr. 1948. "Overcoming Resistance To Change." *Human Relations*, 1: 512–532.

Cummings, T. G. and Molloy, E. S. 1977. *Improving Productivity and the Quality of Work Life*. New York: Praeger.

Dachler, H. P. and Wilpert, B. 1978. "Conceptual Dimensions and Boundaries of Participation in Organizations: A Critical Evaluation." *Administrative Science Quarterly*, 23: 1–39.

Faucheux, C., Amado, G. and Laurent A. 1982. "Organization Development and Change." In M. R. Rosenzweig, and L. W. Porter, eds. *Annual Review of Psychology*, Vol. 33. Palo Alto: Annual Reviews, Inc.

Ford, H. with Crowther, S. 1988. *Today and Tomorrow.* Cambridge, MA: Productivity Press. (Originally published in 1926.)

Franke, R. H. and Kaul, J. D. 1978. "The Hawthorne Experiments: First Statistical Interpretation." *American Sociological Review* 43(5): 623–643.

French, W. 1969. "Organization Development: Objectives, Assumptions and Strategies." *California Management Review*, 12(2): 23–34.

Ghiselli, E. E. 1973. "The Validity of Aptitude Tests in Personnel Selection." *Personnel Psychology*, 26: 461–477.

Glaser, E. 1976. *Productivity Gains Through Worklife Improvements.* New York: Harcourt Brace Jovanovich.

Goldberg, L. R., Greiner, J. R., Guion, R. M., Sechrest, L. B. and Wing, H. 1991. *Questionnaires Used in Prediction of Trustworthiness in Pre-Employment Decisions: An APA Task Force Report.* Washington, DC: The American Psychology Association.

Haire, M., Ghiselli, E. E., and Gordon, M. E. August 1967. "A Psychological Study of Pay," *Journal of Applied Psychology Monograph*, 51(4), Part 2 of 2, Whole No. 636.

Hamper, B. 1991. *Rivethead: Tales from the Assembly Line.* New York: Warner Books.

Homans, G. C. 1950. *The Human Group.* New York: Harcourt Brace & World.

Iaffaldano, M. T. and Muchinsky, P. M. 1985. "Job Satisfaction and Job Performance: A Meta-Analysis." *Psycholological Bulletin*, 97(2): 251–273.

Isenberg-O'Loughlin, J. and Inmace, J. J. 1986. "Full Steam Ahead at Nucor Unlimited." *Metal Producing*, January: 33.

Janis, I. L. 1972. *Victims of Groupthink.* Boston: Houghton Mifflin.

Katzell, R. A. and Yankelovich, D. 1975. *Work, Productivity and Job Satisfaction.* New York: The Psychological Corporation.

Kirtland, R. K., Jr. 1981. "Pilgrims Profits at Nucor." *Fortune Magazine*, April 6: 43–46

Lacey, R. 1986. *Ford: The Men and The Machine.* Boston: Little, Brown.

Likert, R. 1961. *New Patterns of Management.* New York: McGraw-Hill.

Lincoln, J. F. 1961. *A New Approach to Industrial Economics.* New York: Devin Adair.

Locke, E. A. 1976. "The Nature and Causes of Job Satisfaction." In M. D. Dunnette, ed., *Handbook of Industrial and Organizational Psychology.* Chicago: Rand McNally.

Locke, E. A., Feren, D. B., Caleb, V. M., Shaw, K. N. and Denny, A. T. 1980. "The Relative Effectiveness of Four Methods of Motivating Employee

Performance." in K. D. Duncan, M. M. Gruneberg, and D. Wallis, eds., *Changes in Working Life*. New York: Wiley.

Locke, E. A. and Latham, G. P. 1990. *A Theory of Goal Setting and Task Performance*. Englewood Cliffs, NJ: Prentice-Hall.

Locke, E. A., Schweiger, D. M. and Latham, G. P. 1986. "Participation in Decision Making: When Should It Be Used?" *Organizational Dynamics*, 14(4): 125–152.

Maslow, A. H. 1954. *Motivation and Personality*. New York: Harper.

McClelland, D. C. 1961. *The Achieving Society*. New York: The Free Press.

McGregor, D. M. 1960. *The Human Side of Enterprise*. New York: McGraw-Hill.

Meyer, H. H., Kay, E. and French, J.R.P. Jr. 1965. "Split Roles in Performance Appraisal." *Harvard Business Review*, 43(1): 123–129.

Nevins, A. and Hill, F. E. 1957. *Ford: The Times, The Man, The Company*, vol. I, II & III. New York: Scribner's.

Ohno, T. 1988. *Work Place Management*. Cambridge, MA: Productivity Press.

Roethlisberger, F. J. and Dickson, W. 1939. *Management and the Worker*. Cambridge, MA: Harvard University Press.

Sashkin, M. 1986. "Participative Management Remains an Ethical Imperative." *Organizational Dynamics*, 14(4): 62–75.

Schein, E. H. 1985. *Organizational Culture and Leadership*. San Francisco: Jossey-Bass.

Schmidt, R. A. and Bjork, R. A. 1992. "Common Principles in Three Paradigms Suggest New Concepts for Training." *Psychological Science*, 3 (July): 4.

Schmidt, F. L. and Hunter, J. E. 1992. "Development of a Causal Model of Processes Determining Job Performance." *Current Directions in Psychological Science*, 1(3): 89–92.

Schmidt, F. L., Ones, D. S. and Hunter, J. E. 1992. "Personnel Selection." In M. R. Rosenzweig, and L. W. Porter, eds., *Annual Review of Psychology*, Vol. 43. Palo Alto, CA: Annual Reviews, Inc.

Skinner, B. F. 1974. *About Behaviorism*. New York: Alfred A. Knopf.

Staw, B. M. 1984. "Organizational Behavior: A Review and Reformulation of the Field's Outcome Variables," in M. R. Rosenzweig and L. W. Porter, eds., *Annual Review of Psychology*, Vol. 35. Palo Alto, CA: Annual Reviews, Inc.

Staw, B. M., Bell, N. E. and Clausen, J. A. 1986. "The Dispositional Approach to Job Attitudes: A Lifetime Longitudinal Test." *Administrative Science Quarterly*, 31(1): 56–77.

Strauss, G. 1963. "Some Notes on Power-Equalization." In H. J. Leavitt, ed., *The Social Science of Organizations*. Englewood Cliffs, NJ: Prentice-Hall.

Susman, G. I. 1976. *Autonomy at Work: A Sociotechnical Analysis of Participative Management*. New York: Praeger.

Taylor, F. W. 1947. *Scientific Management*. New York: Harper. (Originally published in 1911.)

Twentieth Century Fox Film Corporation. 1969. *M.A.S.H.* Directed by Robert Altman.

U.S. Department of Health, Education and Welfare. 1973. *Work in America*. Cambridge, MA: MIT Press.

Vernon, H. M. 1921. *Industrial Fatigue and Efficiency*. New York: Dutton.

Vroom, V. H. 1964. *Work and Motivation*, New York: Wiley.

Vroom, V. H. and Jago, A. G. 1988. *The New Leadership: Managing Participation in Organizations*. Englewood Cliffs, NJ: Prentice-Hall.

Vroom, V. H. and Yetton, P. W. 1973. *Leadership and Decision Making*. Pittsburgh: University of Pittsburgh Press.

Williamson, C. 1960. *American Suffrage from Property to Democracy: 1760–1860*. Princeton, NJ: Princeton University Press.

Index

About the Author

GLENN BASSETT is Professor of Management and Chair of the Management Department at the University of Bridgeport. For more than a decade he consulted on employee relations practices and employee relations research issues as a member of the General Electric Corporate Staff. This is his ninth published book. His previous Quorum titles are *Management Strategies for Today's Project Shop Economy* (1991) and *Operations Management for Service Industries* (1992).